COMICS AND NARRATION

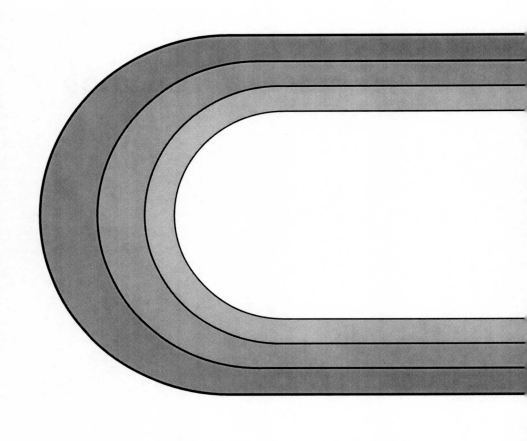

COMICS AND NARRATION

Thierry Groensteen

Translated by Ann Miller

UNIVERSITY PRESS OF MISSISSIPPI • JACKSON

www.upress.state.ms.us

The University Press of Mississippi is a member of the Association of American University Presses.

Publication of this book was made possible in part with the assistance of the Hemingway Grant program.

Cet ouvrage publié dans le cadre du programme d'aide à la publication bénéficie du soutien du Ministère des Affaires Etrangères et du Service Culturel de l'Ambassade de France représenté aux Etats-Unis. This work received support from the French Ministry of Foreign Affairs and the Cultural Services of the French Embassy in the United States through their publishing assistance program.

Originally published in 2011 by Presses Universitaires de France as *Bande dessinée et narration: Système de la bande dessinée 2*

First printing 2013
∞
Library of Congress Cataloging-in-Publication Data

Groensteen, Thierry.
  [Bande dessinée et narration]
  Comics and narration / Thierry Groensteen ; translated by Ann Miller.
      p. cm.
  Includes bibliographical references and index.
  ISBN 978-1-61703-770-2 (cloth : alk. paper) — ISBN 978-1-61703-771-9 (ebook)
  1. Comic books, strips, etc.—History and criticism. 2. Narration (Rhetoric) I. Title.
  PN6710.G757 2013
  741.5'9—dc23   2012036707

British Library Cataloging-in-Publication Data available

CONTENTS

TRANSLATOR'S FOREWORD

Bande dessinée et narration: Système de la bande dessinée 2,[1] published in the original French in 2011, is the long-awaited follow-up to Thierry Groensteen's seminal *Système de la bande dessinée*, written in 1999,[2] in which he embarked on the project of defining the fundamental resources deployed by comics for the production of meaning and aesthetic effects. By making underlying systems visible, Groensteen was able to shed light on the spatial operations of layout and articulation that conditioned the activity of the reader. He now builds on and expands that analysis, refining the concepts set out in *Système 1* by bringing them to bear on new material. He acknowledges the increasingly transnational nature of comics culture by moving beyond the mainly Franco-Belgian corpus on which he had drawn in the first volume and exploring innovative currents that blur and extend the boundaries of the medium, such as abstract comics, digital comics, and shōjo manga. In so doing, he shows how the comics apparatus is put to work by virtuoso practitioners across a spectrum from mainstream to experimental.

In addition, major chapters are devoted to two areas that were not covered in *Système 1*, the question of the narrator and the nature of rhythm in comics: here Groensteen maps out the theoretical terrain rigorously and comprehensively. The value of his approach becomes self-evident through the insights that it affords into the expressive power of artists as disparate as André Franquin, Robert Crumb, and Chris Ware, and, more generally, into evolutionary tendencies such as the recent move away from uniformity of graphic style in the work of exponents like David Mazzucchelli and Fabrice Neaud. In his final chapter, Groensteen poses the question of the relationship of comics to contemporary art: historically the latter has disdained the former, while plundering its resources, formal and thematic, but more recently certain comics artists have chosen to exhibit their work in galleries. The argument returns to the question of narration as Groensteen considers the most exciting work currently being produced by comics artists.

Groensteen also explores theoretical advances made over a decade during which more critical ink has flowed than ever before. He alludes to important work by many French-language researchers, most notably Thierry Smolderen and Harry Morgan, both of whom have offered re-readings of the history of the medium, critiquing approaches that discern only a straightforward evolution towards its present forms and functions, and Jean-Christophe Menu, whose concern, as both artist and theorist, is to investigate the potential of comics, including possibilities as yet unrealized. Groensteen is equally familiar with comics scholarship in English: he engages with the work of Scott McCloud and Douglas Wolk, among others. He also points to recently developing approaches such as the study of comics within media theory, adaptation theory, cultural studies, or cognitive science, all valid, he recognizes, even if it is the task of understanding how the medium works that is primary.

Groensteen himself has hardly been slacking in between the publication of *Système 1* and *Système 2*, having produced a series of books that examine comics from a variety of angles, encompassing analyses of formal features and mechanisms, historical studies of the medium as a whole and of particular genres, and reflections on cultural positioning, as well as a superb textbook. This prolific output (to which should be added a plethora of articles and exhibition catalogues) has been achieved in parallel to his other activities as lecturer, publisher, and curator, not to mention indefatigable traveler, promoter of dialogue and debate on every continent. However, it is with this volume of the *Système* that he completes his general theory of the medium.

Readers of *Système 1* will know that Groensteen's approach, semiotic in the broadest sense, is not to be equated with a dry exercise in taxonomy: on the contrary, it is the pleasures of comics that provide the starting point for his analysis, and, equipped with the rich conceptual framework that he offers, we return to comics as better, subtler, and more demanding readers. Groensteen's prose is elegant and highly readable, maintaining its lucidity however complex or detailed the point being made. The difference between French and English syntax patterns means that it is not easy for the translator to replicate the style of the original, and the text may seem a little clumsy in places as a result. Certain words pose particular problems: "bande dessinée" is an obvious example. I have used "comics" throughout, usually as a singular noun. I have not attempted to harmonize my translation with that of my *System 1* predecessors, Bart Beaty and David Nguyen, not wanting to risk any further stylistic clashes, but where the text refers back to *Système 1*, the endnote gives the page numbers of both the original

French text and its translated version. This will, I hope, facilitate the continuing debates that this book is bound to provoke and nourish among scholars in both linguistic communities.

Finally, I would like to thank two people: Laurence Grove, whose translation of an earlier version of Chapter 5 appeared in *European Comic Art* 3.1 (Spring 2010), and helped me to solve some tricky problems, and Malcolm Hope, who read through every chapter and made valuable suggestions.

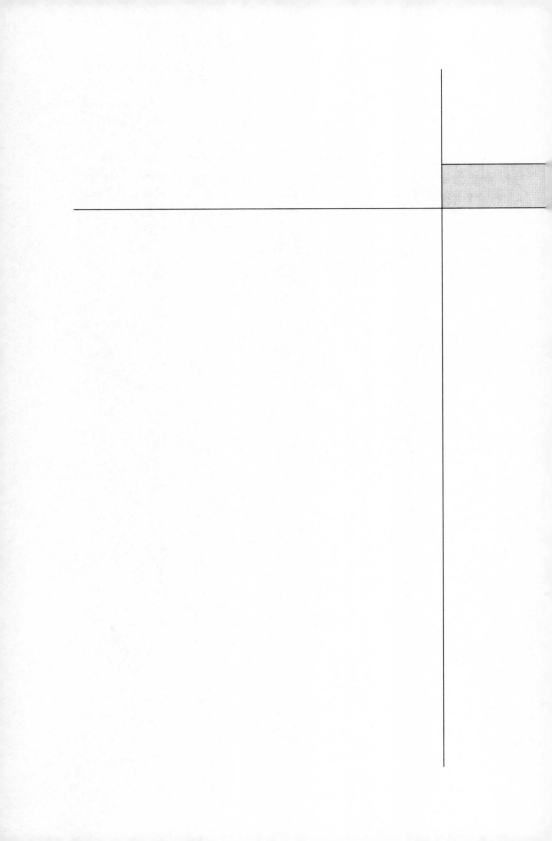

COMICS AND NARRATION

INTRODUCTION

The System of Comics, published in the original French in 1999 and in English translation in 2007, set out to theorize the foundations of the language of comics. This theory was macrosemiotic in its scope: it was not concerned with the details of single images, but with the articulation of images within the space of the page and across that of the book as a whole. The principle of *iconic solidarity* was shown to be applicable to three major operations: breakdown, page layout, and braiding. The book had the further aim of describing the formal apparatus through which meaning is produced, emphasizing the extent to which aesthetic and semantic considerations were interwoven. The image was defined as utterable, describable, interpretable and, ultimately, appreciable—all adjectives that put the accent on the active participation of the reader in the construction of meaning and in the assessment of the work.

Over the twelve years that have elapsed since then, understanding of comics has moved forward. Advances in scholarship have been particularly noteworthy in relation to the history of the medium, largely due to the illuminating research of Thierry Smolderen into the history of the speech balloon,[1] and into competing conceptions of page layout in the nineteenth and early twentieth centuries.[2] This research has been brought together by the author in the form of a thick and beautifully illustrated volume published in 2009 called *Naissances de la bande dessinée*.[3] Smolderen is the first historian to have shown how cartoons served as the "laboratory" wherein comic art was forged, and how comics have subsequently been constantly redefined through "contact with society, with its media, its images and its technologies," leading up to the production of "an (open) family of graphic dialects." He sheds light on the circumstances that led the medium to adopt, in turn, the model of progressive plot structure, tabular page layout, the "cute" aesthetic, decomposition of movement and facial expressions, and the speech balloon as "visual sound track."

As a result, Jean-Christophe Menu's rightful desire that a "*critical history* of the *language* of comics, rather than a history of its best-sellers"[4] should be written, seems, in fact, to have already been partially realized. There remains, however, the task of completing the undertaking in relation to the twentieth century. As things stand, Smolderen stopped after McCay just as, before him, David Kunzle, starting from 1450, had only pursued his investigations as far as the end of the nineteenth century.

Another line of research that has grown considerably is content analysis. Into this vast field there falls anything to do with Gender Studies, the relationship of comics to History and the representation of society, as well as issues raised by autobiography and autofiction.

Harry Morgan has placed his most recent research under the aegis of *Mythopoeia*, or the production of myths.[5] He aims to uncover the formal apparatus that regulates the interaction between the content of comics and the physical, material, technical, editorial, and social constraints that bear upon it. He maintains that it is the study of this "specific connection" that will enable the identification of the essential features of what he calls graphic literatures.[6]

New pathways continue to be opened up in contemporary research. Media theory offers perspectives from which to interrogate the relationships (consisting of filiation, overlap, reciprocal influences, borrowings, quotations, adaptations) between comics and literature, theatre, film, and photography. Within the field of comics itself, the development of another form of comparativism is to be welcomed: this consists of contrasting different traditions of comics production worldwide. Furthermore, disciplines based on cognitive science have cast some light, although still too faint, on the way in which images are perceived, processed by the human brain, understood, and recalled.

While all these types of investigation are flourishing, the same cannot be said of semiotic theory (in the widest definition of the word), which represents, as it were, the very foundations of comics research, and which, by analyzing the formal apparatus that constitutes it, offers the prospect of a more subtle understanding of the medium and its potential. Indeed, there has been relatively little progress in this area.

The intention of this volume is to deepen, extend, and complete the theoretical propositions put forward in *System 1*. It further clarifies the basic concepts of iconic solidarity, sequence, and modes of reading comics. It revisits more specific questions already discussed, such as regular page layout or the threshold of narrativity. It engages with new objects, like children's books, digital comics, or abstract comics. It addresses fundamental questions that had been deferred, like the issue of rhythm and that of the narrator. It ends by situating comics in relation to the contemporary art scene.

To sum up, where the first volume described the foundations and the major articulations of the system, its particular architecture and dynamic, this volume is more concerned to analyze the uses to which it may be put.

It can be distinguished from the previous volume in two other ways.

In *System 1*, my thinking was based mainly on comics from the European, and most often, Franco-Belgian tradition. A choice that seemed normal to readers of the original edition may have been perceived as reductive or problematic in countries where the work was published in translation (particularly the U.S. and Japan). This second volume aspires to be much more open to other comics traditions. It devotes one section of its argument to manga and draws to a much greater extent on examples from virtuoso American comics artists like David Mazzucchelli, Art Spiegelman, and Chris Ware. I also enter into dialogue more often with English-language critics and researchers.

Finally, where *System 1* approached comics from an essentially ahistorical standpoint, attempting to draw out some universals from the language of the medium, *Comics and Narration* is much more closely involved with its recent developments. This is not only because it takes account of phenomena such as abstract comics or digital comics that have only become established in recent years, but also in the sense that it attempts to ensure that theory is always in phase with the aesthetic evolution of modern comics.

The historical studies by Smolderen referred to above have shown comics to be a medium that constantly renews itself. Modern comics have won over a new readership and invented new formats (two evolutions encapsulated by the concept of the "graphic novel," however hard it is to define). There has been a certain feminization of the comics profession. A current of auteurist comics has freed itself from the stranglehold of the series. It has gained ground on the terrain of the intimate, the confessional, and narratives of the self. The Ouvroir de bande dessinée potentielle [Workshop for Potential Comics] has turned experimentation and play on the codes of the medium into a manifesto, and, one might say, into a philosophy of creation.[7] And the very long-standing tradition of wordless comics has been revivified by the innovative work of François Ayroles, Peter Kuper, Shaun Tan, Lewis Trondheim, Jim Woodring, and many others.

Perhaps more interesting than the proliferation of comics lacking any text is the fact that "talking" comics seem to have discovered the virtues of momentary silence, of the withheld utterance, the pause. In the past, comics were very talkative: the image was often submerged beneath the words and stifled by verbiage. Contemporary artists are not afraid to turn the sound off where necessary, to give the drawing some breathing space, to allow for thinking in images, and to engender a visual emotion. Comics have learned to hold their peace.[8]

Another seismic change in comics creation is the abandonment of the dogma of uniformity of style. I will discuss (see below, 5.3.3) the different stages, manifestations, and consequences of this development. An artist can now offer a wide range of different graphic styles within a single work, and, among them, afford a place to the draft, the inchoate, or to graphic lines that seriously disrespect the sacred imperative of optimum transparency and immediate legibility.

As a general rule, the comics industry perpetuates the imperialism of the series and the hero, along with outdated aesthetic standards corresponding to a long-gone classic period, even if, as a concession to modernity, it is prepared to disrupt layouts[9] or to deploy the whole arsenal of special effects allowed for by digital coloring processes (just as most films churned out by the cinema industry are technically well made but lacking in originality). Authentically modern comic art thrives more easily in the margins, either with literary publishing houses that, as latecomers to comics, are less encumbered by the weight of tradition, or with independent or alternative publishers.

Since the 1990s, the gap has become ever wider between the ambitions and the procedures of a formulaic, commercial comics output designed for a mass market, and those of an auteurist comics production more detached from the imperative of maximizing profit margins, more focused on creative individuality and more receptive to artistic influences from outside the "ninth art." (Unsurprisingly, children's comics are still mostly bound by the standards of mass-market series. On the one hand, this is because the output of literary or alternative publishers is essentially aimed at adults, and, on the other, it is because the ideal of legibility imposed on commercially produced comics guarantees their ready accessibility to less seasoned readers.)

Although this book is more theoretical than critical in its scope, it will be more attentive than the previous one to newly emerging formal features: the play between the figurative and the non-figurative, the poetic quality of stories, stylistic patchworks, the exploration of subjectivity, and a certain hybridity arising out of the encounter with the techniques of contemporary art. My longtime interest in forms regarded as marginal and in minoritarian uses of the medium—especially silent comics, minimalist comics, and self-reflexive comics—has convinced me that theoretical elaboration can only be relevant and legitimate if it takes the risk of being responsive to contemporary developments in creative work, and of interrogating them.

CHAPTER ONE

Comics and the Test of Abstraction

It is in the nature of experimental works that they shift the boundaries or contest the usual definition of the medium to which they belong. This general rule is particularly applicable to comics, and I have already discussed the difficulties it poses for researchers (see *Système 1*, 17–21; *System 1*, 14–17).

In that first volume, I did in fact refuse to give a complete and analytical definition of comics, confining myself to the observation that a comic consists necessarily of a finite collection of separate and interdependent iconic elements. In more recent texts, I have taken to quoting the definition proposed by Ann Miller: "As a visual and narrative art, [comics] produce meaning out of images which are in a sequential relationship, and which co-exist with each other spatially, with or without text."[1] An eminently balanced and sensible definition, which, I have written, applies perfectly to the great majority of work produced up until now.[2]

To the great majority, but not to all. The list of experimental comics that give this definition something of a mauling includes works with no characters, no narration, and no drawing (Jean-Christophe Menu, with characteristic wit, suggests a few more possibilities: archaic, infranarrative, pictogrammatic, and extraterrestrial comics).[3]

1.1 A NEW CATEGORY

One part of this marginal comics production has been labeled and in some sense officially recognized as a category, if not a genre, by the appearance in 2009 of the anthology *Abstract Comics* published by Fantagraphics and edited by Andrei Molotiu. What exactly are *abstract comics*? Molotiu distinguishes two types: either sequences of abstract drawings, or sequences of drawings that contain figurative elements, the juxtaposition of which does not produce a coherent narrative. His anthology offers many more examples of the first case than of the second. I would personally reserve the term *abstract comics* for the first type, and would call the second type *infranarrative comics*.

This anthology was not completely unprecedented: in its thirteenth volume, the journal *Bile noire* [Black Bile] (Spring 2003), published in Switzerland by Atrabile, launched a regular feature edited by Ibn al Rabin that was devoted to abstract comics, which had to conform to a rule prohibiting "the representation of any concrete 'object' (i.e., one with an unambiguous meaning) other than those belonging to the semantics of the medium itself, in other words speech balloons and panels." Along with Rabin himself, contributors included Alex Baladi, Guy Delisle, Andreas Kündig, David Vandermeulen, and Lewis Trondheim (only Rabin and Trondheim also appear in Molotiu's anthology).

Trondheim, as is well known, has since produced two small books for the Association in this same vein: the first, *Bleu* [Blue], is in color, ludic in tone, and visually similar to the work of Miró, and the second, *La Nouvelle Pornographie* [The New Pornography], is in black and white and is parodic in tone. This minuscule work (from the 'Patte de Mouche' [Squiggle (literally "Fly's Leg")] collection, 2006, had the particular virtue of proving that the play of abstract forms should not be taken automatically to imply an absence of meaning. In this instance, the artful combinations of black and white graphic forms straightforwardly evoked, even if in a disembodied or metaphorical way, the sexual scenarios promised by the title.

But that is an exceptional case. As a general rule, abstract comics demolish Ann Miller's definition quoted above: they jettison narrative art, sequential relationships, and the production of meaning (subject to some slight reservations that I will mention later).

The text introducing the new regular feature in *Bile noire*, which continued to appear until 2007, also specified that any recourse to a text was "strictly prohibited." This edict was somewhat surprising in that its author was apparently unaware that, if anyone so decides, words, just as much as images, can be put to incoherent use, become incomprehensible, and contribute to the destruction of meaning.

Abstract comics can be approached in a number of ways. We will encounter them later, firstly in relation to the question of rhythm (see below, p. 134–35), and secondly as part of the ongoing dialogue between comics and contemporary art (p. 162). For the moment, my discussion is concerned with them insofar as they re-problematize the very definition of comics.

1.2 THE FORMAL APPARATUS AND ITS PERCEPTION

Let us turn first to comics that are abstract in the strict sense of the word, that is to say composed of a series of drawings that are themselves non-figurative. What remains of the comics medium once it leaves the realm of *mimesis*? There remain, firstly, those elements "belonging to the semantics of the medium itself, in other words speech balloons and panels," to quote the formulation of *Bile noire* (even if the term "semantics" seems inappropriate here). Jean-Christophe Menu refers to the "formal apparatus of comics as a *crude skeleton*."[4] I had used the term "skeleton" myself to designate "the grid whose compartments are left empty" *(Système I, 35: System I, 28)*. Another striking formula is the one used by Adam Gopnik in the catalogue of the MoMA exhibition *High & Low*, when he points out that painters like Jasper Johns, Robert Rauschenberg, and Öyvind Fahlström realized, at the beginning of the 1960s, that "the secondary machinery of the comics—the panels and balloons and onomatopoeia—began to have an iconic force greater than any image they might contain."[5]

It is interesting to note that no single element proclaimed to be constitutive of this "machinery" is in fact indispensable to comics. Many artists never use onomatopoeia, others never use speech balloons—either because their stories are wordless, or because the words are placed beneath the images or "float" inside them—and the drawings are not necessarily framed. It is nonetheless the combination of these elements (frames and balloons in particular) that, in the modern collective imaginary, seems to typify comics, to characterize the formal apparatus of the medium and its language (to the point where this "machinery" should be called *primary* rather than secondary).

Indeed, contemporary artists continue to take their inspiration from the machinery of comics. For example, in the first decade of this century, the Brazilian artist Rivane Neuenschwander has exhibited in a number of galleries[6] her large panels based on *Zé Carioca*, a popular Brazilian comic with a nationalist flavor. Neuenschwander turns it into an abstract comic: she keeps the shapes and proportions of panels and speech balloons, but empties both of their contents, refilling the outlines with blocks of a single color, each one different. Every panel is two meters high: the effect is to cast off the small format of the original printed version and to transmute it into the monumentality of art. Moreover, visitors are invited to draw or write on the surface with chalk, thereby re-creating a new comic of their own. By hollowing the comic out, by reducing it to a skeleton, Neuenschwander has reinvented it as palimpsest.

It is nonetheless true that the majority of abstract comics do not include speech balloons. What exactly is it, then, that we see on a comics page made up of abstract images? Two things—that need to be distinguished from each other.

Firstly, visual content: colors, lines, forms organized into motifs. These abstract "images" interact with each other. They establish relationships of position, contiguity, intensity, repetition, variation, or contrast, as well as dynamic relationships of rhythm, interwovenness, etc. In principle, nothing in this list pertains to narration, which is why I alluded above to a *series*, rather than a *sequence*, of drawings. Unless, of course, it is feasible for a line, a shape, a color, or any kind of graphic entity, to have "adventures" in its own right, as Menu suggests is the case for Baladi's mini-album *Petit trait* [Little Line],[7] given that the "story" recounted is that of the transformations undergone by the line in question, through a kind of *physis*, whereby each new image is generated by the preceding one.

Secondly, what is shown by an abstract comics page is the spatio-topical apparatus of comics (henceforth referred to as *the apparatus*).[8] This is a space that is demarcated and compartmentalized, within which frames enter into spatial relationships and compose an organized totality. The images are con-figured, because this multiframe subjects them to a double movement of junction and disjunction—in other words designates them to the reader as being in solidarity, even as they are separated (by framing lines, gutters, or simply blank space).

In its *Traité du signe visuel* [Treatise on the Visual Sign], the Groupe Mu wrote:

> A work of visual art can be examined from the point of view of forms, from the point of view of colours, from the point of view of textures, and from that of the whole formed by all of these together. It should also be noted that these visual data are co-present, so that the image is, from the outset, always potentially tabular. A comparison may be made with temporal arts (poetry, music . . .), where tabularity can only be achieved by a process of construction.[9]

Comics is an art of space and an art of time: these dimensions are indissociable. To the intrinsic tabularity of the images it adds, by a process of construction, both a linearity and a more encompassing tabularity, that of the page.

But the question posed by abstract comics is precisely this: in the mind of someone looking at a comics page of this type with non-figurative content, does the division of the page into the pattern of a multiframe still immediately summon up the idea of a comic? This is not necessarily the case. The page can be read as a tabular surface, that is to say as a global image, crisscrossed by orthogonal lines (Mondrian-style). In this case, the relationships among the zones (we will avoid referring to "motifs") are merely spatial relationships organizing a visual field.

If, on the other hand, the apparatus is recognized as being typical of comics, then its conventional configuration, possessed of its own potency, will invite a linear decoding, that is to say a reading, even if it is immediately obvious that the images, in this instance, do not represent, and consequently do not recount, anything. The apparatus invites the reader to look at the images one after another; contiguous images are perceived as consecutive, and this ordering constitutes a discourse, the discourse that vectorizes the visual field of a comics page. Instead of being viewed together, the images are caught in an oscillation between a global apprehension and a fragmented, one-after-another apprehension. It is under this condition that, while still not defined as a narrative, the drawn or painted surface ceases to be simply a tabular surface and becomes a comics page.

It is evident that the context in which the abstract work is encountered greatly influences the way in which it is perceived, either as a "tableau" or as a "page." If it is encountered in an anthology entitled *Abstract Comics*, then the second hypothesis is likely to be adopted. However, Molotiu's introductory text is illustrated by the work of artists such as Kandinsky, de Kooning, or Alechinsky, produced in the 1930s, 1960s, and 1970s, in a field far removed from comics. Their reproduction in the context of the anthology allows these "tableaux" to be read today as abstract comics that anticipated the advent of the genre, despite the fact they were never conceived as such (in the same way that books of engravings by Ward or Masereel are now regarded as "graphic novels" *avant la lettre*). Molotiu has similarly "recuperated" pages by Syros Horemis taken from a scientific volume, *Optical and Geometrical Patterns and Designs* (1970) and arranged as a multiframe.

A range of attitudes can be envisaged, from that of Molotiu "reading" a modern painting like a comic, and that, easy to imagine, of the numerous lovers of traditional comics who would reject the idea of abstract comics as a contradiction in terms, even when it is taken up by authors already familiar to them, such as Trondheim, Baladi, or Delisle.

The difference between these standpoints resides precisely in the identification of the apparatus as the foundation of the comics medium, as the cardinal element of its "primary machinery." If the apparatus is spontaneously perceived as necessarily pertaining to comics, then it becomes a symbolic structure, a discursive operator—something, in fact, of the order of the *concept*. But if the reference to comics does not automatically come to mind, then this same apparatus is understood as no more than a mechanism for organizing space, and its visual elements become mere *percepts*.

So, the pages collected by Molotiu can only be responded to as "abstract comics" on condition that the apparatus is identified as belonging to the realm of comics, which is far from self-evident; it is a question of context, personal culture, subjective perception.[10]

It is clear that responding to an abstract work as a comics page is equivalent to asserting that the spatio-topical mechanism of comics exists in its own right, independently of any condition concerning figurative representation or narration, and that this mechanism, this apparatus, is sufficient to establish that the work belongs to the field of comics. Logically, then, the apparatus should be recognized as constituting the central element of a definition of comics.

The problem of definition has been called into question by recent developments within the comics field. Statistically, abstract comics represent only a minute proportion of production as a whole, but they bear considerable symbolic weight because they suggest that comics can banish narration and figuration without ceasing to be comics; at the same time, digital comics, a rapid and more substantial growth area, have banished paper. In the face of these developments, what remains of traditional definitions of comics? Nothing more than the sharing of a space for inscription or display—in other words, the apparatus, the "plurality of images in solidarity."

Before moving on I would like to mention some brief considerations about the actual abstract images. Two types can be distinguished. In those of the first type, the abstraction is "indigenous"; in the others it has been achieved, the result of an operation of erasure, blurring, covering over, or distortion applied to an image that was originally figurative. An example of de-figuration is presented in *Abstract Comics*, "Flying Chief," by Derik Badman, based on *Tarzan and the Flying Chief*, a story by Jessie Marsh published in 1950 (fig. 1). Badman explains: "I redrew the story, ignoring text, balloons, captions, and characters, taking only the backgrounds and transforming them into abstracted shapes, marks and textures."

Between 2006 and 2008 Molotiu himself produced a comic called *24 x 24: A Vague Epic*, the pages of which incorporate elements, rendered unrecognizable, of artists such as Poussin, Fragonard, or Goya.[11] It is also worth mentioning the

Fig. 1. Derik Badman, "Flying Chief," in *Abstract Comics* (Seattle: Fantagraphics, 2009).
© Derik Badman.

work of Thomas Higashiyama, a graduate of the University of Decorative Arts in Strasbourg, who has researched abstract comics for several years, and who, before moving on to a simple play on forms and colors, went through a phase of reworking existing drawings taken from manga.[12]

In the October 2010 issue of the magazine *Étapes* [Stages], Higashiyama declared that he approached comics not as an artist but as a graphic designer. The practice piece presented for his final degree is a book, approximately one hundred pages long, untitled, and still unpublished. As I write these lines I have in front of me a copy that he kindly sent me. He explains that he wanted the reader to be "caught up in the movement of a story, without having to read a text or decode images." Out of a small number of elements—panels, empty speech balloons, circular or star-shaped forms, single or multicolored backgrounds—he assembles and reconfigures, page upon page, playing on repetition, superimposition, rhythm, changes in scale, and other visual surprises. One of the most original aspects of his work is the occasional reification of the apparatus into a grid whose frames seem to have been emptied (or whose contents have become transparent), with the result that colored shapes seem to have slid *under* the orthogonal network of gutters. Higoshiyama thereby introduces into abstract comics the notion of multilayer, which I will refer to later (4.2.2) in relation to manga.

1.3 FROM THE AMALGAM TO THE SEQUENCE

The practice of juxtaposing on the same page figurative drawings with no logical or semantic continuity has a long history. In the nineteenth century it was not unusual for a humorous artist to fill the page space with an array of drawings whose only relationship to each other was the fact that they had been produced by the same hand. These sheets were called "macédoines" [medleys].

Abstract comics belonging to the second type identified by Molotiu, those whose images are figurative but do not amount collectively to a coherent whole, are of a different order. This is because they are not the result of a collection or assemblage of random drawings, but of the intention to produce a comics page devoid of any narrative project. A string[13] of images in an abstract comic can be created through a process of improvisation, following the whim of the pencil, or it can, alternatively, be planned and its outcome premeditated.

In 1987 at the Cerisy conference on the theme of "Comics, Narrative and Modernity," I demonstrated that the juxtaposition of drawings within a multiframe does not automatically lead to a narrative; there are other principles according to which images may be related to each other. I had called these amalgam, inventory, variation, inflection, and decomposition.[14] These categories (initially referred to as "primary distributive functions") were alluded to again in *Système 1*.[15] It seems to me today that two supplementary cases could be added to this taxonomy: in the first, the same image would be repeated in every panel of the multiframe, producing a kind of "wallpaper effect," and in the second, the page would consist of a single large image occupying the whole surface artificially divided up by the superimposition of a grid. These two supplementary theoretical cases could be termed respectively *seriation* and *fragmentation*.

In his 2008 doctoral thesis, Harry Morgan judiciously noted a similarity between two of the infranarrative functions I had proposed in 1987, and two of the six types of transition—"closure"—identified by Scott McCloud in *Understanding Comics*.[16] The transition that he calls "aspect to aspect" does indeed correspond to what I had called "decomposition," and his "non-sequitur" to my "amalgam." But McCloud, who goes on to examine[17] the frequency of each of these categories in the work of thirty-three American, European, and Japanese artists, finds only a single occurrence of the "non-sequitur," that is to say the case where there is "no logical relationship between panels whatsoever."[18] This happens to be taken from a short comic by Art Spiegelman, *Ace Hole, Midget Detective*, which forms part of his experimental collection, *Breakdowns*.[19] A very narrow corpus, then, given that McCloud does not seem to take any account of abstract comics (moreover, Spiegelman's story cannot, in fact, be categorized either as abstract or as infranarrative).

And yet, the definition of comics offered by McCloud ("juxtaposed pictorial and other images in deliberate sequence," usually abbreviated to "sequential art") makes no specific reference to the idea of narration. Everything depends on what is meant by the concept of sequence. In this respect, McCloud's stance lacks precision; however, the fact that he includes the "non-sequitur" as one of the possible types of transition implies that he may have a wider conception of the notion of sequence. My own concept, *iconic solidarity*, intentionally stops short of considering whether comics have any "narrative purpose."

Between February and November 2009, Daniel Blancou produced an exciting series of strips in numbers 37 to 40 of the journal *Lapin* [Rabbit] under the title *Samuel Limpinski*. His declared objective was "to write, in three panels, strips whose meaning was not 'nailed down.'" We understand by this that the causal links between the three panels are sometimes stretched so far or are so ambiguous

Fig. 2. Daniel Blancou, "Papa," from *Samuel Limpinski*, in *Lapin* no. 37, February 2009.
© Daniel Blancou.

that they demand much work of the reader, who is left to construct logical inferences and, ultimately, to produce meaning.

We can take the example of the strip called "Papa" [Dad] in *Lapin* no. 37. The
first panel, which is silent, shows tadpoles swimming in a pond. The second is
a medium close-up of a man gazing downwards (a tree, viewed from beneath,
is visible in the background) saying: "You're not going to bring that home?!"
The third and last panel, again silent, transports the reader to an exhibition of
modern art. A somewhat perplexed man is contemplating an abstract canvas,
while, to his right, a woman moves away, adjusting her shoe as she does so. It is
not difficult to make a link between the first two panels, even if the child that
"Dad" is addressing is not represented in either of them. In contrast, the situation represented in the third panel seems completely unrelated to the incipient
story. Two interpretations seem possible. *Either*: whether or not s/he brought the
tadpoles home, the child examined them sufficiently closely to enable him/her,
many years later and having become an artist, to produce canvasses inspired by
their form. It is not possible to base a judgment on the section that appears in
the frame, but the black circular shape represented in the picture could be taken
as a detail from the head of a tadpole, massively blown up. *Or*: the two situations
bear no relationship to each other but the indecisive man has perhaps intimated
that he is thinking about buying the picture, and his partner has replied: "You're
not going to bring that home?!"

In order to make the first interpretation hold up, we have had to presuppose
a leap in time (a temporal hiatus) and to extrapolate an entire image from an
indeterminate detail.[20] To shore up the second interpretation we have had to du-
plicate a line of dialogue from panel 2 (situation A) and to assume that it applies
equally well to panel 3 (situation B). In other words, it is only by carrying out in-

terpretative work that relies on making narrative hypotheses, and by taking much of the initiative that the reader can reduce the apparent incoherence of the strip.

The comics reader takes semantic and narrative coherence for granted. S/he presumes that "the positioning of any panel necessarily has some point"[21] When images set out consecutively fail to offer any immediate coherence, the reader is naturally inclined to minimize what seems like a "breach of contract" by formulating hypotheses intended to confer intelligibility on the string of panels—to convert an *amalgam* into a narrative sequence. It is only when these attempts fail that s/he makes the decision to assign these images to the always improbable category of infranarrative comics.

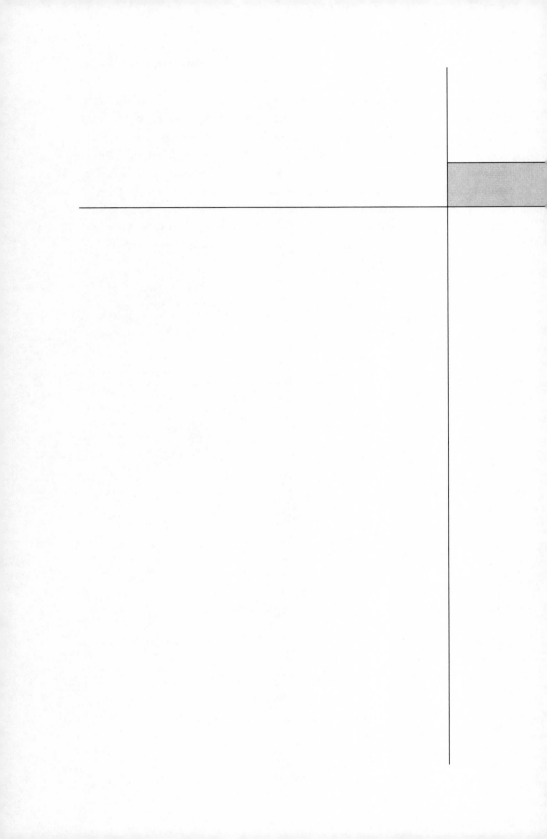

CHAPTER TWO

New Insights into Sequentiality

Several authors who have tried to apply the concepts defined in *System 1* to a particular comic or to a larger corpus have taken me to task for the fact that they could not find in it adequate tools to describe certain specific mechanisms that had caught their attention. This does not surprise me as *System 1* was never intended to be a textbook offering a ready-to-use analytical grid. And neither did it offer a research methodology. Its goal was to interrogate the basic principles of the language of the medium, to identify its functions, to study its articulations, at the most general level possible. It is obvious from the example of Daniel Blancou's strips discussed above that authors have potentially infinite resources for inventing new, and ever more original, varieties of this language. There could be no question of drawing up some kind of predetermined list.

It is in the same spirit of broad generality that I pursue in the following pages my investigations into comics as a "sequential art," in Will Eisner's formulation, subsequently adopted by Scott McCloud. Having discussed the borderline cases of abstract and infranarrative comics, I now return to my central subject, which is, precisely, narration.

2.1 SITUATION AND STORY: QUESTIONING THE NARRATIVE POTENTIAL OF THE SINGLE IMAGE

Can an isolated image narrate? Can it, on its own, tell a story? In *Système 1*, 121–26, *System 1*, 103–7, the question was posed in terms of the ontological difference between the still image (such as a drawing or a photo) and the moving image (the film shot). Some film theorists, most notably André Gaudreault, have asserted that an intrinsic narrativity is associated with movement, because it implies a transformation of the elements represented. Obviously, the same cannot be said of the still image. Given that its narrative potential is not intrinsic, it can

21

only arise, where it does arise, out of certain internal relationships between the objects, motifs, and characters represented.

My own position was intended to be open and anti-dogmatic. It was summarized in a dual conclusion: "if we cannot dismiss the hypothesis that an isolated [still] image can [also] be intrinsically narrative, we can, conversely, be certain that the juxtaposition of two images [. . .] does not necessarily produce narration."[1]

Rereading this today, I am aware that I introduced a certain confusion into the debate by surreptitiously changing its terms; by referring to page 125 (106), it can be seen that I slid from the question of narrative potential to that of meaning. No longer: *can a single image, on its own, contain a story*, but instead: *how does the single image produce meaning*—which, as I now acknowledge, is not quite the same thing.

However, the issue of the narrative potential of the single image was taken up later, on page 130 (110). The analysis of a page taken from *Alack Sinner* enabled me to infer that certain images can easily be translated into utterances of a narrative type ("Alack lights a cigarette") whereas others can only be read in narrative terms if they are considered within a wider plane of meaning-production: "the triad composed of the panel that is currently being read, the panel that precedes it, and the panel that immediately follows it,"[2] or even a still more complete sequence.

I realize that these observations, however useful they may be for understanding the meaning-producing mechanisms at work in comics, do not settle the issue. This is because "Alack lights a cigarette" is, undoubtedly, an "utterance of a narrative type" (it expresses an action), but it is not, in itself, a *narrative*. Something like "Alack lights a cigarette, takes a few short drags, and then stubs it out in the ashtray" would look more like one (and it is obvious that a single image would be incapable of translating the whole of this utterance into visual terms).

I am taking the subject up again here not only in order to clarify or complete what I wrote back then, but also to respond to Harry Morgan. In *Principes des littératures dessinées* [Principles of Graphic Literatures],[3] Morgan made a case for the inclusion within the field of literature of works limited to a single image: "a daily panel, a humorous cartoon, or a single engraving from a cycle by Hogarth."[4] And Morgan goes on to recognize the "narrative potential of the single image," which, according to him, was taken for granted by a nineteenth-century reader, given that "at that period, painting [was] essentially narrative."[5]

The author of the *Principes* adopts a radical position on the matter. Having quoted a few authors for whom "an isolated image can narrate if it contains relationships of causality and consecutiveness," he goes on: "We will go further than our predecessors and we will recognize the narrative potential in an isolated image where events before or after (the cause or the effect) *can be deduced* from the scene that is shown."[6] And so to his conclusion: "We must therefore embrace within graphic literature both narratives in a single image and narratives in multiple images."

Morgan puts forward the view that a daily panel can be described as "a daily strip reduced to one panel." However, the examples that he calls upon, taken from Brad Anderson's *Marmaduke* panel, do not seem convincing to me. When, for instance, having described the August 10, 1999, offering ("[The dog] Marmaduke is watching, through the glass door of the oven, a joint that is roasting. The little girl tells us that he would rather watch this show than the television"), he comments: "A strip would include two preceding panels in which the dog would be watching television, would get bored with the show, and would come and sit in front of the oven." But these two variations on the same theme are not at all equivalent—that is the whole point. Recounting the same thing differently never means recounting the same thing. In the panel, we have a situation but no narrative. In the virtual strip we would have had successively: an initial situation, its abandonment (or rather transformation), then a second situation. Undoubtedly, the global, anecdotal meaning would not have been substantially altered, but its perception by the reader would have been very different. What disappears in the single-panel version is the unfolding, the rhythm, the payoff. These are precisely the signature features of a narrative.

The defining quality of a narrative—forgive me for bringing up this banal point—is that it necessarily includes a beginning and an end, or, to put it another way, an element of development of the action, of evolution of the initial situation, from state A to state B.

I concur, then, on this point, with the ranks of theorists (the majority) who, like Aron Kibedi Varga,[7] feel that a single image can *evoke* a story, but that this does not mean that it *tells* one. It is "the juxtaposition of images [that] generates narratives."[8]

The exception to the rule occurs when the single image encompasses several different scenes, that is to say that it plays on juxtaposition within its own space. This is the case of the "narrative images" of which François Garnier has tracked down many occurrences in medieval iconography:

The narrative image consists of a set of elements and relationships that present an incident or tell a story. It reads like the account of an incident, like a story.[9]

The unfolding of the action is conveyed by the "simultaneous figuration" of several distinct moments, the character or characters involved in the story being gifted with a kind of ubiquity because he or they appear(s) in several different parts of the image. Other examples of a similar order have been discussed by Wendy Steiner, who notes that the events are often set out like waystages, as in the picture in the National Gallery of Art in Washington, representing *The Meeting of St Anthony Abbot and St Paul the Hermit* (Studio of Sassetta, c. 1440), or depicted in adjoining rooms of the same building.[10]

Steiner notes that, in a visual narrative, it is principally the repetition of the subject that informs us that what we are seeing is a story. "If a figure appears more than once in a painting, we automatically assume that it is shown at various distinct moments."[11] Nonetheless, she observes that this is not always the case, and mentions the lithographs of M. C. Escher as instances where the repetition of a character can simply be a matter of design, devoid of any narrative intent. It follows that for this kind of simultaneous presentation of figures to be construed as a narrative, there must be a "realist interpretation": "To read a painting narratively we must see the repeated shapes as people, their body postures as gestures, their background as a spatial environment, and the scene represented as a pregnant moment expandable into entire temporal sequences."[12]

As we know, this mode of representation disappeared with the Renaissance. When Alberti speaks of *istoria*, he is referring to a theme or composition rather than to a narrative in the strict sense. From then on, the image (in painting or sculpture) would condense the story on which it was based into a single, synthetic scene.

In the eighteenth century, Gotthold Ephraim Lessing established a clear boundary between painting and poetry, which, in his view, were not suited to imitate the same objects. "Actions are the peculiar subjects of poetry," whose "consecutive signs can express only objects which succeed each other." Whereas painting is static, made up of "signs arranged side by side," and "(c)onsequently, bodies with their visible properties are [its] peculiar subjects."[13] Lessing does not say that it is impossible to "bring together into one and the same picture two points of time necessarily remote," but he maintains that this is something that "good taste can never sanction."[14]

He adds this remark, which touches directly on the issue that concerns us:

Painting, in its consistent compositions, can use but a single moment of an action, and must therefore choose the most pregnant one, *the one most suggestive of what has gone before and what is to follow.*[15]

The German philosopher offers few details about the mechanisms that enable the moment represented to suggest what has gone before and what is to follow. But in the example of the *Marmaduke* strip quoted above, it is clear that it is the observation made by the little girl, a verbal utterance, therefore, that enables Morgan to extend the panel into a sequence—the image itself is static and does not invite this treatment.

In the time of Nicolas Poussin, history painting was the most prestigious of all genres. Louis Marin summarizes the question that was posed to all artists: "How is it possible to tell a story when the formal and structural constraints of the painted work can only represent a single instant of it?" For Poussin, the solution was to increase the density and complexity of the crucial moment represented by portraying it as "an accumulation of simultaneous actions, hierarchized by an organizing principle that renders them both intelligible and essential." The emotions attributed to each of these characters are translated into postures, gestures, and facial expressions. Marin's conclusion is that "the arrangement of figures in the space represented corresponds to the writing of the story in this same space, according to the constraints that arise from the principle of the crucial moment represented."[16]

Personally, I believe this arrangement both reveals the logical connectedness of the scene and enriches its meaning. In fact, though, this is simply an episode extracted from a story that was already familiar (Poussin's subjects were mainly taken from mythological or Old or New Testament sources). The story is not recounted—it is evoked, and this evocation is readily comprehensible only because the subject matter is already well-known. The spectator is at liberty to use the image as a starting point for summoning up the story as a whole, by recalling from memory the episodes that come before and after it.

It seems undeniable that a clear difference has to be established between images that refer to already-known stories and those (like the humorous daily panels or the Rockwell covers that I allude to below) that are invented by the artist. Most single images belonging to the second category—and those that come under the conventional heading of narrative painting are no exception—are not sufficiently explicit for it to be possible to attribute a scenario to them, however minimal.[17]

I have in front of me the forty-odd reproductions in the volume *Victorian Narrative Painting*,[18] and in this collection put together by Julia Thomas, I can see hardly any images that allow for a story to be surmised. Let us take as an example the canvas by William Quiller Orchardson called *The First Cloud* (1887): it shows an upper-class woman leaving a drawing room under the gaze, half submissive and half dumbfounded, of her husband. Since the woman is represented from behind, her expression is not visible. The clenching of her right hand and the briskness of her step are the only indications of the anger that we attribute to her. Of course, the title constitutes here, as often elsewhere, the main explanatory feature of the work. But Orchardson merely offers us a *situation*. And since he denies us any glimpse of what has provoked this marital tiff, it is impossible for us to unravel the situation and extrapolate a story.

Julia Thomas acknowledges that the expression "narrative painting" was very little used by the Victorians: it is a category that she herself has fashioned to allow for the inclusion of works that were, at the time, described as "scenes from everyday life," "literary painting," "genre painting," "anecdotal," or "domestic" painting, etc.[19] She also notes that these paintings, which, in the tradition of William Hogarth, often had a morally improving purpose, aspired to emulate the novel, and that many of the canvasses were directly based on a text, with the aim of making the story explicit; long quotations often appeared in exhibition catalogues or on the frame surrounding the work.

Moreover, two centuries after Lessing, painting with narrative pretentions was still getting a bad press. In a study of the covers produced by Norman Rockwell for the *Saturday Evening Post*,[20] Morgan describes them as "a picturesque example of single narrative images," and notes, enlisting the support of a *New Yorker* critic, that their status as essentially "narrative images" debarred Rockwell's works from "serious painting." The problem is that, here again, I cannot personally see these images as authentically "narrative." Morgan writes: "In *The Flirts*, a truck driver (an Oliver Hardy lookalike) picks the petals off a daisy as if to say 'She loves me, she loves me not', watched by his pal (a Stan Laurel lookalike), for the benefit of a blonde whose convertible has pulled up alongside the truck. A reflection in the side-view mirror of the truck indicates that this brief encounter is taking place at a red traffic light. This amounts to the integration of before/after or cause/effect relationships into the image. The narrative is, then, as follows: a truck driver who looks like Oliver Hardy, finding himself next to a pretty female driver at a red light, takes advantage of the situation and flirts with her."[21] At the risk of being repetitive, I believe it is not a narrative that we have here, merely a simple anecdotal situation. The red light is one feature of the situation, but it is not a narrative agent. There would be a narrative if the pretty driver followed the trucker into a milk bar.

Every situation has narrative potential. But that does not mean that it fits neatly into a precise and predetermined script; there is not one and one only *before* scenario, any more than one and one only *after* scenario, that can be deduced from it. A vertical strip by the cartoonist Bosc provides a perfect illustration of this limitation (fig. 3). It appeared in *Paris Match* in 1964 and offers a parody of Millet's famous work *The Angelus* (1857–1859). By disclosing the before and after of the painting, Bosc reveals that the brief pause observed by the farm-laboring couple when the village church bell rings merely interrupts their incessant quarreling.

The Angelus, a painting of very wide popular appeal, is generally regarded as a symbol of piety and reverent contemplation. In comparison with this traditional reading, Bosc's strip obviously has a transgressive dimension. The cartoonist develops an alternative scenario in which the saying of prayers is just a fleeting interlude in a life that seems to be otherwise dominated by aggression and conflict. But this axiological reversal, generated by what Christian Moncelet has called "a diegetic overflow"[22] into earlier and later time frames, is, after all, a perfectly admissible scenario, which neither infringes logic nor offends reason. It is, moreover, a scenario that uses humor to illustrate the fluidity of any situation, or, one might say, its fertile narrative potential. From this seed, different stories can germinate in the human mind, which never lacks in imagination.

Just as, between the beginning and the end of Mr Natural's meditation session (see below, p. 140–42), unexpected events occur that neither the character nor the reader could anticipate, so Bosc demonstrates that a situation can always be overturned or shown in an unexpected light by anyone who decides to have a little fun by expanding on the original.

Since 1999 *The New Yorker* has featured the "Cartoon Caption Contest," where readers are invited to invent a caption for a drawing. Prizes are awarded to several entries, which are then published. These captions make it possible to assess the extent to which the same visual starting point can be interpreted as quite different concrete situations. The caption (usually a line of dialogue attributed to

Fig. 3. Bosc, *La Dispute à L'Angélus*, 1964. © Estate of Bosc.

one of the characters) clearly fulfils its *anchoring function* here: it confers a single meaning onto an image that, without it, would remain open to multiple interpretations. There is no need to think in terms of a before and after—it is in the context of a simultaneous relationship among the elements of the situation that the nailing down of the meaning comes into play.

The meaning of a single image is not necessarily indeterminate (with or without a caption, cartoons have a meaning intended by the artist; the joke only works if all the readers interpret it in just that way), but it is unusual, exceptional even, for it to be possible, on the basis of a single image, to infer one—and only one—scenario once it is projected backwards or forwards in time.

Conversely, the hiatus between two consecutive images, in a sequential narrative, can be programmed so that all readers will necessarily reconstruct the virtual content of the narrative ellipsis in exactly the same way. Take the example, already cited in *Système 1*, 155, *System 1*, 131, of the arrival of the doctor on the eighth page of *Les Bijoux de la Castafiore* [The Castafiore Emerald].²³ Let us recall the scene: Haddock has fallen down the stairs. Tintin rushes over.

—"Nothing broken, I hope?"
—"No," replies the Captain. "Luckily not. Though I might easily have sprained something."

At that point, the unfortunate Captain feels a sudden sharp pain, making him cry out, and the following image shows the doctor giving his diagnosis.

—"It's a bad sprain . . . and you've pulled the ligaments."

Following Benoît Peeters, I used the expression *suturing function* to designate the way in which the word "sprain" builds a bridge between the two images. For the purpose of the argument that I am putting forward here, one thing should be emphasized: the unnecessary episodes that this repetition enables Hergé to omit (you have to imagine Tintin getting the Captain to sit down, looking the doctor's number up, calling him, waiting for him to arrive, showing him in, being there as he examines Haddock's ankle) constitute the only possible scenario. You do indeed *have to* imagine all that. I do not mean that these exact episodes, as they logically unfold, necessarily reach the conscious awareness of the reader, but rather that the reader, confronted with the need to explain the sudden presence of a new character—the doctor—who has been conjured up from nowhere, can do so only by reconstituting that particular scenario, and no other. This is because this transition corresponds to a stock sequence of events, or "script." We all know how these things would happen in everyday life in similar circumstances. So it is not just the repetition of the word "sprain," but the familiar, routine nature of the events that have been expunged that allows the narrative to "leap from one situation to another," in Peeters's term.

2.2 THE POETIC USES OF SEQUENTIALITY

Three general conclusions can be drawn from the observations above:

1. Some uncaptioned (silent) images only lend themselves to one reading and carry a perfectly clear and unequivocal meaning. In others the meaning is indeterminate, and only the addition of a verbal element reduces their polysemy.

2. Some images (whether or not they include text) are self-sufficient, in the sense that their meaning is intrinsic to them. This still applies when an image of this type is wrenched away from the context of the sequence; even in isolation, it would still be readily understood. In other cases, the secure semantic anchoring of the image is dependent on its placement in the sequence and can only be interpreted correctly if the reader takes account of what has come before and what goes after.

3. Some ellipses between two immediately consecutive images can only be closed up and interpreted in a single way: others represent a more open transition, whose meaning can remain suspended and indeterminate.

Classic comics, forced to submit to the imperialism of narration, were confined to explicit images and transitions (even if they did on occasion overuse captions that redundantly reaffirmed the meaning already obvious from the image) and most panels were self-sufficient. In contemporary comics, in contrast, there is an innovative current characterized by a poetics of reticence, ambiguity, and indeterminacy. Some authors prefer to stray off the narrow path of "narrative and nothing but." They are attracted to gray areas, images that are cut adrift, message-jamming strategies of all kinds, and, in general, create connections between panels that work through harmonies, resonances, correspondences, eschewing the kind of relationships that are immediately decodable in terms of narrative logic and meaning.

The anthology *Le Coup de grâce* [The Death Blow],[24] a collective work published in Brussels in 2006 by La Cinquième Couche, includes the following proclamation: "We long for startling transitions, improbable links, new kinds of narrative associations. We find conventional narrative functions boring and stifling." On the publisher's website (www.5c.be) the ambition that inspires the authors is described in more detail: they aim to invent "new proposals for narrative articulation" between the images. These transitions will not be "functional" but will operate on a poetic, visual, and formal level through likeness or metaphor . . . "Because meaning is not a matter of cause and effect leading up to narrative resolution. Because meaning does not lie in clarification."

These words summarize, in exemplary fashion, the historical situation as experienced by many young artists today. This conjuncture has produced heightened awareness that comic art is not ontologically destined only to perpetuate a canonical model dominated by the categories of narration and legibility, but that its constituent features—the association of text and image, the spatio-topical apparatus for the display of images—lend themselves to the exploration of new forms, new configurations, new ambitions.

(I will not dwell here on the fact that this opening-up of the medium should be interpreted, essentially, as one consequence of its—relative—legitimization as an artistic form, of the dialogue that the "ninth art" has begun to engage in with other areas of contemporary art, and of the fact that increasing numbers of comics artists have received art school training.)

This new kind of comic art disrupts the expectations and habits of readers of traditional comics;[25] it is, quite clearly, still awaiting a new readership. Its minority and economically marginal status qualifies it as experimental, but it would be more apt to describe it simply as *poetic*.

I have selected here, as a very convincing example of a poetic comic, an extract from the album published in 2003 by Ilan Manouach called *Les Lieux et les choses qui entouraient les gens, désormais* [The Places and the Things that Surrounded People, Henceforth], also published by La Cinquième Couche. A summary of this work would probably describe it as the story of a tiger that terrorizes a village. But is it really a story? It is not told in linear fashion. It is difficult to establish the chronology of what takes place, and the book seems to progress instead by a succession of variations around the theme, with numerous digressions and interludes. The text—which consists of snatches of dialogue and interventions from an anonymous narrator—is very sparing, disappearing for whole sequences, like the one from which the page reproduced here (fig. 4) is taken.

The title of this two-page sequence (of which the second is shown here), "The tiger walks through the empty streets," announces quite clearly that it will do nothing to move the action forward nor to propel the story towards anything resembling an outcome. The animal's aimless strolling produces narrative stasis. On the page that particularly interests us, the tiger stops for a moment in front

Fig. 4. Ilan Manouach, *Les Lieux et les choses qui entouraient les gens, désormais* (Brussels: La Cinquième Couche, 2003), p. 51. © La Cinquième couche.

of a house where a pregnant woman can be seen at a window; it exchanges an insistent look with her before continuing on its way.

Apart from this free-ranging exploration of the margins of the plot, what is extraordinary here is firstly the reduction of representational elements to those that are necessary for the intelligibility of the scene. There is no trace of street life, of the facade of this private house, or of the decor of the rooms where this woman lives. Objects and characters seem tenuous, fragile, always threatening to fade into the whiteness of the page (the outline of the tiger in the fifth image is barely visible). Manouach skillfully makes the panel frame border coincide with the uprights of the window. In the first four images, he creates a rhythmic and visual movement, as the shot/counter-shot effect interacts with the dialectic of closeness and distance. The placing (the siting) of each of these panels is dictated by a concern for graphic equilibrium, not by the need to align them into some causal chain of events.

It is not surprising to learn that Manouach is also a jazz musician. His comics are composed like a succession of tenuous sounds, melodic lines, breaks, syncopations, improvisations around a theme, riffs.

Following the example of work by Bertoyas, Coché, Duba, Fortemps, Goblet, or Killoffer—to name but a few French-language authors—*Les Lieux et les choses qui entouraient les gens, désormais* is a book in which the narrative framework is loosened in order to give free rein to these "new associations" among images demanded by poetic comics, and, in particular, the deployment of all kinds of seriality effects.

2.3 THE MODALITIES OF ICONIC SOLIDARITY

The explorations of new relationships among the images draws out the full meaning of the concept of iconic solidarity, a concept that encapsulates the ineluctable basis of any definition of comics (see *Système* 1, 22; *System* 1, 17). This "solidarity," permit me to remind you, inheres in this: the images are "visually and semantically over-determined by the fact of their coexistence *in praesentia*" (*Système* 1, 21, *System* 1, 18). By bringing into play the notions of *string, series,* and *sequence* (*Système* 1, 173, *System* 1, 146), I distinguished among several different regimes of solidarity, with the *sequence* corresponding to the most integrated level where the panels make up a narrative in the traditional sense of the term. It would seem that the preferred level at which poetic comics operate is that of the *series*: the images are "linked by a system of iconic, visual or semantic correspondences" that do not pertain directly to causality and are not under the sway of the logic of the action or the tyranny of the plot.

I judge it useful to introduce here a fresh distinction between the different modalities of the apparently simple state of coexistence *in praesentia*, of coexistence before the reader's eyes. There are four modalities.

From the synchronic point of view, co-presence takes the form of *spatial complementarity*: the page must be filled, the whole of the area made available for graphic inscription by the hyperframe must be occupied (even when the hyperframe is not actually drawn onto the page and so remains purely virtual). Just as a missing piece of a jigsaw leaves a very visible hole in the middle of the puzzle, so the comics page is a compartmentalized space that risks looking incomplete unless each of its sections contains an image.

From the diachronic point of view, that is to say before the eyes of a reader deciphering the page according to a predetermined protocol (an order), co-presence is firstly, prior to any semantic grasp, a matter of *perpetuation*. The flow of images, which catches the attention of the reader and vectorizes his/her eye movements, continues without interruption; it just keeps going. If this flow produces meaning, then its perpetuation sets up expectations. It promises new twists and indicates that the discursive activity of the images will follow its course until it reaches some kind of conclusion.

From the musical point of view, co-presence creates *rhythm*. I will return at more length to a discussion of the different rhythms engendered by the division of the page into a multiframe and by the dynamics that emerge from it.[26]

Finally, from the visual point of view, the solidarity of the images across the surface of the page marks out a *configuration*. This configuration (etymologically configurare = to give shape to) concerns both the positioning of the frames, which adjust to each other on the model of fractured bones knitting together, organizing themselves into the page layout,[27] and the distribution over the page of the iconic content of each panel, linked by effects of resonance, counterpoint, symmetry, extension, etc. The impact of the contents can potentially be aggregated, producing the kind of global image that Benoît Peeters refers to as a "tableau effect."

It is clear that the notion of iconic solidarity gains significantly in precision once it has been established that it comprises four modalities (spatial complementarity, perpetuation, rhythm, and configuration) and three regimes or degrees (string, series, sequence).

Spatial complementarity, perpetuation, and sequence are the key determinants of conventional narrative comics. Conversely, in poetic comics, it is rhythm, configuration, and seriality effects that are the most salient.

Given that it had been established that iconic solidarity, the founding principle of comics, presupposes the coexistence of a number of images *in praesentia*, it is reasonable to ask whether graphic narratives that proceed at a rhythm of one image per page (for example the novels of Frans Masereel or Lynd Ward composed out of woodcuts, Chinese *lianhuahuas*, Moebius and Jodorowsky's *Les Yeux du chat* [Cat's Eyes],[28] Sempé's *M. Lambert* [Mr Lambert], Martin Vaughn-James's *The Cage*,[29] or Vincent Perriot's *Entre-Deux* [In Between][30]) accord with the characteristics detailed above, and even whether they belong in the field of comics.

In works of this type, there are never more than two images visible to the reader at any one time, split across two pages—one on the left-hand and one on the right-hand page (although sometimes only the latter is used). The space within which iconic solidarity comes into play is less that of the page—a flat surface immediately accessible at a glance—than that of the book, a foliated space that must be discovered progressively. The dialogue among the images depends on the persistence of the memory of pages already turned. There is a stronger appeal to the "dialectic of repetition and difference"[31] (which Sempé resolves in a radical way by keeping the same "still image" throughout the book). The braiding effect that operates between spatially distant images can, as in the case of Vaughn-James, assume as much importance as the friction between adjacent images orchestrated by breakdown.

There is no compelling reason to ostracize these works and consider them as falling outside the domain of comics. They do, undoubtedly, exemplify a particular usage of the spatio-topical system, and indicate one of its limitations—the page can no longer be described as a multiframe. The page (or, more precisely, the available surface of the page, delineated by the hyperframe) coincides with the panel. But these whole-page panels, or "monoframes," still follow each other in a predetermined order and invite a reading. The main mechanisms for the production of meaning associated with graphic narratives are fully activated and operational.[32]

2.4 THE SHOWN, THE INTERVENED, THE SIGNIFIED

Let us return to Lessing for a moment. The German writer and critic may have defended the idea that painting should restrict its ambition to the representation, through bodies, of a single moment of an action, but he goes on to add:

> All bodies, however, exist not only in space but also in time. They continue, and, at any moment of their continuance, may assume a different appearance and stand in different relations. Every one of these momentary appearances and groupings was the result of a preceding, may become the cause of a following, and is therefore the center of a present action.[33]

It is difficult for us not to read retrospectively into these lines an appropriate description of the narrative mechanism of traditional comics. Comics of this type do indeed rely on a *narrative scheme*, one characteristic of which is its anthropocentrism, the priority it gives to the character, the agent of the action, to the extent that the panel appears to be a space that is tailor-made for him/her, his/her "natural habitat."[34] From one panel to the next, the main character is generally repeated, remaining the *center of the action*. The very progress of the action depends, however, on changes in the character's appearance and relationships. "Appearance" refers mainly to bodily posture and facial expression; "relationships" are interactions with other characters and with the surroundings. The nature of these relationships tends to be, in Van Lier's term, "intergestural" ("by analogy with "interlocutory").[35]

The discontinuity that is the basis of the language of comics forces the reader to make inferences in order to interpret each new image appropriately, that is to say to ensure that it correlates with the previous one and to the wider context of the whole text within which it occurs. This operation was described in *System 1* as the conversion of an *utterable* into an utterance, taking account of the fact that it is semantically determined not only by what went before it but also by what comes after it, and thus draws upon *three planes of meaning-production* (see *Système 1*, pp. 126–31, *System 1*, pp. 108–10).

I propose to complete this descriptive framework by introducing three new complementary notions: the *shown*, the *intervened*, and the *signified*.[36] Once the part played by the reader's cognitive activity in the construction of meaning is accepted, it follows that what can be read in the image does not necessarily coincide with what can be seen, and frequently exceeds it. I will henceforth call what can be seen what has been *shown*; and I would suggest that the (relative) complexity of the language of comics arises out of the fact that what is read sometimes needs to be thought of in terms of what has *intervened*, and other times in terms of what has been *signified*.

In traditional comics, the shown—that which the *monstrator*[37] displays to us—normally serves to convey what has intervened, that is to say whatever is supposed to have taken place between the preceding image and the one we are reading. The reader spontaneously converts the inter-iconic space into a temporal interval. S/he makes the supposition that succession in space (between two panels positioned one after the other) indicates succession in time. And this consecutive relationship is, in turn, equated with a causal relationship. *Post hoc, ergo propter hoc*. It would be interesting to determine how far this spontaneous intellectual schema is based on experiential learning and how far it arises out of an innate cognitive predisposition.

The time gap between two images can be very wide; this is the case of Hogarth's cycles of engravings, where each one represents a different stage in the life of the protagonist, whose entire "career" is recounted in six or eight images. But this gap can also be very narrow, as in the example of the verbal ping-pong between the two characters portrayed by Jason in the page reproduced on page (150). Or it can be indeterminate, as is the case between many of the images in "Mr. Natural's 719th Meditation" (see below, pages 140 to 142). And, occasionally, we have to suppose that it is non-existent, as in the case of the first four images on the page by Manouach reproduced above, which seem to dilate the same, single, significant moment. In each of these instances, it is left up to the reader to gauge, at least approximately, how much time has passed.

When consecutive images are part of a kind of "sequence shot" with a fixed frame, as in *Mr Natural*, or involve cutting between one fixed-frame series and another (shot/reverse shot) as in the extract from Jason's work, the temporal hiatus is immediately obvious (even if the reader has to conclude that the amount of time passed is indeterminate). Making sense of the hiatus becomes a more complicated if substantial changes occur between the iconic contents appearing in consecutive panels. When the action or the scene shown is transformed, its interpretation has to draw on at least one, and potentially three, new elements—most often, this entails either noticing a movement (the characters move, change their position, and this changes their appearance as well as the relationships between them) or deducing a whole script, that must have taken place between two disjointed images (like the arrival of the doctor in *Les Bijoux*), or, sometimes, identifying a change of location.

Out of these three elements, it is clear that the first two necessarily combine with a temporal factor (they specify how the interval between frames has been filled), while the third can either combine with it ("elsewhere, later . . .") or be substituted for it ("elsewhere, *meanwhile* . . .").

The notion of what has *intervened* only becomes meaningful if it supposed that time has passed. We are teleported to the aftermath of events, and we have to link this aftermath to what we have read before; in a perspective based on classic narrative logic, that is to say on a causally linked chain of events, the operation of reading consists of inferring, from what we can see, what occurrence(s) must have intervened. *Adventure* in English, like *aventure* in French, both come from the Latin *adventura*, itself derived from *advenire* and devised to designate, precisely, "things that must happen."[38]

I ask the reader to refer, once again, to the page by Jason (page 150). Between the panels containing the conversation that the little girl strikes up with the stranger, the *shown* consists of the alternation of close-ups, and the *intervened* is the same in each image, so crystal clear that the reader does not even need to make a mental representation of it: *s/he has heard what has just been said and has decided to keep the conversation going by speaking in his/her turn.* But the last panel on the page introduces a break. This is what is *shown*: the three characters taking part in the scene are featured together, having a meal. They are not talking. This is what has *intervened*: a script that, plausibly, can be reconstituted as follows: *the mother left the kitchen, announcing that the meal was ready, she put the dish on the table, they came and sat down, took a helping of food and began to eat.* I am spelling out at some length here a transition that poses no problem of interpretation only to underline the point that the *shown* presupposes the *intervened*, but that the two notions do not completely overlap.

Moreover, these two notions (*shown/intervened*) cannot adequately account for what happens in a modern (or more exactly, postmodern—I am not interested in going down that road now) comic like Chris Ware's *Jimmy Corrigan*,[39] or in a poetic comic like the one by Ilan Manouach. This is because the discursive activity of these comics cannot be reduced to a causal chain of events, and that is precisely the level at which the reader can identify what has *intervened*.

So, on one page of *Jimmy Corrigan* (see page 49), the reader can note three apparent contradictions among the different iconic contents that are shown. *Firstly*, Jimmy sometimes appears as an adult and at other times as a child; *secondly*, he sometimes converses with his mother face to face and at other times over the telephone; *thirdly*, the scene is set sometimes on a station platform and at other times in the hospital ward where the preceding pages had taken place (the hospital context now only alluded to by the inclusion of the bed-ridden patient visible in the bottom left corner and the white-coated doctor who appears in the small image against a brown background). Jimmy's posture and the verbal content of the page imply continuity in the sequence—there is no isotopic break. This apparent continuity renders the interpretation of incompatible data highly problematic. The reader can only resolve the paradox by separating out what belongs to "reality" and what belongs to the phantasmatic scenarios engendered by Jimmy's fertile and somewhat obsessive brain.

Let us consider only the two images on the top right-hand side of the page: Jimmy makes successive appearances, identically dressed and adopting the same posture, first as an adult and then as a child. If, on the basis of what we see, we try to work out what has *intervened*, we would be forced to conclude that Jimmy has suddenly and inexplicably got younger, about a quarter of a century younger, in fact. The reader quickly rejects this hypothesis as absurd and realizes that a different cognitive schema is necessary to understand what is happening in the gap between these two images. The blank space that separates them is in this case the locus not of a temporal and causal articulation, but of a transformation on the ideational level. Without warning, Chris Ware has shifted from an objective to a subjective regime.[40] That being the case, the *shown* no longer offers a means of understanding what has *intervened*, but, instead, what is *signified*. Jimmy's reverie had begun on the previous page, triggered by something the doctor had said:

"Where you should be right now is with your family."

Jimmy then hallucinates the unexpected apparition of his mother and imagines the two of them having a frank conversation that was never possible in reality. His unease makes him feel as if he is regressing, becoming as helpless and dependent as he was as a child—which is what the image conveys by representing him in his younger incarnation.

The scene is riddled with incoherences that can only be dispelled if the reader abandons the traditional mode of reading an *adventure* comic (in the etymological sense) in favor of a different reading protocol that goes beyond the simple production of logical inferences and positions itself from the outset against a much wider horizon of interpretation.

In modern or poetic comics, then, what is shown does not necessarily pertain only to the level of the action, but can bring two new categories into play: the subjectivity of the protagonists in all its varying forms (dream, emotion, fantasy, hallucination, projection, etc.) on the one hand, and/or, on the other hand, the deployment by the author of stylistic features such as analogy, metaphor, or allegory—or even graphic rhythmic and visual effects that exceed a strictly narrative intent.

To summarize, we need to have recourse to the notion of what is *signified* every time a reading based on the assumption of what has *intervened* leads to an aporia. But it is important to be aware that this is a quite different route to the determination of meaning. In fact, given that Chris Ware and his contemporaries are still telling us stories, they have not abandoned the terrain of the adventure story. They have simply made it more complex, transcended it, introduced polyphony into it, and interwoven it with other levels of discursive activity. The reader must, therefore, be open to and accepting of this heterogeneity of the discursive texture, and, when necessary, to employ a different kind of logic. Jacques Samson has very aptly observed that Ware's work calls for a "new reading competence": "reading becomes more like a deliberate act than a reflex activity. The reader must cooperate so that what is revealed [as if by photographic developing fluid] achieves maximum sharpness."[41]

To synthesize: the conversion of the *shown* into either the *intervened* or the *signified* represents the two concrete forms that can be taken by what I described in *System 1* as the conversion of the *utterable* constituted by the image into a meaning-bearing *utterance* (assuming the context of a sequential narrative where every image is interpreted in the light of those that have gone before). Of course, the difference between the intervened and the signified can be considered as only a matter of degree—the former is a simplified version of the latter. My claim is that, on the one hand, there is the classic type of comic that is guided by an ideal of legibility and that can be roughly described as belonging to the realm of the adventure story: saving exceptions, the meaning of each image is exhaustively accounted for by the evidence it displays of what has *intervened*. The reading process therefore does indeed approximate what Samson has called "a reflex activity." And on the other hand I am claiming that there is a type of comic whose composition is more sophisticated or which operates in a register that is more poetic than narrative: these comics can be identified precisely from the fact that the category of the *intervened* is no longer sufficient to account for what is happening. The "deliberate act" of reading has to become a work of interpretation in which the category of the *signified* comes into play.

The above reflections can be compared to those set out by Scott McCloud in *Understanding Comics*. McCloud defines comics as an art of "closure" and postulates that the reader is called upon to cooperate actively with the author in order to "read" the ellipses as indicative of time and movement. But, having stated this, he does not further interrogate the nature of this cooperation.[42] The six types of "panel-to-panel transitions" that he identifies do not lead to any distinction among modes of reading. When McCloud interrogates the nature of the link between two consecutive images, he is concerned only with the relationship they may or may not have with a common referent. Whether the transition is from "moment-to-moment," "action-to-action," "subject-to-subject," "scene-to-scene," "aspect-to-aspect," or whether it is a case of "non-sequitur," is, as he himself emphasizes, a matter of narrative technique, from which he ultimately draws few conclusions of any greater scope and which seems to have no relevance to artistic achievement.

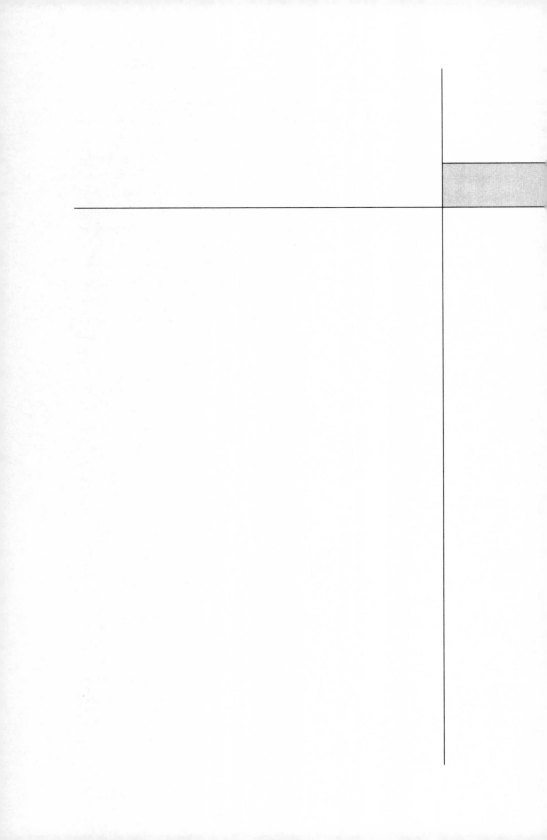

CHAPTER THREE

On a Few Theories of Page Layout

It was established in *System 1* that page layout is, along with breakdown, one of the two fundamental operations of the language of comics—it comes into force at the level of the panels, defining their surface area, their shape, and their placement on the page. In other words, it establishes the relative position and proportions of panels that are co-present on the same page and assigns compatible shapes to them.

Layout in comics has accommodated, and still does accommodate, many kinds of configuration. There is, nonetheless, an objective criterion that makes it possible to classify all existing and possible pages into two groups: frame regularity. It is, in fact, possible to make a distinction between regular layouts (where all the frames are identical; this is the model usually known in the Franco-Belgian context as the "waffle-iron") and all the others that, over and above their dissimilarities, have irregularity as a common feature.

3.1 DEGREES OF REGULARITY

We will see later[1] in what ways regularity or irregularity in the arrangement of frames is pertinent to the question of rhythm—the rhythm of narration and the rhythm of reading.

But it is important here to interrogate the criterion itself. There are in fact different degrees of regularity of page layout, and I should have made this clear in *System 1*. I propose to rectify that omission now.

A first element of regularity can be assessed at the level of the album as a whole: we need to know whether all the pages are divided into a preset and equal number of strips, established from the outset. When this is the case, the narrative is propelled onward by means of a kind of scrolling ribbon, maintaining a constant height (comparable to a film strip).

However, within this system based on three or four strips per page (these being the most frequent options in a book with a French-style format), there is no obligation for strips to be the same height as those above or below them. For example, In Christophe Blain's work, the height of the strips is not necessarily uniform: every page of *La Capitale* [The Capital][2] has three or four strips, but they are of uneven height. When strips do conform to a standard height—as in the case of Hergé—that constitutes a second degree of regularity.[3]

There is also a third degree of regularity that affects the panel. Within a strip of uniform height, panels can adapt to the content by narrowing or widening, or they can themselves maintain a uniform width. Only in the last case do the vertical and horizontal gutters meet at right angles, producing the orthogonal grid known as the *waffle-iron*. We need, then, to distinguish three levels, or degrees, of regularity.

The waffle-iron is itself a matrix that can be applied strictly (all the pages contain, say, nine or twelve images of an identical format) or more flexibly. Flexibility allows for the inclusion of larger images that are multiples of the standard frame size; the simple "elimination" of one vertical frame division produces an image that is twice as big; the elimination of two will produce a full-width panel,[4] but these multiples fit into the grid without disrupting its geometrical regularity or altering the dimensions of the matrix.

A further criterion for the critical appreciation of page layout needs to be introduced. This is *density*, alluded to above. By this I mean the variability in the number of panels that make up the page. It is obvious that a page composed of five panels will appear less dense (as potential reading matter) than a page that has three times as many.[5]

In this respect, it may be noted that the comics medium is ruled by fashion cycles. In 1970s French comics, density had considerably diminished, and six or seven panels per page was becoming the norm. We had entered an era of comics production in which the reading experience was increasingly being overwhelmed by spectacular effects—and the standard-bearer for this change was the magazine *Métal hurlant* [Heavy Metal].

In contrast many current young authors opt instead to confer increased density on their narratives—while remaining within the bounds of an album in the classic hard-cover 48- to 60-page format. Thus we have witnessed a strong revival of the four-strip page in, for example, the work of Larcenet, Blain, Tarquin, or Dumontheuil (in *Le Roi cassé* [The Broken King][6]), a standard format used in the past by Hergé, but that had been gradually marginalized in favor of the three-strip model, which had become ultra-dominant in recent decades. Nonetheless, several authors are running counter to this tendency by returning to the 1970s norm. For example, Loisel and Tripp, co-authors of *Magasin général* [General Store],[7] offer expansive layouts, favoring wide open spaces and emphasizing decors and atmospheres. The pages of *Face de Lune* [Moonface][8] drawn by Boucq contain an average of five panels. And Bilal holds the record for the lowest density with just four panels per page (on average) in *Le Sommeil du monstre* [The Sleep of the Monster].[9] Bilal compensates for the paucity of panels by offering an abundance of speech balloons and narrative voiceovers. These are driven out to the edge of the images, often invading the frames, the interframe space, and the margins, producing an effect of proliferation (considerably attenuated in the following album, *32 Décembre* [32 December]).[10]

The "graphic novel" format, smaller than the traditional French hard-cover album format, naturally tends to reduce the number of strips, which rarely exceed three.

One of the most marked tendencies in recent comics production is the increased frequency of full-width panels,[11] which could also be called "landscape panels,"[12] panels that extend across the whole page and so coincide with the strip. The next size up, the panel that occupies half a page, is also much in evidence. And there are numerous albums in which, every three or four pages, an oversized panel breaks up the rhythm of the layout, creating a small visual surprise, obviously intended to give extra pleasure to the reader.

Henceforth, most young authors lean toward a basic layout pattern, but use it unsystematically, constantly varying it. In several of his albums (for example *Le Minuscule Mousquetaire* [The Tiny Musketeer],[13] Joann Sfar alternates for no apparent reason pages with three strips and pages with four. I believe this practice is quite disruptive from the point of view of the reader. It suddenly breaks from a convention that has been perceived and recognized as a stable feature of the work, expected to be as immutable as the size of the screen during the projection of a film. I know that comics do have the "advantage" over film that the size of the "screen" can be instantly altered at any point. But the choice of either three or four strips is precisely the constant background against which these stylistic variations will become meaningful; it is this choice that gives the work its basic beat, its fundamental rhythm, which structures the narration.

Even more surprising than Sfar's sporadic impulses is an album like *Prosopopus* by Nicolas de Crécy,[14] which "changes gear" half way through, as if the author suddenly realized he was running out of space. Just over half of the album is dominated by the three-strip system that the artist habitually favors (apart from a few odd pages that have four strips), and then four strips becomes the rule in the last part of the book, with the exception of a few pages that increase the density of the narration still further by moving to five strips. The reader is continually disconcerted by these infringements of the principle of uniformity.

3.2 RHETORICAL USES

A reminder that, following Benoît Peeters,[15] I use the term *rhetorical* for the technique that molds the shape or size of the panel to the action that it encloses: a vertical frame for a lone, standing character, a wide frame for a crowd scene, and so on.

In relation to this rhetorical aim, I think that contemporary French comics production can be divided into three main schools. In order of increasing complexity, the first of these would consist of all the proponents of simple rhetoric (too numerous to mention, and, by definition, not displaying, in this respect, any salient feature making them worth singling out). This group are devotees of a second-degree regularity: the number and height of the strips is preset, and the only question to be resolved is the width of panels, all rectangular, which stretch or shrink according to the needs of the story. This school can be called classical, and the layout of the pages that typify it is discreet and non-ostentatious.

An author like Ceppi illustrates in exemplary fashion a slightly more sophisticated option, which I shall call *elaborated rhetoric*. This consists of multiplying, within a system based on three strips of varying heights, vertical stacks of two or sometimes three panels. This configuration does not breach the regularity of the outline of the strips, but it subdivides them lengthwise, thereby obtaining a smaller panel format that is suited, for example, to an exchange of dialogue between two characters facing each other. The horizontal vectorization that the strip, by its nature, promotes, is confounded here and, dialectically balanced, so to speak, by these small vertical syntagms that fit inside a tier of predetermined height, but which also constitute local infractions to the supposed linearity of the reading process. Within the strip, the alternation of vertical panels, horizontal panels, and stacks of this type continually break up this linearity. Ceppi takes on the mantle of Edgar P. Jacobs, whose layouts approached the intricacy of marquetry, part of a strategy (also evinced by the abundant texts) designed to detain the reader's gaze.[16]

Finally, a third school, perhaps influenced by manga, but mainly motivated by the desire to break with a classicism viewed as outdated, exacerbates the rhetorical intention, resulting in a new conception of the page that I have termed "neo-baroque."[17] New, because Philippe Druillet, back in the 1970s, had already inaugurated and exemplified, almost single-handedly, a baroque conception of the comics page, which was characterized by the breaking up of most of the panel frames in favor of the interpenetration of images, the abandonment of the canonical rectangular shape, the creation of an overall "tabular effect," the extension of certain compositions across a double page, and a magnification of the decors in relation to the characters, producing an effect of monumentality.

The "neo-baroque" permanently deploys a whole arsenal of unsystematic effects, allowing for some images to be highlighted and so to escape the monotony presumed to be the inevitable consequence of any form of regularity. This tendency pervades a considerable proportion of the output of publishers like Soleil or Delcourt to the point where it has become a kind of "trademark." The effects that the specialists of "neo-baroque" favor and indulge in at every possible opportunity are: the destructuring of the hyperframe by images that bleed off the edge of the page and intrusions into the gutter, the use of multiple insets, the maximization of the contrast between large background images and the inset panels, the vertical or horizontal elongation of panels (as if to achieve a shape as far removed from the square as possible), and the frequent stacking of very narrow horizontal panels, resulting in what I will later designate as *stanzas*.[18] It is as if the simple succession of panels was no longer deemed sufficient to ensure the production of meaning: the apparatus must become more sophisticated (or more hysterical) by piling special effect upon special effect, frames interwoven and overlapping to suggest various degrees of subordination, independence, contrast (I could go on . . .) among the images.

The prominence of the "neo-baroque" can be attributed to a generation that has turned its back on the ideals of simplicity and transparency that permeated classic Franco-Belgian comics, whose leading practitioners strove above all to tell a story as legibly as possible.

3.3 PAGE LAYOUT IN THE WORK OF CHRIS WARE

Chris Ware is one of the most celebrated authors of the last few years. It is appropriate to accord him special treatment here, given that layout is quite evidently one of the foundations of his poetics and one of the areas in which he has been particularly innovative.

However, even if the odd album here and there has taken him as a model, it does not seem that Ware has attracted any more imitators than a Crepax or a Toppi did in their day. This is probably because his inventions, like theirs, are too distinctive to be easily appropriated unobtrusively. They are his stylistic signature. Perhaps Ware's influence has taken, in the case of some authors, the more positive form of a "permission to innovate," an encouragement to imagine non-traditional layouts.

At the furthest possible remove from the "neo-baroque," Ware founds his conception of the page on geometric regularity, but escapes monotony by inventing configurations and constantly renewing them. The thickness of the panel borders further reinforces the internal structure of the pages, giving them an almost carceral appearance.

The graphic and architectonic dimension of the page is also emphasized by Ware's use of axonometric or isometric perspective for bird's-eye-view (high-angled) images in place of the conical perspective that artists have used since the Renaissance, the perspective that approximates most closely to what the eye sees. In Ware's panels the lines of flight do not converge and distances are extended in the same way in all three spatial directions, taking no account of the apparent reduction in the size of objects as their distance from the viewer increases.

The density ratio is particularly high on Chris Ware's pages. It is not unusual to find more than fifteen panels on one page of *Jimmy Corrigan*, despite the album's small format. This density arises out of the proliferation of extra-small panels. It is these that actually constitute the building blocks out of which the others are mathematically constructed. In fact, all Ware's images correspond to one of three or four standardized formats, and it is readily observable that they are perfect multiples of each other—a medium panel is equivalent to four small ones, a large panel is worth two medium-sized ones, etc. This is, then, a case of graduated regularity, or rather of nested regularity. The page appears to be structured by an orthogonal lattice, a tight grid, deployed in modular fashion. On closer inspection, however, it becomes clear that the dimensions of the basic cells in the grid can vary from one part of the page to another.

The geometric perfection of all the compartments of the multiframe has the effect of inscribing major horizontal axes across the page (the traditional divisions between strips), but also vertical axes that are just as imposing, partitioning the page from top to bottom. The habitual direction of reading, along a horizontal

Fig. 5. Chris Ware, *Jimmy Corrigan, The Smartest Kid on Earth* (New York: Pantheon Books, 2000), unpaginated. © Chris Ware.

linear axis, is confounded, or at least subjected to powerful tensions. Rather than resembling ribbons or friezes laid out one above the other, the page looks like a combination of quadrangular blocks. Any given large image constitutes a single block, any mosaic of four, six, eight or twelve small images together constitutes another.

The pages are structured around the large images. It is therefore not surprising that they occupy privileged sites on the page, which correspond with each other from one page to the next. Whether these sites are identical, symmetrical, or opposing across two or more pages, they are always likely to be overdetermined by braiding effects. The page reproduced in fig. 5 appears on a right-hand page in the album. It opens, top left, with a large panel that has a symmetrical correspondence to a panel of the same size that appears top right on the left-hand facing page.

Symmetry, in particular, is used by Ware to heighten the legibility of the binary oppositions that structure the spatio-temporal development of the story, such as interior/exterior, past/present, or day/night. But when two large images mirror each other on facing pages, this can also signify other oppositions or correspondences. For example, in the sequence where Jimmy is invited to the home of an Italian friend, two images enter into a dialectical relationship on the sole grounds of their locations on the page: on the left-hand page, the women are all in the kitchen, while on the right-hand page the men are in the workshop. This says everything about the position and role of the two sexes in the social order. In an earlier example, the death of the grandmother is marked by a large silent image of the death bed drawn from a high angle. The body lies with hands clasped, covered in flowers. In the corresponding position on the facing page, an image of the same size, similarly drawn from a high angle, shows a little girl who laughs as she runs around. Life and death could not be more clearly counterpoised: one existence has come to an end, another is just beginning.

No other author has offered such an illuminating demonstration of comics as a system in which the constituent elements, orchestrated together, work in such close solidarity and "are inter-regulated" one by another.[19] Nor has any other author founded his or her poetics so conspicuously on a reflective and original deployment of the spatio-topical architecture of the medium.

CHAPTER FOUR

An Extension of Some Theoretical Propositions

In *System 1*, I devoted myself at some length to the description and examination of the basic units of comics language: the balloon, the panel, the strip, and the page, analyzing how they are deployed and interact with each other; the actualization of these units in the spaces, frames and sites of the album makes up what I have proposed to call a spatio-topical system. When I drew out those observations, I claimed only that they applied to comics, more specifically to Western comics, and to comics appearing in the sole format that we were familiar with at that time, namely print.

The evolution of the medium, along with the fact that some of the concepts elaborated in *System 1* have been appropriated for the description of objects of study outside my original corpus, have led me to reflect on the limits of the field of application of the concepts I put forward back then. In this chapter, I will widen my investigation to include three specific areas I did not take account of in the previous book: children's comics, manga, (particularly *shōjo* manga), and interactive digital comics. Through a close investigation of these three new corpora, I will seek to identify what makes them distinctive, and to arrive at any new concepts that are necessary for their understanding; but it is highly likely that through their very differences, these new branches of graphic literature will shed new light on the "classic" comics that already have a complete descriptive framework. Implicit in this new endeavor is a reexamination of those classic comics, conducted from the margins and the borders.

4.1 ILLUSTRATED CHILDREN'S BOOKS

From a publishing perspective, the illustrated children's book sector is, in many countries (from France to South Korea), easily as dynamic as the comics sector, even if it is of lesser concern to theoreticians of the medium. As well as sharing the "album" label,[1] these books are similar to comics in that they tell a story by harnessing the power of both text and drawings; where they differ is in their slimmer pagination and lesser narrative breadth, which are adapted to their younger readership, and in the fact that they do not normally feature either the partitioning of space typical of comics (the division of the page into strips and strips into panels) or the integration of dialogue into the image by means of speech balloons.

These differences can sometimes be attenuated, as there is a certain permeability between the two areas. Some illustrated children's books could quite reasonably be called comics;[2] if they are not regarded as such, this is solely on account of their positioning by the publishing industry (inclusion in a children's series, on the list of a specialized children's publisher, and, consequently, in the children's section of bookstores). A book like *Rupert Bear*, in England, seems to fall into an intermediate category, characterized both by the sequential apparatus that typifies comics and by a dissociation between text and image that realigns it with the illustrated book. Moreover, it is possible to trace a lineage of first-rate artists—from Peter Newel and Tove Jansson right down to Dave McKean, Posy Simmonds and Richard McGuire—who have put their talents to use in both areas.[3] It should be acknowledged that the children's literature sector is artistically very rich, with a diversity of styles and graphic techniques that matches that of comics, as well as a great variety of formats.

The report entitled *Lire l'Album* [Reading Illustrated Children's Books][4] by Sophie Van der Linden, who for many years played a key role at the Institut Charles Perrault in Eaubonne in the Greater Parisian region, gives an excellent overview of the particularities of this sector of the publishing market. Van der Linden is kind enough to mention *The System of Comics* as an "influential guide" and to take on board some of its analyses concerning, for example, the functions of the frame. I note, however, a general convergence between her approach and mine, especially when she writes that critics should "take as their starting point the particularity of the work, and understand how it forms a coherent whole in which all the elements, combined together, are meaningful."[5]

With the aid of judicious borrowings from comics theory (Fresnault-Deruelle, McCloud, Morgan, and Peeters are also cited), Van der Linden sets out to show that "the illustrated children's book does indeed constitute a specific form of expression."[6] Even if special formats like animated books, object books, activity books, or picture books are left out, we can find examples of works that demonstrate real originality in their use of layout, in the sequencing of images, and in the relationship between text and image. I will summarize below her observations on these three aspects and include my own comments.

Van der Linden notes that the illustrated book "does not exhibit a regular layout that is immediately obvious, unlike a comic book."[7] Indeed, it is true that the pervasiveness of the "waffle-iron" model in comic art—whose varying degrees of regularity I have detailed above[8]—does not extend to illustrated children's books. This is particularly noteworthy, because it indicates a fundamental difference in the way that artists approach the blankness of their raw materials (the page or the book) and mentally project their visual ideas onto it. From the broadsheets known as *images d'Épinal* [popular prints from Épinal] to modern comics albums, via the Sunday newspaper pages from the beginning of the twentieth century, the regular page layout, with its strict geometry and its rhythmic scansion imposing a steady beat, extends through the history of comics like a canonical model. It constitutes a preferred response, an immediate formal resource, convenient, orderly, and remarkably efficient, to the initial gesture of appropriation of space at the stage of gridding,[9] and sets up a powerful matrix whose frames, as they generate and contain images, seem intrinsically likely to give rise to narration.

The illustrated children's book is an exception to this dominant model; it is, in contrast, consistently, and from the outset, the double page that constitutes the "elementary, preferred, unit of design."[10] Moreover, and Van der Linden perhaps does not give sufficient emphasis to this point, images that bleed to the edge of the page, and even panoramic images that encroach right across the central gutter to cover both pages, are extremely frequent. In the children's illustrated book, the artist's goal is to offer the reader, at the turn of each page, if not something spectacular then a visual thrill, a little pictorial excitement—at the very least the chance of absorption in the image and so a projection into the fantastical world of the fiction.

Each double page, endowed with a strong identity and coherence, is a moment of stasis that interrupts the story. This is why, when an adult reads an illustrated book to a child who listens to the story and looks at the pictures, the adult will often ask permission before turning the page to ensure that the child has covered every last detail and is steeped in its atmosphere.

Thus, children's book illustrators' main concern is not layout (in the sense defined by *System 1* as an arrangement and mutual adjustment of frames) but rather *composition* (*cum ponere*: to put more than one element together).

Van der Linden identifies three categories of image.[11] As part of a string of images, they are caught between contradictory tendencies towards "autonomy and dependency." The first category is that of the *isolated image*, which appears alone on a double page, whether covering its whole surface or with text on the facing page. By virtue of the autonomy of each double page, an image of this type is independent and does not interact, or interacts only faintly, with those that precede and follow it. Conversely, the second category is that of *sequential images*, which, as on a comics page, are juxtaposed iconically and semantically connected, unmistakable links in the chain of narrative discourse. There is also an intermediate category: *associated images*, which are "neither completely independent nor completely interdependent." In such cases it is often the text that takes the lead in carrying the narrative, even if a minimal "visual or semantic" continuity is apparent.

The author and illustrator Nicolas Bianco-Levrin, interviewed by Van der Linden,[12] makes the interesting observation that illustrated children's books and comics have, in general, a different way of "conveying time. In the illustrated book, it is the text as much as the image that will give indications about time. In comics, the time that has elapsed between two images is often determined by the action, and, most often, it is the image that carries temporal indicators." This observation can be compared with my own reflections about the shown and the intervened.[13]

In a discussion of the role of text in the illustrated book and its importance relative to the image, Van der Linden rightly notes that there is no set rule: "Every book opens either on text or image, and either can carry the narrative."[14] Text and image can, on a case-by-case basis, take on the status of *primary* or *secondary* narrating instance.

In material terms, the spatial distribution of text and image and how far they interlock is also highly variable.[15] They can remain separate if, on the model of the old-fashioned children's book, a page of text (often verso) and a page of images (often recto) alternate. The most frequently encountered layout is the one that Van der Linden calls "associative": at least one group of words and one image share the space of the page. In the case where there are several texts and images, the authors can opt for a compartmentalization similar to that of a comics page, although with a lesser density of panels; but the illustrated book is at its most distinctive when "texts and images are not partitioned off into reserved spaces [but] articulated into a global composition." Texts and images are thereby "intermingled," and their presentation "is based more on contiguity than on continuity."

The psychoanalyst Serge Tisseron, also the author of several essays on comics, has insisted on the reassuring aspect of the comics multiframe, with its "multiple containers," for the child reader. For Tisseron, a comic works to "contain and reassure," presenting itself to the child as "a privileged space where a psyche that has not yet become stabilized within its own boundaries can find confirmation and reinforcement."[16] Within this perspective, the much freer page configurations in numerous illustrated books, where frames are absent and indistinct spaces emerge from the co-presence of textual and iconic information whose reading order is often uncertain, must surely lack any such calming effect. But as far as I am aware, educationalists have not looked into the issue.

If some general notions like iconic solidarity, or arthrology (restricted and general) find a field of application in illustrated children's books, it is clear that this is not the case for other more specific operations described in *System 1*, which cannot be brought to bear on an area of literature encompassing such a disparate range of works. The tremendous freedom that creators of children's books enjoy brings out, by contrast, how rule-governed the sphere of comics is, showing it up, in fact, as a system.

Despite the differences between comics and children's books, certain areas of artistic inquiry are common to both—particularly the subordination of the image to the authority of the text. Claude Lapointe (born 1938), a highly renowned children's book illustrator who taught this discipline at the Strasbourg Art School, insisted in all his pronouncements on the particular properties of what he calls the *narrative image*, the image that has to "be subservient to the cause of the most effective transmission of the story." As well as requiring it to be accurate and precise, he long believed that this type of image should be "transparent": "no graphic or aesthetic 'effects', no interpretation. . . ." Subsequently, he modified his conception of the image, favoring one that was "more formally ambitious and offbeat, one that imparts a slight graphic or aesthetic *frisson*, an original idea. . . ." But he continued to lament the excessive valorization of illustrators with an "academic style" by critics and judging panels who paid little attention to "narrative criteria" (which stage of the action to represent, framing, distinctiveness of characters, accuracy of their gestures and expressions, etc.)."[17] Back in 1987 he was already contrasting the "communicative image" with the "expressive image." Lapointe, the illustrator of *La Guerre des boutons* [The War of the Buttons] and *L'Appel de la forêt* [The Call of the Wild], declared that communicative images, images that "tell a story," put their creator under the obligation of telling that story well and making it interesting. Their very legibility makes them more fragile, more vulnerable than gallery-hung paintings that benefit from the rarely disputed cultural indemnity afforded by the mastery of academic techniques and a wider thematic resonance.[18] Behind the polemical dimension of his words, there can be discerned a stance that both professes humility (in relation to the text), and at the same time vaunts his expertise, a stance that is typical of the illustrator, in the classic sense of the word.

One could cite the counter-example of a more modern tendency in children's illustrated books by author-artists who render into images not a preexisting text, but a story of their own invention, and who, while most probably valorizing the "mastery of academic techniques" mentioned by Lapointe, give priority to the image as the driver of the narrative.

Albums of this type are closer to the artist's book than to the traditional illustrated book. The Belgian artist Anne Herbauts represents this trend perfectly. Interestingly, alongside her books for children, she has published five comics albums,[19] all of which fall into the category I have called *poetic comics*.[20]

The contemporary comics field seems itself to be riven by the same tension between classic albums entirely subservient to demands of legibility and transparency and dedicated to the omnipotence of the narrative[21]—and a freer, more poetic current, comics whose images are charged with affect, that have the quality of an epiphany, a graphic event. We have seen that these comics are characterized by a variety of operations of articulation and association between images, neither directly narrative nor chronological. What they demonstrate is that without repudiating the spatio-topical apparatus of comics (multiframes divided into strips and panels), it is possible to introduce some play into the system and thus escape its rather normative and mechanical quality, and discover within its formal constraints a new freedom of expression.

4.2 MANGA

My comments regarding manga will be limited to page layout. In this respect as in many others, it is immediately clear that there is very great heterogeneity. Many manga, regardless of genre, are hardly distinguishable from Western comics in their page/panel layouts. This assertion would apply to at least half of the twenty-five artists who were the object of detailed analysis in my book *L'Univers des mangas* [The World of Manga][22] (particularly to Fujio-Fujiko, Mizuki, Ōtomo, Chiba, Taniguchi, or Tsuge). Other manga, in contrast, differ very clearly from the model familiar to us. This is the case of, among others, the robot stories of Gō Nagai and even of some of Tezuka's works, which seek to make the page more dynamic by replacing as many straight lines as possible by diagonals—or, in a different respect, by the manga of Hiroshi Hirata or Ryoichi Ikegami, whose images systematically bleed on at least one side, and sometimes on all four sides, scorning both hyperframe and margins.

There is no correlation between the originality of the theme and the exoticism or extravagance (to my European eyes) of the layout. So genres that have no equivalent in the West can be very conventional in their form; I am thinking, for example, of *EroGuro*, a cross between the erotico-grotesque and the extremely violent, a genre that is astonishing for the frankness of its bizarre, often terrifying fantasies. These are portrayed graphically, but the images are arranged on the page in a relatively (in the case of Suehiro Maruo) or absolutely (in many of the collections of Shintaro Kago) classical way.[23]

The type of manga that features the most unusual layouts, those that diverge the most emphatically from Western conventions, is without doubt *shōjo manga*, that is to say manga for teenage girls (usually drawn by women). Because it is precisely this divergence that interests me here, the following pages will focus exclusively on *shōjo*, and in particular on its most salient distinctive features.

According to Yukari Fujimoto, a specialist in *shōjo*, the first work to stand out, in terms of its page layout, was *Arashi o koete* [After the Storm] by Macoto Takahashi (a male author), which began publication in January 1958 in the magazine *Shōjo*. It is notable that this story introduced the stylistic device of a full-length image of the main character "above" the panels or in the side margins of the page. In *L'Univers des mangas*, I made the following comment: "This device seems to have the sole function of enabling the reader to take in all the details of the elegant costume, whether contemporary or traditional, designed to arouse her envy: the heroine, temporarily sidelined from the plot (which continues meanwhile, in the spaces that she leaves unoccupied), has become a fashion model." This technique—which, by analogy with fashion shows, I will call the *catwalk effect*—was widely imitated and spread rapidly through the whole range of magazines intended for a readership of teenage girls. Even if it has somewhat fallen out of favor, it has not completely disappeared; its historical accomplishment has been to liberate the layout of *shōjo* manga.

The aesthetic peculiar to *shōjo* was fairly well established as from the middle of the nineteen seventies through the work of female authors like Moto Hagio, Yumiko Ōshima, Keiko Takemiya, and Riyoko Ikeda. It varied, of course, according to the individual style of the artists, but it is striking to note the mass occurrence, almost to the point of institutionalization, of certain recurring features. Apart from the catwalk effect, these are:

- a tendency to elongate the panels, either lengthwise or widthwise, and to prefer long narrow frames to more balanced rectangles;

- the creation of dynamic tension between closed panels and others that either extend on one side to the edge of the page, or consist of an unframed drawing, in a spaced delimited by the borders of adjacent panels;

- a marked taste for small inset panels superimposed on a larger panel,[24] partially masking it, and often overlapping onto an adjacent panel; also frequent are a series of three or four panels in a row, making up a narrative syntagm (and what we will refer to below as a stanza) overlaid onto a large unframed or full-bleed image;

- a division of the page space into two kinds of zones: those (not always closed off) that contain images, and those left blank; the whiteness of the paper thereby comes into play between the images. It is no longer the "white nothingness" (as Henri Van Lier described it)[25] onto which is imprinted the compact multiframe that dominates Western comics, it becomes a background against which an irregular configuration of panels, scattered like an archipelago, stands out, a conspicuous void, a visual echo chamber where the images can resonate; it is also noteworthy that, in the same way, the words have a tendency to "float" in balloons with expansive outlines, providing them with their own echo chamber;

- sometimes, the page is prettified by decorative elements, intended to be romantic, like flowering branches, showers of stars or twists of hair, that substitute for the frame and surround an image or a whole page.

4.2.1 An Emotional Rhetoric

These seven elements of layout[26] work together with choices at the level of mise en scène and representation, including in particular very sketchy or almost absent decor (the character is often set against a black or white background) and a predilection for close-ups, a concentration on faces and eyes.

It is well known that the *shōjo* is less concerned with portraying an action than with creating an emotional climate in which the expression of feelings is uninhibited; the reader is constantly invited to scrutinize the heroine's face and to decipher from it—sometimes with the help of an internal monologue—evidence of the passions that ravage her heart and soul. It is for this reason that the eyes, "mirrors of the soul," are doubly highlighted, both by recurring close-ups on them (to the point where certain pages contain virtually nothing else) and by the graphic convention of enlarging them, transforming them into deep wells or blazing lamps.

This visual trope is also coupled with another, an emphasis on hair. In recent years, the characters usually sport unisex haircuts; locks of hair tumbling over the eyes and forming an unkempt mass around the face connote not a boy or a girl, but youth itself, wild and free—rebellious, romantic, and seething with powerful emotions.

The strangeness of *shōjo* for a Western reader resides in this dialectical—and paradoxical, according to our criteria—relationship between, on the one hand, minimally differentiated characters and very repetitive images and, on the other hand, a page layout that, in contrast, sets out to be inventive and constantly changing throughout the narrative. This conception of layout could not be further from the canonical model of the waffle-iron. The matrix-like dimension of the multiframe is therefore very much diminished in the *shōjo*, and the hyperframe is perforated, dismantled, or even completely renounced. The page is less a closed space that invites reading than a lower-density open space,[27] its emptiness allowing for the circulation of feelings, energy, dreams—a space that stirs up strong emotional involvement in the reader.

With the exception of the catwalk effect and the use of decorative elements, all the techniques described above are also found in manga for boys or adults, but in these cases (with the image taking up a whole page or a double page), their effect is to add emphasis, accentuate a dramatic moment, a sudden reversal, a rapid movement, or an outbreak of violence. This more sparing use makes them stand out as departures from the standard layout; whereas, in *shōjo*, these techniques are used without restraint and are combined together, resulting in pages where it is precisely irregularity and ostentation that become the norm.

This aesthetic has a cost: *shōjo* artists have few "special effects" left to call on, and it is more difficult for them to mark the high points in the story other than

Fig. 6. Miwa Ueda, *Peach Girl*, vol. 1 (Paris: Panini Comics, 2002), p. 21. © All rights reserved.

by ramping up the same dynamism-generating techniques that already pervade the work.

We note that most of the techniques typical of *shōjo* (with the exception of the catwalk effect, the ornamental motifs, and the heavy use of empty space) can be found in the work of French artists belonging to what I have called the "neo-baroque" school.[28] There is no doubt that in their desire to rejuvenate the Franco-Belgian tradition, these artists have drawn on the range of techniques already tried and tested by mangaka—as well as by the cartoonists who emerged onto the American comic book scene in the 1980s (Miller, Sienkiewicz, Chaykin, etc.).

Here is a page (fig. 6) from a *shōjo manga* originally published in 1998: *Peach Girl*, by Miwa Ueda. Although the layout is not especially frenetic, many of the techniques mentioned above are in evidence: the absence of a hyperframe delineating the page surround and separating the drawn surface from the margin; borderless images, the absence of decor, a heroine drawn full-length, facing the reader—the *catwalk effect* in its purest form; the use of a close-up (even if, on this occasion, the eyes are closed, expressing contentment, or indeed bliss).

In addition to these elements, our attention is captured by other formal parameters, which concern the frames and superimposition effects. In this particular case, two frames are discernable, but neither is closed: the top one is open along two edges of the page, while the horizontal rectangle that can be seen lower down not only exits from the page on the right-hand side, but seems to fade in to the white background.

Can a frame that is partially open and on the verge of dissolution still be called a frame? Certainly, insofar as it is still possible to attribute to it five out of the six functions conferred on the frame in *System 1*, that is to say the separating, rhythmic, structuring, expressive, and readability functions.[29] As regards the sixth function (which was first on my original list and in my own thought process), that of closure, it could be considered that it is still operative, if we allow that the edge of the page can act to segment and to frame, thereby collaborating with the part of the frame that is visibly drawn. We could then refer to a hybrid frame, consisting partly of ink lines and partly of a physical boundary. But in fact, the virtual impression that remains uppermost in the reader's mind, it seems to me, is more that of an escape to the outside world, an exit from the page (or, conversely, a frame introduced from the outside, which has forcibly encroached onto the territory of the page without completely entering it). This permeability of boundaries suggests that the fictional world can communicate with the world inhabited by the reader. Whereas the hyperframe habitually found in European comics implies a watertight division between reality and fiction—by assigning a tangible limit to the latter, the layout here seems to invite the reader to project herself into the unreal world of the heroine and to identify with her.

On this page the drawn sections of the frames have the effect of dividing the space into four vertically aligned zones (for only three images). The top zone focuses on Toji, the boy whom Adachi, the heroine, observes from a distance of a few meters, unbeknown to him. She is in love with him and has just heard him come to her defense against other boys. This is a subjective vision—we see Toji from Adachi's optical point of view. The second frame isolates the happiness on Adachi's face and encases her emotion. By containing this precious moment, it transforms it into an experience that is not merely evanescent; it both emphasizes and, symbolically, eternalizes it.

There is no action on this page. The images resonate against each other, diffracting a significant moment, a realization (Toji is interested in me, perhaps he will return my feelings if I declare them . . .), a sudden illumination that is materialized by the radiant sun in the middle of the page.

Benoît Peeters distinguished, the reader will recall, four conceptions of page layout. He used the term "rhetorical" to describe the instance where the panel "adapts its shape to the action portrayed," accentuating narrative effects. We are certainly dealing here with a layout conceived as rhetorical, with this one difference: where Western comics favor the rhetoric of action, *shōjo* is all about the rhetoric of emotion.

4.2.2 Multiframe and Multilayer

We now come to the final noteworthy aspect of this page, which is, again, typical of the general aesthetic of *shōjo*. I refer to the superimposition of different graphic elements. If we take the face represented in close-up on the bottom right-hand side of the page, we can see that, although it is incompletely drawn, the hair encroaches on the gray-colored sky that occupies the adjoining zone. The horizontal frame separates the two zones, but it is itself superimposed onto the drawing, especially the bottom line that runs level with Arachi's mouth and cuts her face in half. And the full-length drawing of Arachi is, in turn, superimposed over all four zones.

The Japanese critic Fusanosuke Natsume has analyzed this kind of arrangement as a multilayered page layout, a description that, interestingly, sounds not unlike the Photoshop stencil system. In the book *Manga no yomikata* [How to read Manga], Natsume puts forward a schema that decomposes the entire contents (iconic, graphic, textual) of a double page of another *shōjo manga* into three superimposed layers.[30]

To summarize Natsume, the notion of the *multilayer* is combined with, and sometimes substituted for, that of the *multiframe*. Depending on the examples chosen for analysis and the zones under consideration, prominence would be given either to the segmentation of space into clearly delimited contiguous zones (resulting in a framing effect) or to the penetration of space by means of superimpositions and encroachments that create the illusion of a staggering of elements from surface to depth (resulting in a layering effect).

According to another specialist in Japanese comics, Jaqueline Berndt, the technique of the catwalk effect can be analyzed as a particular instance of the inherent ambiguity of manga—many of them, she writes, "provide the readers with an enjoyable uncertainty as to whether the single panel or the whole page is to be treated as the main visual frame."[31] It can be seen how this "ambiguity" is articulated around the notion of the multilayer: the panel is the most prominent unit when it is the framing effect that prevails, while the page emerges as the "frame of reference" when it is the layering effect that stands out. But, personally, I would, here again, refer to the two dimensions as "under tension," adding to existing tensions alluded to above. It is the dialectical play between these alternative options that gives *shōjo manga* its particular dynamism.

4.3 DIGITAL COMICS

The writing of this essay coincides with a historical turning point. We are at a conjuncture in which the comics sphere has been forcefully challenged by the huge growth in digital comics online called webcomics (after the relative flop of earlier experiments with interactive comics on DVD). The computer screen, a new way for readers to access the ninth art, has given rise both to original creations and to adaptations (or simple transpositions) of existing print versions. Some publishers have chosen to develop their own platforms, but most sell the rights for the digital exploitation of all or part of their list to specialized sites, but in either case a major concern is the preemption of illegal digitalization, or piracy. As things stand at the moment, everyone is struggling to find a viable economic model that will preserve the legitimate interests of the authors—who, in France, are actively defending their cause.

It is clear that this book, which is steering a path between semiotics, aesthetics, and narratology, is not an appropriate forum in which to conduct a debate about the economic, legal, and commercial implications of digital comics, however pressing and legitimate these concerns may be. I will adopt a similar line to the small number of researchers who have begun to investigate the theoretical and artistic aspects of this ongoing technological revolution. The major question to be addressed seems to be whether tomorrow's interactive online comics can still be defined as comics, or whether—either because of their potential for radically new forms of expression or because of the changes they bring to the very experience of reading—we are witnessing the birth of a new medium. Attempting to assess the compatibility of the newly arrived digital formats with the theoretical framework set out in *System 1* will perhaps help us answer this question. That is the purpose of the next few pages.

We will begin with a reminder that over the last twenty years computers have gradually become omnipresent in comics production as a tool for creation, for transmission (the manuscript sent to the publisher is not a batch of originals but instead files sent electronically), and for preparation for publication (by means of a software package). A graphics palette, a scanner, and software for graphic design and coloring are now standard equipment for most artists. Whether the artists create their images on the screen or simply use it for arranging them on the comics page, or for introducing heterogeneous elements from various sources in among them or for coloring them, these applications can alter the surface features of the image, its visual qualities. But they do not inherently run counter to defining elements of the medium; notably, they neither affect the spatio-topical system nor the various operations of sequentiality.

From the theoretical point of view, the main change brought about by the use of digital tools is that the term "editing,"[32] whose usage in this context I denigrated in *System 1*,[33] is now fully justified as a description of the operations carried out on the screen by certain artists. I made the point that the operation referred to as "editing" in the vocabulary of cinema "is an operation that takes place after the filming and that is brought to bear on already existing material," whereas comic art is a matter of page layout, which "is usually devised at the same time as the drawings take shape on the paper," or even preexists them.[34] However, in January 1999 in a review of two albums published by Enki Bilal and by Yslaire,[35] I noted that both artists had broken with normal practice by first producing the whole set of images intended for inclusion in their respective albums as separate works, distinct and autonomous objects. After digitalization, at the next stage of the creative process, the images are assembled on the screen, and the texts are positioned. In this sense, it could be claimed that the era of editing in comics was inaugurated by these two works, along with a few others.[36]

In the case of any work created or edited on the screen, the disappearance of the emblematic object known as the "original" obviously poses the problem of the future conservation and management of the comics heritage. What will comics archives consist of? Can a gallery collect computer files? What will be left for it to exhibit in times to come? Almost certainly there will no longer be paper originals (or there will be paper versions that have been digitally printed), but, for some works at least, only disparate, autonomous panels, "source images." This is exactly how Bilal proceeded when he exhibited ninety-nine images in a Paris gallery, framed like artworks, to accompany the launch of *Le Sommeil du monstre*. Since then, he has maintained this strategy, which has opened wide the doors of the art world to him. The autonomous images, "uncontaminated" by speech balloons and extricated from the narrative flow, secure admission into an art gallery; once edited into comics format, their status changes and they take up their place on a publisher's list.

Back in 1996, Schuiten and Peeters wrote:

For a computer-generated work, the notion of the original makes no sense. [. . .] In one way, the digital revolution signals both the end of the "era of mechanical reproduction" described by Walter Benjamin and its apotheosis. One of the innovations brought in by digitalization is the effective abolition of the very idea of reproduction. However many generations of successive copies are produced, the quality of the data remains unaffected. [. . .] The final glimmerings of the aura have been extinguished.[37]

Having established itself as an indispensable aid to artistic creation, the computer—and more generally the digital screen in its various formats and functions—seems well on the way to becoming a new channel through which the public can access works of art. This phenomenon is usually referred to as a change of platform. This term makes sense if the change is measured in relation to what was done previously. But in the case of a work largely created on a computer, the fact that the computer should then be used to deliver it is, on the contrary, a mark of continuity. We used to have comics produced on paper and printed on paper, and we are now entering an era where digital technologies can come into play both at the initial stage of the work, its conception, and at the final stage, its distribution.

4.3.1 The Experience of Reading from a Computer Screen

How does reading from a screen differ from reading from the printed page? It entails the loss of a very strong, affectively charged object relation: the physical handling of the book, which involves both arms, or even the entire upper body, is replaced by intermittent pressure on the mouse from the reader's index finger. There is certainly a loss, in relation to motivity, participation, tactile (and occasionally olfactory) sensations, and even interactivity. "The book," as the publisher Pierre Marchand pointed out not long ago, "is also a wonderful interactive object, which can be leafed through, handled and read from front to back or back to front."[38]

Programmers seem, moreover, to be very aware of this loss and of the attachment of readers to the book as an object that can be picked up; after all, have they not invented interfaces that imitate the flipping of "pages" that appear to be lifted and turned over?

However convenient the reading experience that it offers, the computer screen is not a "new book-object" because it has none of the qualities of that object. The iPad-style tablet, that new "reading machine," or the cell phone certainly qualify as objects that can be manipulated, but in terms of their ergonomic features they are fundamentally different from books.

The preceding observations were worthy of mention, given their importance, but they do not of course have any claim to originality. What is more crucial is the idea of self-containment in relation to a work. Reading a book in print format is an all-absorbing activity that cannot accommodate any other parallel or subsidiary activity, with the possible exception of listening to music *in the background*. This does not apply to reading on the web, where one is never more than a few clicks away from any other site, and so, inevitably, permanently tempted by the attractions of digressing, surfing, zapping. Indeed, the younger generation, who have grown up as digital natives, have developed a way of using computers that is not monofunctional but plurifunctional—they consult a site while simultaneously listening to music and visiting their friends via electronic messaging, social media, or chat rooms. In short, they are well-trained in multitasking.

What disappears along with the self-containment of the work is the spatial memory that was associated with it. This type of memory is extremely active in the case of comics, where every panel occupies a specific site, not only on the page but also in the book.[39] A printed comic can be perceived as a collection of images spread out across the page, arranged according to a positional logic that is easy for the memory to retrieve. Apart from the fact that digital media are characterized by the removal of content from a surrounding context, when a comic is read on the screen, as each page succeeds the next it also replaces and effaces it, precluding the mental retention of the arrangement of panels.

For all these reasons,[40] it is tempting to conclude that the screen lends itself less to a *reading* of comics, in the full meaning of the word, than to a *consultation*. Numerous commentators have already made the point that screen-based reading is less well suited to large-scale works like *War and Peace* or *À la recherche du temps perdu* [In Search of Lost Time]. Similarly, one may find it practical to read an ordinary thirty-page comic book on a computer or tablet screen[41] but be much less inclined to embark on a screen-based encounter with comics that require lengthy immersion such as *Maus, From Hell, Cages,* or *Jimmy Corrigan* (not to mention the eye strain from prolonged viewing of a light-emitting screen).[42]

There is no longer only one type of screen. The "landscape" aspect ratio of the computer screen allows for the display of a double comics page; the comic can also be navigated half a page at a time, with a format that appears enlarged in comparison to its print version. The cell phone screen, in contrast, which is much smaller, can only display one panel at a time. But not all pages can be so easily divided across the middle into two equal halves, and not all panels necessarily fit into a rectangular format that approximately corresponds to the shape of the cell phone screen. The web publishing of a comic originally intended to be read on the printed page can, then, prove to be inadequate and damaging to the format of the work by forcing it to fit into a frame of arbitrary size and shape that bears no relation to its original proportions.

As long as the principle of the page is maintained, all the relationships of juxtaposition, organization, and mutual adjustment that it entails, and all the effects of dialogue, braiding, and seriality among panels are also safeguarded, and the comic is still displayed within its own spatio-topical system. In contrast, when it is displayed panel by panel this edifice falls apart, the images are deterritorialized, and all the linking threads woven across the surface of the page are masked or destroyed. There are a number of different display modes (rate of scrolling, use of fade-in fade-out or not, static, or with slide show from one image to the next—the "mobile window" can be dragged across the page—with the possibility of exploring the image zone by zone, etc.), which can be optimized to varying degrees (the rhythm may be imposed or under the control of the reader, and additional functionality may allow for going backwards or zooming in). Whatever the exact form taken by this "cinematic reading," the result will always be a hybrid, not to say a mongrel medium. It resembles cinema in that consecutive images are revealed one by one on a screen with fixed dimensions; however, the text is still usually accessed through speech balloons rather than through sound, and the scrolling does not bring persistence of vision into play, or even elementary animation techniques.

As far as I can judge, the appeal of web-based delivery of comics[43] depends on factors such as portability (I can read a comic on my cell phone wherever I am), cost (the cost of a digital download is significantly cheaper than that of a print version), the impression of receiving a kind of "home delivery," the sense of security that comes with the subscription (not only the impossibility of missing any episodes, but the privilege of being among the first to see them)—acknowledging the almost magical allure the luminous screen seems to hold for some, just because it is a screen, and this applies to any screen: the computer screen, the cell phone screen, just like the television screen before them. All these factors can explain the growing popularity of webcomics (although it is too early to say whether it will last), but, as we have seen, none of the factors actually enhances or enriches the work itself. For the informed reader attached to the linguistic and aesthetic properties of comics, a sense of depletion and deterioration must logically be uppermost.

For publishers, in contrast, the digitalization of their back catalogue offers the hope of new financial gain. It fits with the cross-media strategy that currently obsesses the leisure industry—in other words, how to maximize the commercial potential of a work (although the word used is "product") by licensing it for exploitation across different platforms.

4.3.2 Hypermedia and Immersion Fantasy

So far we have only concerned ourselves with comics designed for print media and subsequently made available online. Digitalized rather than digital comics, then. We must now come to digital comics in the strict sense of the word: comics originally conceived for cyberspace. Everyone interested in the issue has concluded that computers offer two new kinds of potential to comics: the access to multimedia content and interactivity. Comics is thereby redefined as an interactive hypermedium, orchestrating heterogeneous elements (text, still image, moving image, sound) and transforming the reader into an active user, a "readeragent"[44] according to the neologism coined by Anthony Rageul.[45]

As Pierre Fresnault-Deruelle's very accurate definition states, print-medium comics are polysemiotic, in that they bring together text and image, but mono-sensory, calling upon sight only. Comics designed for digital media can benefit from a wider semiotic range—they are plurisensory once they involve sound, and they can, in addition, be interactive.

While the screen-based delivery of a comic conceived for a print medium is most often assumed to imply *deterioration* of the work, one could make the assumption that, in the case of a work designed to exploit the potential of multimedia, the deployment of sound and motion represents an enrichment, an *enhancement*. But the reality is perhaps not so simple, and we should look more closely before deciding whether the addition of sound and motion really is a plus. And we should begin by realizing that this interpretation rests on an implicit ideological view of art, based on the assumption that certain media are handicapped at birth by built-in imperfections, but that, thanks to technological progress, they can eventually overcome their limitations. We seem to have hit upon two fallacies, rightly identified by Harry Morgan: "the evolutionist fallacy, which consists of describing the history of the medium as a series of obstacles overcome, or as uninterrupted progress, and the teleological fallacy, often associated with the evolutionist fallacy, which consists of writing the history of the medium retrospectively, as a process of gradual approximation towards the perfection of its current form."[46]

A historical comparison can be illuminating. Even if photography and film are both derived from the same principle of the capturing of reality via the action of light on a sensitive surface, the arrival of cinema cannot be described as an enrichment of photography by the addition of motion: photography remained what it was, and cinema took up its own place, a new place, in the media landscape. On the other hand, the transition from silent film to talkies (*The Jazz Singer*, 1927) can undoubtedly be considered as a crucial enhancement and even as the achievement of the potential of cinema as a medium. The objective of capturing the spectacle of human activity in its entirety, and of giving the spectator the illusion of enjoying reality itself, implied from the outset the incorporation of sound recording into the project. It simply took some time to resolve the main technical problem, the synchronization of sound and image. It is also worth noting that sound did not detract from the image, it did not take away any of its prerogatives or counteract any of its specific dimensions (framing, camera movements, editing, etc.).

It is important to be aware of the fact that all means of expression are per-fectly capable of "immersing" their audience, of involving them in a story to the point of attributing a kind of virtual reality to fictional characters and made-up situations. In this respect, the novel form suffers from no deficit, despite its reli-ance on words alone (the tradition of illustrated literary texts, very fashionable in the nineteenth century, has, moreover, fallen out of use, except in children's literature). Comics suffer from no deficit either: the reader will readily imagine him/herself riding alongside Blueberry, flying through the air with Astro Boy, or climbing up a skyscraper with Spider-Man. If this was not the case, if the com-ics medium was inherently impoverished, incomplete, or deficient, is it credible that it would have survived the arrival of cinema, television, sound recording, and the internet, and that it would still be manifesting so much very obvious vitality, relevance, and popularity?

There is, then, no need to "bring comics to life," since it is an art form that is already complete. Any reader looking at a comics page will imaginatively com-pensate, easily and spontaneously, for the absence of real motion or sound.

McCloud goes further and sees a contradiction between motion and sound, which represents "time through time,"—and the comics multiframe, which rep-resents time through space. In McCloud's view, in this cohabitation comics' "multi-image structure [. . .] becomes superfluous, if not a nuisance."[47] I would not formulate the issue in exactly these terms, since there can be complemen-tarity rather than opposition between time and space. The contradiction lies instead between two types of temporality: the concrete, measurable time of mo-tion and sound, and the indefinite, abstract time of comics narration. Comics readers generally set their own rhythm, with no constraints; as soon as they have to make allowances for the exact length of an animated image or sound, the reading process must be synchronized with these additional factors, and read-ers' freedom is sacrificed—or else this synchronization may already have been programmed by the author, who therefore also imposes the rhythm at which the images scroll.

One remark in passing: when synchronization is left to the reader (who clicks to activate sound or animation), the sounds that punctuate the narration tend to be short and sharp (the noise of a fall, a shout, a gunshot); when sound, im-age, and motion have been pre-synchronized, lengthy musical accompaniments often determine the rhythmic shape.

Should we go as far as to argue, with Magali Boudissa, that "there is a fun-damental narrative incompatibility between motion and sound, both temporal objects, and the spatial nature of comics"?[48] Must the introduction of motion and sound necessarily come at the cost of a "regression in terms of representation?"[49]

This much is certain: in print-based comics, the two components that come into play, the text and the image, enter into an intimate, almost fusional relationship. We know that the seasoned reader never asks the question posed by the adult newcomer: "What should I look at first?" The experienced reader moves between text and image fluidly and unconsciously, bouncing one off the other. Once motion and sound are thrown into the mix, it becomes much harder to achieve this perfect degree of integration: often, they remain disparate elements, aggregated but not fused, unsystematic.

Multimedia comics (sometimes called "motion comics") seek to immerse the reader more completely in the fictional world. But, apart from the fact that this is a wholly unnecessary, not to say absurd, undertaking for the reasons set out above, it manages only to evoke a kind of "virtual reality" that it fails to bring into being. When McCloud writes that, in this respect, "the art of film already does a better job than any tricked-up comic can,"[50] we have to understand this "better" not in the sense that comics (any more than the novel) is not a completely satisfying art form in its own right, but in the sense that motion and sound are an integral part of the cinematic work, whereas, in the case of comics, they will never be more than add-ons. (The concept of "customization"[51] is not really appropriate here because "to customize" means to personalize a standard product; for the reader, a comic "enhanced" by sound and motion is in no way customized. Instead these add-ons tend to curb the reader's imagination and, in any case, to impose an extraneous rhythm on the reading process.)

Given all this, it is reasonable to agree with Boudissa that the deployment of multimedia resources does not really work to the advantage of comics and that, rather than strengthening the hold of the fictional world, their effect is to destabilize that world[52] or to transform it into something else.

As Anthony Rageul points out, the introduction of sound and motion poses the problem of the right dosage, the correct ration—with the twin hazards of overdoing it or undercooking it:

A comic that flirts with animation is faced with two options: it can either settle for being a glorified slide show, or it can make every single element move, and end up by turning into an animated cartoon.[53]

The hypermedia graphic narrative as such seems, then, condemned to remain a hybrid form, unsatisfactory from the reader's perspective and characterized only by a trivial "surface playability."[54] But what happens if real interactivity is added?

4.3.3 Interactivity, the Gateway to the Gaming World

We have reaffirmed above the important truth that the book is already, in its own way, an interactive object. It becomes so in a still more obvious way when it has a format that enables physical manipulation by the reader. One example would be books whose pages are cut into horizontal strips that invite the reader to re-combine them into a vast number of new texts (as in Raymond Queneau's *Cent mille milliards de poèmes* [Hundred Thousand Billion Poems], 1961) or images (as in Edmond-François Calvo's *Anatomies anatomiques* [Anatomical Anatomies], 1945). Another is the Oubapo concept, based on refolding or turning upside down. We can also add, for the record, postcards, birthday cards, and advertise-ments from the beginning of the twentieth century with drawings that included an invisible element that appeared only when the card was held in front of a heat or light source (usually revealing the answer to some question set on the card).

Interactivity—in the sense of physical manipulation—is, then, nothing new in itself. However, with the advent of digitalization it has taken on manifold new forms. We will list some of these. The first is scrolling, in the sense that this requires the user to click or to use a scroll bar. (I will note in passing that the fact that a strip, or string of images, scrolls vertically—on the model of a page unfurl-ing—rather than horizontally makes little difference. Japanese newspaper com-ics have always been set out as vertical strips, known as *yon koma manga*, in the style of *Sazae-san*.) Interactivity is far more pronounced if the user has to choose among several pathways. I will return to this point.

There is a second procedure, which is the possibility of zooming in on an im-age. It is rarely used for narrative purposes, such as making a tiny detail visible. It works more like a magnifying glass, enabling the drawing to be seen on a larger scale and homing in on the graphic line. But the zoom presupposes a prolonged pause over an image and so breaks the rhythm of reading. In this sense, immer-sion in the drawing and immersion in the fictional world seem to enter into contradiction.

One form of interactivity allows a new element to appear in the visual field with a single click—an additional panel (or several panels), an object, a character, a graphic motif, or a speech balloon. This effect is not a feature of print comics, except at the turn of the page. Once the spread is opened, the entire contents are displayed simultaneously. The interactivity of digital comics allows for the emer-gence, at a given moment, of an element that had been masked, playing on the effect of discovery or surprise. The result is a certain modification of the visual field, which therefore occurs in the form of successive states, to be read on the mode of before and after.

In this respect, one possibility that has as yet rarely been exploited consists of offering access to alternative versions of each image (or certain images). Thus the reader could elect to see the same panel in color, black and white, or even in draft form. The artist's work can be viewed at a still-earlier stage if a click gives access to an archive photograph or document that was a source of inspiration. This allows for the possibility of a critical edition, hidden within the work itself.

The most significant mechanism is, undoubtedly, multipath storytelling that requires the user to choose among different pathways for the story to progress. S/he must, at almost every step, decide whether to go left or right, to follow one narrative thread rather than another, whether the hero catches his plane or misses it, whether the villain is killed or just arrested, and so on. Following the craze for *Choose your own Adventure* books,[55] there were attempts to apply a similar format to print comics ("if you choose this option, turn to page XX") with little success. The principle works much better online.

Multipath storytelling necessarily negates the notion of the page. On a page, the only available reading path is from point A to point B. The introduction of plurilinearity, that is of trajectories that intersect, frees the operation of breakdown from the close interaction that it normally maintains with page layout.[56] The whole organizational logic of the spatio-topical system is upset, apart from those parts of the system concerned with the properties of the panel and its frame.

In practice, plurilinearity can take two different forms. The first consists of the choice between two links opening two different narrative possibilities. The one to appear on the screen will be the one that the user has clicked on.

The other possibility is the "infinite canvas," or at least the network that is multiply extended in different directions. All these potential narrative tracks are co-present and simultaneously displayed, like highways crisscrossing on a map, collectively tracing out a spatial configuration on the mode of the rhizome, going way beyond the limited format of the page. By choosing to follow one or other pathway, the web reader uses the screen like a moving frame, a mobile windowing system that gradually reveals, as it moves, new twists and turns and, in some cases, new forks in the road.

Even if one believes this possibility is indeed potentially one of the most fruitful, it is nonetheless surprising to see McCloud, having formulated severe reservations about most of the other specific features of digital comics, getting suddenly excited about a type of comics "that can take virtually any size and shape."[57] As if, in the closing pages of his essay, he had discovered the Holy Grail, McCloud finds in this "essential" technological development nothing less than the possibility of "reinventing comics!" This U-turn can perhaps be explained, as Rageul judiciously observes, by the fact that McCloud seems to have a nostalgic attachment to an "original form" of comics—for a time when adjacent images followed on one after another in an unbroken line on the model of Trajan's Column or the Bayeux Tapestry. This linear model, this ideal reading path, was, he claims, broken down by the invention of printing. We have had to learn to live with the comic book where the comics narrative becomes "a landscape of tiny cul-de-sacs, asking readers to adapt to new paths every few panels based on a complex protocol."[58]

I do not believe that the comics reader feels driven into a cul-de-sac at the end of every strip, and it seems to me that the book is a model that has over many years demonstrated its effectiveness, including the comic book. In *System 1* I myself described the infinite ribbon of images as an "ideal form," but, on the one hand, I was putting myself in the place of the author (who has to accommodate to the page from the earliest stage of conception of the work), not of the reader, and—on the other hand, I noted that if the organization of the page is subordinated to an "architectural design," then "material constraints can help to engender an artistic success."[59] Theories of page layout, in which most French-language theoreticians (Fresnault-Deruelle, Peeters, Baetens and Lefèvre, Smolderen, Chavanne, and myself) have taken a close interest, seek to conceptualize the various possible creative uses of this constraining format. It is striking to see that McCloud, in *Understanding Comics*, takes scant interest in the page as a unit whose format is perfectly suited to the capacity of the human eye, which can form an overall impression of its relationships of composition and proportion from a comfortable reading distance of thirty centimeters. This is, in fact, the major blind spot of his theory. It then becomes easier to understand why he greets the advent of the potentially infinite canvas as liberating.

Interactivity can take other forms, and Rageul's comic *Prise de tête* offers a kind of catalogue of the most inventive of these. In this case, the narration remains linear, with the result that the interactive narrative cannot be described as hypertextual. But, as the chapters go on, the participation asked of the "readeragent" becomes more and more substantial. The images slide, overlap, metamorphose, while the frames move, separately or in concert, by means of various simple but ingenious techniques. The problem posed by this work is that interaction and reading are two different modes of attention, and they soon begin to compete with each other. Not only, as Boudissa notes, can "the search for screen hotspots turn out to be tedious" (and the search for the type of action to be taken: should the user click on the image, and if so where, exactly, or should s/he hover over it with the cursor, drag it, use the horizontal and vertical scroll bars, and so on; at every step the "user's manual" has to be reinvented), but, conversely, the story can be pushed into the background by the pleasure of navigating. The reader no longer asks "What happens next" or "How is this story going to end," but "What new actions will I be asked to perform?" It is no longer clear whether the author has set out to tell a story or to display the entire contents of a box of tricks. Rageul declares that what he "is precisely trying to do, is to produce meaning not just from the story being presented, but also from the interactive mechanisms" that each bring "an additional layer of meaning" and "play a full role in the construction of meaning."[60] What he fails to see is that there comes a moment when this meaning no longer has much importance, because the experience undergone by the "readeragent" is less like reading than playing a game.

Rageul defends the principle of game-playing. He describes *Prise de tête* as a "playable comic" and quotes Jean-Louis Boissier: "What is interesting in a game is the idea of practice, the performative dimension."[61] But the "schizophrenia" that he invites from the readeragent, half reader, half agent, is an unstable state that is not necessarily pleasurable, and the constant "disconnects" that interrupt the activity of reading not only create a "distancing effect" from it, they can actually prove fatal to it.[62]

4.3.4 More Than a New Medium, a New Culture

Interactive digital comics present a wide-open range of possibilities, far from exhausted by the reflections above—they will continue to evolve as the technology advances. The field is too vast for it to be referred to as a "genre," still less as an autonomous medium. Digital comics are intrinsically hybrid, cross-fertilizing the comics system with elements borrowed from animated cartoons, video games, computer technology (mouse, keyboard), and web navigation. Given that everything can be digitalized and that any content can be distributed via the internet, the digital environment is by definition a site for exchanging, mixing together, and perpetually reconfiguring. The codes that comics are founded on, because they have a kind of all-purpose productivity that makes then readily appropriable, or misappropriable, are available as ingredients. However, the transformation of the ninth art into a hypermedium seems to run counter to one of its founding principles, which is the simultaneous display, and, therefore, immediate accessibility of its component parts. The mechanism that allows for the *sudden appearance* of a new element, mentioned above, quite obviously contradicts this, and seems likely to open up new possibilities. But these are above all different kinds of *effect*, and so operate through a logic that is more akin to film, where the image perpetually emerges anew.

Comic art is fundamentally a form of literature in which nothing is hidden, which can be possessed in its entirety, with nothing left out—the reader can discover it simply by leafing through it, can browse over its surface without obliterating what has gone before, and while glancing ahead to what comes next. A hypermedium, with its complex procedures for revealing new material in stages and its forked pathways, deprives comic art of its qualities of transparency and immediacy, which, for me, are bound up with the very particular pleasure it induces.

I do not deny that my sensitivities concerning digital comics, and, therefore, the general tenor of my reflections, are "idiosyncratic," partly because I belong to a generation whose love for comics was indistinguishable from a love for the stories that they told. For readers of my age, reading comics has always meant being exposed to a certain type of fiction, divided into genres and series, and being hooked on adventure stories. It went without saying for us that comics, like the novel or film, was "a narrative type within the narrative genre."[63] Of course, we have to acknowledge that comics is now put to many other uses, and arouses, among certain groups of younger readers, different expectations. To be convinced of this, one needs only to consider the phenomenon of "cosplay" (derived from "costume play," originating in U.S. science fiction conventions but subsequently appropriated by manga fans worldwide) to realize that these young people who dress up as their favorite hero have little interest in the story—what they are seeking in comics is the hero or heroine with whom they identify. The emphasis is on the characters themselves, their costumes, their attributes, possibly the values that they incarnate, but not at all the context in which they appear or the adventures that they have had. This phenomenon of identification is difficult for readers of my generation to understand—we were also crazy about heroes, but what mattered to us was how they gained hero status through their actions and how they swept us up in the excitement of their adventures.

If cosplay points to a new relationship with comics and the imaginary world that they conjure up, there is every reason to think that digital comics, as an interactive hypermedium, are also likely to give rise to new ways for readers to position themselves in relation to comics, new expectations, and new practices in which the idea of game-playing may become key. Since my personal comics culture is far removed from that, I can conceptualize that other mode of appropriation/consumption theoretically, but I will never make it my own.

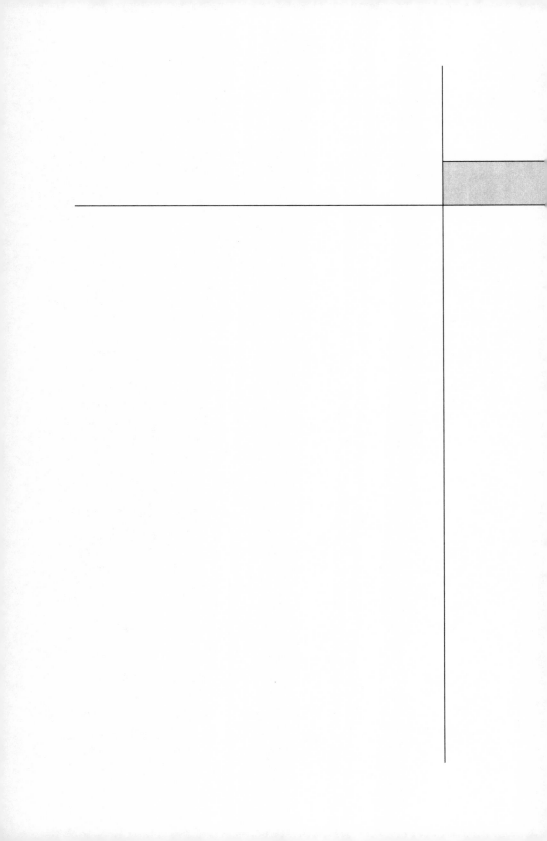

CHAPTER FIVE

The Question of the Narrator

"In literature, things are not recounted because they happen;
they happen because they are recounted."
—**Alberto Manguel**, *L'Angoisse du lecteur* [The Anxiety of the Reader] [1]

I consciously and deliberately left aside the question of "different instances of enunciation" in the first volume of *The System of Comics*.[2] I will now introduce it here.

Moreover, it has to be said that up until now, comics theory has had very little to say on the subject. This near-silence may be read either as an acknowledgement of the difficulty of the question when applied to the Ninth Art, or as a sign that it has not so far been deemed to be of primary importance.

5.1 INSTANCES OF ENUNCIATION IN THE GRAPHIC NARRATIVE

It is well-known that the narrator—the teller of the story, the source responsible for the enunciation of the narrative discourse—is a key concept in literary narratology, which takes great care to distinguish it from the real-life author. The narrator is an instance constructed by the text.

The narratological theories that have so far been put forward, in France and elsewhere, disagree over a central issue. Some maintain that there can be no story without a narrator, and that any such hypothesis is impossible, unthinkable. Within this perspective, story and narration are, then, more or less synonymous, or at least presuppose each other.

In the view of Sylvie Patron,[3] these "type one narratologies" (at the front rank of which is classic French narratology, as exemplified by Tzvetan Todorov, Gérard Genette, or Paul Ricoeur) adhere to a communications theory model of the narrative, that is to say they consider that the story is necessarily and in every case a message delivered by an enunciator to a recipient. This interpretation is open to question, however, if the author can be considered as the emitter of the "message." I do not see any automatic link between the approach to narrative within a communications theory framework and the postulation of the presence of a narrator. Establishing that link in fact demands a conceptual leap.

Other theories allow that some stories seem to tell themselves, stories in which no trace can be found of the intervention of any narrator and therefore argue that there are no grounds for decreeing that there must be one. It follows that the existence of a narrator, rather than being assumed as a matter of principle, can only be deduced from the observation of a certain number of markers of narration discernable in the text.

The narrator, whether regarded as a compulsory agent or as optional, is defined in every case as an intermediary between the story and the reader, an instance that expresses a point of view on the events recounted. This point of view is referred to by Todorov as a *vision*, by Genette as a *focalization*, by Franz Karl Stanzel as a *Mittelbarkeit* (an indirect transmission, or mediacy), and by Ann Banfield as a *subjectivity*.

Can narratological theories, initially conceived to account for literary texts, be extrapolated to domains not based on writing? Film theorists were the first to attempt this, but, there too, the question of the narrator is contentious. While most film semiologists (particularly André Gaudreault, François Jost, André Gardies, Jacques Aumont) have adopted the following credo: "there is no story without a narrator," others (such as Christian Metz, Raymond Bellour, Gilles Deleuze and, following him, André Parente) have freed themselves, in different ways, from this tenet of poststructuralist semiological orthodoxy.

In any case, no extrapolation from literary narratology can be envisaged unless the concepts are revised. Given that the "explicit traces of the narrator" identified in literary works were necessarily linguistic traces, an author such as Schaeffer, for example (like Todorov before him), came to the conclusion that "the application of the technical notion of 'narration' should be restricted to the verbal sphere."[4]

If one wishes to pose the question of the cinematic narrator, it is, then, important to arrive at a different definition of this "technical notion" by identifying specific markers of cinematic enunciation. Idem for comic art.

In other words, I do not believe in the possibility of establishing a general science of narratology that would be valid across all types of narratives in whatever medium. I believe that the issue of the narrator can legitimately be raised in relation to any type of story, but that the question should be posed afresh for each medium, because each has its own enunciative mechanism and, consequently, a distinct narratalogical configuration.

Furthermore, when I speak, out of convenience, of the "issue of the narrator," I have no illusions about the difficulties associated with this term, which excessively personalizes what it refers to—that is to say, the way in which the narrative function(s) is/(are) carried out. Words such as *narrator, enunciator*—or *monstrator*, which I will use later, have the same suffix, which refers to a person who performs the action in question. This choice of vocabulary may cause a misunderstanding or may even be downright misleading. It is clear that only the author is a real live person, an individual, and no one is postulating the existence of spooky presences taking over from him/her or sitting at his/her side. These words have to be taken as metaphors that personify various functions that come into play in the work. Theory isolates, names, and defines a number of functions (enunciation, narration, monstration) and credits them to an instance, a virtual entity, the fictitious agent of various concrete operations.

My postulate is, therefore, that each medium heightens or diminishes awareness of the intervention of one or other of these instances by seeming to give substantial embodiment to some narrative functions to the detriment of others, and by distributing them differently.

Certain modes of expression tend, then, to make their recipient forget that "someone" is addressing him/her, either on account of their power of illusion (this is most obviously the case of cinema—it would be trite to emphasize that filmic monstration, by giving the spectator the impression that the events are taking place before his/her very eyes, tends to make him/her forget the presence of a narrator and so obliterates it) or because they are based on a performance that seems in-mediate, that is to say without mediation (this is the case of theatre and performing arts in general).

It should also be said that any effects arising out of the medium-specific apparatus can be stronger or weaker according to the awareness the recipient has of the technical resources of the medium in question. A true cinephile will be attentive to framing, lighting, depth of focus, and editing, while a younger or less-experienced viewer will only be interested in the twists and turns of the plot, or how photogenic the actors are and how well they can act.

It follows from these preliminary remarks that I will not deal in abstractions by committing myself either to the theories of the "narrator at all costs" or to the empirical theories that identify a narrator only when traces of its presence can expressly be found in the work. In line with my usual procedure, I will begin by interrogating the specificity of the medium in order to draw out relevant narratological concepts on an ad hoc basis.

This research, of course, concerns only comics that tell a story. Even if these are in the immense majority, it is still important to note the existence of a number of experimental comics that are not at all, or only slightly, narrative. I have shown elsewhere that the juxtaposition of drawings within a multiframe did not automatically produce a story, and that the resulting page could belong to an infranarrative category such as the *amalgam*, the *inventory*, the *variation*, the *inflection*, or the *decomposition*.⁵ And in the first chapter of this book I referred to the anthology *Abstract Comics*, which has, in a sense, given official recognition to these non-narrative formats.

Even so, these formats remain marginal and occur infrequently. The dominant comics format is narrative, and the remark formulated by Roger Odin in relation to cinema can be applied to it; it is precisely this that "makes it sociologically grounded." Indisputably, the reader who opens a comic does so to "be exposed to a story."⁶

5.1.1 For Every Image, a Perceptual Source

Unlike those in a film, comics images do not create the illusion that the events are taking place as we read. Several factors work against this—in particular: the visible discontinuity of the sequential flow of the narrative; the fact that readers cannot forget the physical, concrete situation in which they find themselves, that of having a book in their hands (or in front of them), and turning the pages, at a rhythm that is not imposed but under their control; finally, the fact that each new image does not obliterate the previous one, does not take its place, but is added to it on the mode of accumulation, collection, with the totality of images remaining easily accessible at any time. For all these reasons, graphic monstration, in contrast with filmic monstration, does not create the impression of a story unfolding before our eyes. It is not therefore possible to invoke any effect of erasure of the narrator, which is normally the consequence of this "happening as we watch" impression. It remains to be seen whether, conversely, the enunciative mechanism of comics actually calls forth the notion of a narrator, and in what way.

The difficulty of elaborating a narratology for comic art arises out of its polysemiotic nature. It combines text and image in varying proportions. It is essential to start with the assumption that both play a full part in the narrative process. There is not, on the one hand, a text that tells (and which would be *diegetic*) and on the other, images that show (and would be solely *mimetic*). All my efforts in *The System of Comics* were directed towards demonstrating that a substantial part of the narration is carried by the images, both within them and through their articulation at different levels. To put it another way, there is undoubtedly a dissociation between the *told* (with words) and the *shown* (by drawings), but the *shown* is itself a *told*. I had, moreover, defined comic art as *a predominantly visual narrative form* [within the "narrative genre"].[7]

The few authors who have ventured into the narratology of comic art have approached the question from the opposite direction. They have investigated how far a conceptual framework drawn from literary narratology, notably that of Genette, could be applied to comics, and have supplemented this with borrowings from film narratology.[8]

For Genette, narratology has to address two questions: "Who is speaking?" and "Who can see?" These questions define narrative perspective, which Genette describes as *focalization*. He speaks of *zero focalization*, when the narrator is omniscient and gives us access to the thoughts and emotions of all characters; *internal focalization*, when the story adopts the viewpoint of one character; and *external focalization*, when the characters are presented from the outside, with no access to their inner selves.

The film theorist André Gardies has posed the problem in slightly different terms, by recognizing three possible types of polarization: the polarity is with the character if, as a spectator, I know as much as s/he does; it is with the spectator if I have the impression of being omniscient; and it is with the enunciator if the instance telling the story knows more than I do.[9]

Other film specialists (above all, André Gaudreault and François Jost) have also underlined the necessary distinction between seeing and knowing.

The question of the knowledge possessed respectively by the narrator, the character, and the reader must, indeed, be distinguished from that of the perceptual source. There is no such thing as zero focalization in cinema because everything shown on the screen is seen through a lens, and the camera always takes up a particular position. François Jost has formulated the concept of *ocularization* to take account of camera positioning and the viewpoint that that positioning represents or suggests.[10]

I take it as given that the notion of perceptual source is not restricted to cinema, even if the involvement of camera movements confers specific features on it.

The source is inherent to any image and cannot be dissociated from it. Although the comics image is not seen through a lens, it nonetheless emanates from a viewpoint on the action or the subject represented; we necessarily apprehend it from a particular angle and at a particular distance. In the terms used by Henri van Lier, the image necessarily contains *indices*, that is to say telltale signals, which include its framing or placement within the field of vision.[11]

Nor is the application of the categories of focalization and ocularization particularly problematic. Ann Miller has shown that "In the case of heterodiegetic narration, *bande dessinée* allows for zero, internal, and external focalization"; she suggests, moreover, that ocularization in comics can include "not only images representing the ocular viewpoint of a character," but also images that "bear traces of subjectivity through deformation" and "wholly subjective images."[12]

Despite the pertinence of these analyses, I will not adopt the term "ocularization," which seems to me to be too closely linked to the technical apparatus of cinema, the viewfinder, the lens, the "camera-eye."

Furthermore, I will emphasize that even if every image supposes a perceptual source, this may either be personalized, by expressing the viewpoint of a character (we have access to the action "with him/her" or through his/her eyes") or remain impersonal. This fundamental distinction has been noted and commented on by Kai Mikkonen, who writes: "The non-character-bound perspective, generally speaking, is coded for transparency: while showing and framing a field of vision, it does not presuppose a human narrator or a reporter."[13]

5.1.2 The Monstrating Instance

Like theatre, which preceded them, cinema and comics can be classed as mimetic, or dramatic, arts, insofar as they present characters in action. The term *monstration*, which has gained wide currency, was proposed by Gaudreault "in order to characterize and identify that mode of communication in a story that consists of showing characters who act rather than recounting the events that they undergo, and in order to replace "representation," a term that is too marked, overused, and too polysemic."[14]

According to Gaudreault, an "instrinsic narrativity" inheres in cinematic images, arising out of the fact that they are moving images "in the process of transformation."[15] It follows that shots, the basic units of film, are always already narrative.

The same cannot be said of the images that make up a comic, which, far from being the "movement-images" in Gilles Deleuze's term, are, by definition, still images. Even if one can argue that certain panels can be said to possess a narrativity internal to them (this point has been discussed in chapter two), comics narration is essentially founded on the articulation of images within a sequence.

Whether or not the possibility of immanent narrativity in a graphic image is acknowledged, it presents, in any case, a further distinctive feature. It has often and quite rightly been emphasized that the graphic image, insofar as it is hand-made, has to be read in reference to the signature of its maker. Any drawing is by its nature a codification and a stylization of reality, the result of a reading of the world. Therefore, a drawing cannot be dissociated from the hand of a specific enunciator.

Philippe Marion has suggested differentiating two distinct operations in graphic enunciation: monstration and what he calls *graphiation*. Monstration is transitive, directed towards figuration, whereas graphiation is reflexive, directed towards the graphic act. A "graphic trace effect" can be discerned in any drawing, he claims, through which the drawing designates itself as such, and resists the referential illusion.[16]

Thus for Marion there are two enunciating instances in drawing, a monstrator and a graphiator. To my mind this is a redundant distinction. The phenomenon highlighted by Marion is nothing more than the unavoidable presence of style (a term that should be understood here as synonymous with a particular graphic hand) in any drawn narrative. In my view, graphiation is not a supplementary and distinct layer of enunciation—all that needs to be said is that graphic monstration is never neutral, given that any drawing is necessarily signed and marked by a considerable degree of uniqueness. (It is impossible to imagine a zero degree of style—even the drawings available through generic image banks for web-publishing software, which are neither signed nor hand-drawn, use a specific system of codification.)

In *Reading Comics*, Douglas Wolk makes the excellent point that cartooning can be read as a metaphor for the subjectivity of perception.[17] Instead of saying "This is what I've seen," the artist says "This is what it meant to me," that is to say: this is *how* I saw it.

Paul Valéry used to quote Degas's axiom: "Drawing is not form, it is a way of seeing form."

Readers who are confronted with a comic, whether or not they perceive the presence of a narrative agent, of someone telling them something, cannot, in any case, fail to be aware that the images that they are looking at *have been drawn*, that they are artifacts.

I will keep the term *monstrato*r to designate the instance responsible for the *rendering into drawn form*[18] of the story. As Gardies has pertinently remarked, the term *monstration* underlines the fact that what is *seen* is the result of what is *shown*, and therefore of a decision at the level of enunciation.[19] Asserting the material existence of a monstrating instance within a narratological theory means isolating, in the process of comics creation, what pertains specifically to the drawing inasmuch as it is driven by a narrative intention[20] and imbued with subjectivity.

5.1.3 Present-Tense Images in a Past-Tense Narrative: A Degree of Temporal Imprecision

Questions concerning narrative time have traditionally constituted another important topic in narratology. I will now digress, so as to put forward a few hypotheses on the relationship between comics and temporality. Indeed, the following considerations do not have any direct impact on the validity of my other propositions.

One consequence of the fact that film images seem to be unfolding before our very eyes is that the image has only one tense: the present. (Within a flashback, the present-tense cursor has been moved backwards but we are plunged once more into a fusion with the moment, an immediate communion with the events recounted, even if they logically precede the main story or other events previously recounted.)

Comics images do not seem to have the same kind of deictic link to the present. On this point, the English comics specialist Paul Gravett made a very pertinent comment during a conference presentation.[21] For him, in a Western comic we read what happened next, whereas in a manga, we read what is happening at the moment. The narrative techniques peculiar to manga create, he argues, a sense of immersion in the action that Western comics do not achieve (and do not necessarily set out to achieve). This opposition between two aesthetics would naturally be nuanced according to different schools, authors, and works, but it seems to me to be valid in general. And if we accept this to be the case, we must conclude that in a Western comic, the story tends to be narrated in the past.

In reality, any comic should be seen by its very nature as being in the past, on account of the panoptic display of the images. "(T)here is no present that is not haunted by a past and a future" wrote Deleuze in *The Time-Image*.[22] In comics, at the moment when our attention is focused on one panel, the preceding ones have not yet disappeared (they remain available, retrievable at any time), but, above all, we already have sight of the following panels, and we can see that the future is *already there*. If the future that pulls our reading towards it is already present, then the present inevitably tends to slip back towards a past to which, in fact, it already belongs. The idea that successive presents can coexist is paradoxical: unlike the past, the present cannot be cumulative.

To put this another way, in cinema, the future destiny of the image seems, at every moment, to remain open, because it is hidden from us—but in comics, the image does not surge up from nowhere. The next stage is already accessible, and it is possible for us to glance ahead and catch a glimpse of events yet to take place—or even to go straight to the end of an album and start by looking at its final page.

I would therefore be inclined to say, following Gravett, that to the opening panel of a comic there corresponds an implicit "that's how it all began," and to each subsequent panel an "and this is what happened next."

Manga are not completely exempt from this rule, but they try to challenge it through devices such as the fragmentation of the instant, the multiplication of inserts, the proliferation of onomatopoeia, speed lines, in short by making use of anything that can pitch readers into the heart of the action, fully involving them.

Nonetheless, even if we admit that the comics narrative is inherently in the past, that does not mean the reader necessarily perceives it that way. This is because, even if graphic images do not have the deictic attachment to the present that seems inherent to film images—the image, any image, at the moment we are looking at it, places before our eyes a scene set in the *here and now*. So that, even if we are not completely in the *present time frame* of the characters and the locations depicted, at least they are offering us their *presence*.

To summarize, it can be said that comics stories have a kind of built-in imprecision (or something along the lines of what Genette elegantly calls "a very subtle friction effect"):[23] this produces a narration that tends overall to be read as if in the past by aligning images that, taken one by one, are read as present.

When responsibility for the story is attributed to a narrative voice, this instance can modalize the relationship to time by choosing to deliver the narration in the present or the past (see below, 5.3.1). The use of a specific verb tense (most often the preterite, the fictional tense *par excellence*) will make it possible to tip the uncertain balance between past and present in one or other direction.

5.1.4 The Reciter

Let us now turn to verbal enunciation, which can be added to iconic monstration in the form of a *voice-over*. The site where this voice most often finds expression is conventionally called the *recitative*, but it may not always occur in the
form of a caption box—an area within or above the panel frame may simply be
set aside for it.

To maintain coherence with the canonical term "recitative," I propose to call
the instance responsible for this narration the *reciter*. The reciter will, then, be
for the narrative text the equivalent instance to the monstrator for the drawing.

In French, the voice of the reciter is often called a "voice-off," but the expression is ambiguous, as it can also designate a speech balloon emitted by one of the
characters taking part in the action, while s/he is temporarily out of the frame, or
masked within it. That is why it seems preferable to keep the expression *voice off*
for cases of this type, and to use instead the equivalent English expression *voice-
over* for verbal contributions whose reciter does not belong to the fictional world
(the extra-diegetic reciter).[24]

As an example, I will examine the different ways in which the reciter intervenes
in the album by Franquin, Jidéhem and Greg, *L'Ombre du Z* [The Shadow of Z].[25]

The first page is introduced by a block of text whose function is to establish a
link with the previous adventure in the series, *Z comme Zorglub* [Z for Zorglub].
This recitative functions as a reminder of events previously recounted, and the
final five words, "our friends return to Champignac," allow the story to begin *in
medias res*.

This kind of recitative, with a narrative function, recurs at regular intervals all
through the album. For example, on the fifteenth page: "For hours and hours,
the gigantic operation continued"; or on the eighteenth: "Once he was some way
from the grounds, the stranger sent the car away."

Other interventions by the verbal enunciator, or reciter, usually very short,
merely perform what we have called elsewhere a management function.[26] They
are simply intended to provide a temporal link between two sequences of events
(fifth page: "Meanwhile . . ."; thirty-fourth: "An hour later . . .") or a spatial link
(seventh page: "At the chateau . . ."; eleventh: "Not far away . . ."). In some cases
they combine both types of coordinates ("Meanwhile, in town . . ." on the sixth
page).

A third type of intervention, which occurs five times in the album, consists
of references back to previous episodes in the same series. In this case, the refer-

ences are marked by their use of the imperative: "Read: *Z for Zorglub*"; "See the episodes: *Spirou and the Heirs—The Dictator and the Mushroom*" or "Remember *Z for Zorglub*." These references all involve allusions to events recounted in previous albums. Their intention is to situate the current episode within the memory of the collection as a whole, and so to emphasize the coherence of the series. They can be read as bids to substantiate the claim that this is a *body of work* (although in fact neither *Spirou and the Heirs* nor *The Dictator and the Mushroom* were scripted by Greg: the first was written by Franquin himself and the second by Rosy) and viewed at the same time as a kind of advertisement, an inducement to buy and read the other books if the reader does not yet know them. Interventions of this type are more like footnotes than narrative indicators (indeed they are asterisked, like notes); it would be possible to attribute them to the publisher and it is clear that they constitute a different category of *voice-over*.

The same can be said of the interventions that involve translation or "subtitling." In the album that concerns us, a few fragments of dialogue are spoken in Spanish and others in an imaginary language, the famous "Zorlanguage," which consists of reversing the order of letters in each word ("Eviv Bulgroz!" for "Vive Zorglub! [Long live Zorglub!]"). The French translation is given in or under the panel, preceded, here again, by an asterisk.

Although disparate, the different kinds of verbal interventions identified thus far all belong, fundamentally, to the same register, that of information-giving. They all provide the reader with the keys necessary for full understanding of the narrative.

It was not the examples quoted above that attracted my attention to this particular album, but the moments when the reciter drops the neutral register in favor of a tone expressing empathy with ongoing events. Early in the story (from the fifth page), the reciter feigns surprise: "Well well . . . the object that Fantasio is nervously clutching in his right hand is Dupilon's lighter!!" The same amazement recurs later, on the twenty-third page, in a rather exaggerated tone, as if deliberately over-acted: "But what's going on?!? Does Spirou not recognize Zorglub, the ex-dictator of the Zorglommes?!? And is he letting Champignac's arch-enemy into the chateau??!?" Still further on, the tone becomes fearful, even terrified: "Aaaaaargh! Zorglub's rage will be terrible! . . . And he has not come alone . . ." Another intervention of this type (on the twenty-third page) serves emphatically to underline the solemnity of the moment represented, and tries to weight it with *suspense*: "Look at Zorglub: in a few moments, he is going to make a date with destiny."

In all these cases, the reciter no longer takes the form of a neutral, purely informative voice that restricts itself to dispensing, whenever necessary, elements that the reader needs in order to understand events. With of the additional punctuation marks, the voice takes on emotional coloring and becomes the voice of a sentient human being that, in its own way, takes part in the story by expressing its feelings—even while remaining extradiegetic, the reciter attains the status of an individual, and therefore that of a character.

Even more astonishingly, on the fourteenth page, out of the blue, the reciter expresses itself in a quite unexpected, and, it must be said, somewhat surprising way, in the first person: "The stranger on the back seat could not be identified; but the driver's strange staring eyes reminded *me* of something . . ." Behind the *Shadow of Z*, the shadow of a narrator suddenly looms. (This single occurrence of a personal pronoun referring to a speaking subject brings to mind Flaubert's famous *we* on the opening page of *Madame Bovary*.) Nevertheless, the sudden personalization of the reciter does not remove its anonymity—this "I" does not refer to an identifiable person. The reciter reveals itself but does not name itself.

5.1.5 Stances[27] of the Reciter and the Monstrator

Whether this surprising (and sole) incursion into the text of the first person should be attributed to the scriptwriter's carelessness or whether it was a conscious choice matters little. What this album by Franquin and Greg shows is that the reciter can adopt different attitudes in relation to the story for which it shoulders part of the responsibility.

More specifically, the stance of the reciter can vary according to three criteria:

1. It sometimes stays *in the background,* and is sometimes *interventionist.* When "in the background," it lets the sequential unfurling of the images do the talking (whether or not they contain dialogue) without feeling it appropriate to intervene. Unless I am mistaken, in the album in question twenty-two pages (out of a total of sixty-one) do not include any contributions that could be credited to the instance of the reciter. In its "interventionist" mode, on the other hand, the reciter superimposes its voice-over on a entire sequence of which it becomes the principal narrator, in the sense that the images are no longer even necessary for understanding the action. A sequence of this type can be found on the thirty-ninth and fortieth pages of the album.

Here is the narrative text that accompanies that sequence, divided up into eight segments spread over a page and a half:

The inhabitants of the southern district of Chiquito seem to have gone mad: they are all descending on the shops, waving money around and shouting the name of a brand of toothpaste! The Perez supermarket, for example . . . / . . . a mob is charging towards the toiletries counter . . . /There's complete chaos, the saleswomen want to buy up the entire stock of Zugol toothpaste themselves . . . / at last, some soldiers have appeared on the scene: order is going to be quickly restored . . ./A curious detail: three bandits, who have just pulled off a hold-up in the banking district . . . / . . . have now come under the influence of zorglonde waves . . . / . . . and they are paying one million two hundred and sixty thousand six hundred and thirty seven palombos for the last three tubes of Zugol in a nearby shop . . . /Calm has been restored in the Perez supermarket . . .

This sudden and massive interventionism changes the whole mode of operation of the narration, as if a television news report had intruded into the fiction.[28]

2. The reciter is sometimes *neutral*, and sometimes *involved*. In the sequence cited above, the tone is objective. The facts are reported without the reciter divulging its feelings. The adjective "curious" ("A curious detail . . .") is itself remarkably neutral, as it draws readers' attention to the incident without dictating what they should think. I have mentioned above moments when the reciter is, conversely, involved. This involvement takes the form of solidarity with the characters whose fate seems to be a matter of personal concern to the reciter and/or of solidarity with the reader, as the reciter expresses "out loud" what are supposed to be the reader's innermost thoughts and feelings. There are two possible strategies: the reciter can become the reader's mouthpiece (for example, letting slip a simple "Aargh" to mark the perception of imminent danger; the reciter behaves in this case as if it were the first reader of the story that it is actually partly responsible for enunciating), or it can interpellate them directly ("Look at Zorglub . . ."). In short, the reciter "directs the readers" in the same way that Hitchcock used to say that he directed the spectators.

3. In principle, the reader has confidence in the narrative voice, s/he presumes it to be credible, to say nothing that is not certain, nothing that might be undermined by future events. To this presumed *reliability* can be opposed an

alternative attitude: *deception*. When the reciter feigns surprise ("But what's going on? . . ."), it is, of course, as I have just argued, empathetically giving voice to questions supposedly asked by the reader, but it also plays a role that cannot logically belong to it. By definition, the reciter cannot be surprised, because it is the instance that possesses and imparts information. In order to tell the story, it must already know the story. In consequence, any utterance that can be attributed to the reciter and that takes the form of amazement, doubt about the direction of a plot twist, or wondering what will happen next, can only ever be pretence or deception.

The way in which the reciter fulfils its function, whether it remains in the background or is interventionist, neutral or involved, reliable or deceptive, defines what I will call a *stance* in relation to the narrative.

The next question to be decided is whether any specific resources are available to the graphic enunciator or monstrator to enable it to take up stances analogous to those of the reciter. A response to this question necessitates a widening of the corpus, for it is immediately obvious that in *L'Ombre du Z*, in conformity with the stylistic norms of classic Franco-Belgian comics, the monstrator does not display the same range of registers as the reciter. But we can find examples elsewhere within the history of the Ninth Art that attest to the fact that the monstrator also has the potential for adopting one or another of these attitudes.

It would be tempting to believe that, whereas the reciter can choose whether to speak or remain silent according to the needs of the moment, it is a matter of principle that the monstrator, in contrast, cannot remain in the background. Indeed, once the monstrator declines to play its part, the visual channel of the storytelling is interrupted, and there is a break in narrative continuity. And yet, it can happen that the monstrator remains silent. When a recitative takes up the space of an entire panel, and so a block of text is intercalated between two images, the monstrator stays momentarily in the background and hands over the driving of the narrative to words alone. The monstrator also retreats into the background when it proposes a *blind* image, an entirely black or white image to signal a loss of consciousness and, therefore, of sight (the character falls asleep, faints or is knocked out), or the refusal to reveal a scene. A famous example is the fourth page of Gustave Doré's *L'Histoire de la Sainte Russie* [The History of Holy Russia] (1854), composed of five empty frames, accompanied by this caption:

Fig. 7. Franquin, Greg and Jidéhem, *L'Ombre du Z* (Charleroi: Dupuis, 1962) half-page 31C. © Éditions Dupuis.

As the following century carried on throwing up a series of equally dull events, I would be concerned, dear reader lest I turn you against my work, from the outset, by overwhelming you with excessively tedious images. However, my publisher, like the conscientious man that he is, has urged me to accord it the space shown above, in order to prove that a skilled historian can mitigate everything while omitting nothing.

The question of the neutrality or involvement of the monstrator is posed in terms of homogeneity or heterogeneity of graphic style. The monstrator remains neutral if it adopts a consistent style all the way through the story. When, in the scene cited above, the reciter of *L'Ombre du Z* feigns shock ("Aaaaaargh! Zorglub's rage will be terrible! . . ."), an involved monstrator could display the same emotion by means of a wavy line, a drawing that seems hesitant or blurred. But homogeneity of style is canonical in the classic comics of the 1950s and 1960s. This is no longer the case in contemporary comic art, a point to which I will return.[29] So, when Edmond Baudoin represents a rape scene ("Quartiers Nord" [Northern Districts] in *Salade niçoise*),[30] his drawing itself becomes frenzied, brutal, and seemingly out of control—each brushstroke is a gash, a scar, and the image seems about to descend into chaos. Albums such as those by Fabrice Neaud (especially his *Journal*

4)[31] or Dominique Goblet, to give but two examples, show that breaks in style are now accepted, and have indeed become an integral part of the artist's array of rhetorical resources. This achievement by modern comics facilitates, it would seem, the involvement of the monstrator. And as regards the interpellation of the reader, which we have acknowledged as another mode of involvement, it will suffice, here again, to return to Gustave Doré and *Sainte Russie*—on the second page of the book Doré offers a close-up of the supposed reader's face, embellished with a self-satisfied expression.[32]

It remains to ascertain whether the monstrator can be lacking in reliability and dupe us in some way. A typical case of deception immediately comes to mind—the failure to signal a transition from images supposed to represent "reality" to dream images. It is only afterwards that the reader understands that what s/he has just been shown "was only a dream," a fantasy, a reverie. As a general rule I will class as deceptive all images that initially mislead the reader and whose meaning is retrospectively readjusted.

I had analyzed one such example in *The System of Comics*.[33] On page two of an episode from the Alack Sinner series by Muñoz and Sampayo, entitled *Rencontres* [Encounters], we see Alack leaning forward slightly with one hand clutching his stomach and the other in front of his mouth. As he has just taken a drag on his first cigarette of the morning, we have no hesitation in arriving at a reading of this wordless image: Alack is coughing. It is only after having turned the page, when we find him leaning over a bidet and vomiting that the real meaning of the drawing becomes apparent. The monstrator had momentarily duped us.

Given that both the monstrator and the reciter have at their disposal specific resources for creating more or less comparable effects, we need to ask whether, in the course of the narrative, the respective stances of the monstrating subject and the reciting subject are always and inevitably in harmony. Does the degree of intervention, emotional involvement, and reliability between the graphic and the verbal enunciator always coincide, or can there be a disjunction? We already have the answer to this question, since, in *L'Ombre du Z*, the monstrator remains neutral whereas the reciter is strongly involved. In the pages where the reciter remains silent, its level of involvement is zero, whereas the monstrator is hard at work. And it is clear that the monstrator can always deceive us or demonstrate its involvement without any intervention whatsoever from the reciter.

The respective stances of the reciter and the monstrator can, then, coincide, but they very often diverge. The coordination of these stances depends on the authority of a higher enunciating source, the very source for which we have chosen to reserve the name of *narrator*. The narrator is the ultimate instance responsible for the selection and organization of all the types of information that make up the narrative. The reciter and the monstrator are merely delegated to exercise some of its prerogatives.

From Genette to Stanzel, the question traditionally posed in narratology has been that of perspective: who sees, who speaks, and with what authority (omniscience versus limited perspective)? The concept of *stance* is a little different. As we are faced, in comic art, with a split narration, we should investigate the procedures enabling cooperation and reciprocal impetus between the verbal and visual enunciators. Even if they express a single perspective (which is logical, since the perspective is necessarily that of the fundamental narrator), it can be seen that their modes of intervention and the way in which they carry out their respective functions can be examined separately and compared.

I announced earlier in this chapter my disinclination to come down on the side either of theories of the "narrator at all costs" or of theories that identify a narrator only when traces of its presence can expressly be found in the work—and my desire to investigate first of all, without preconceptions, how that question is posed in the field of comic art. The necessity of separating the enunciating instance responsible for monstration from the instance responsible for verbal utterances may seem debatable—we could instead have attributed the whole process of transmission of the story to a single narrator or to the author him/herself. The fact that we have identified the respective postures of two different instances by showing that they do not coincide establishes the pertinence of the categories of monstrator and reciter, which, in turn, have to be understood in their hierarchical relationship to the overall narrator for which they act as delegates. The empirical study of the mechanisms at work in comic art does indeed confirm the value of these theoretical instances, which have been shown to be defined both by the narrative functions to which they correspond and the roles that they take on.

5.1.6. The Competences of the Fundamental Narrator

I will not go any further in indentifying multiple enunciating instances. The narrator/monstrator/reciter trio is sufficient for an adequate description of the communicative process that is at work in comic art. And I would prefer not to get embroiled in an unwieldy taxonomy, like that of Gaudreault, who distinguishes in the case of cinema a scriptural narrator, a filmic narrator, a filmographic narrator (responsible for the articulation of shots), a filmic mega-monstrator (the instance that co-ordinates the pro-filmic event with framing), and a mega-narrator (the instance that is hierarchically superior to both of these, and co-ordinates them), etc.

But, like him, I nonetheless recognize the existence of a "*primary, fundamental* narrator, a truly *supra-diegetic* (and always already *extra*-diegetic)" (150), also described as "an im-personal (or rather a-personal) instance, which, because it was never given the status of a character within the fictional world, cannot manifest "its" presence (156), an instance that Gaudreault calls the *narrator*, but which, in my terminology, simply corresponds to the *narrateur* [narrator].[34]

I cannot see why this same instance should not be held responsible for a number of operations, which are, moreover, closely correlated. The narrator can, in fact, be regarded as simultaneously responsible for breakdown, page layout, and, where relevant, braiding; or, more generally, held accountable for the distribution and organization of information throughout the narrative, a distribution and an organization that involve the bringing into play of a number of operations, both correlated and complementary, that come under the heading of arthrology.

In order to maintain coherence with *The System of Comics*, I could also, somewhat pedantically, confer on the narrator the title of "great arthrologist," or master of articulations.

One point needs to be emphasized. If I attribute the the responsibility (among others) for the layout to the narrator, this is because I see it as an operation that plays a full part in narration, and not only a matter of aesthetics, technique, or ornamentation. The narrative properties of layout arise most notably out of the fact that it imposes its own rhythm on the reading process and therefore also on the unfolding of the story—that one of its functions is to focus particular attention on certain moments of the action by manipulating framing (by using an extra-large frame or an unusually shaped one) or siting on the page; or that it can set up, by means of an inset, for example, a privileged and dialectical relationship between two images. I wrote in *The System of Comics*: "The page layout does not operate on empty panels, but must take their contents into account. It is an instrument that serves a global artistic project, and is frequently subordinated to a narrative aim, or, at least, gives overall coherence to the narrative discourse . . . ."[35]

But I have not yet said anything about a very important component of the discourse of comic art and of narration: dialogue.

The narrator leaves to the monstrator the task of representing what the characters are up to. Whether they are running, driving a car, eating, fighting, making love, sleeping, meditating, or walking their dog, the drawing will take care of things. There are nonetheless two human activities that cannot easily be reconstituted in the form of a drawing: speaking and thinking. I have previously written that the image "is unable to translate (them) and can only quote (them)."[36]

It is as if the narrator had "recorded" the words that the characters are supposed to have pronounced and *reported* them to us: *Such-and-such a person said this,* or *Someone else replied that.* The narrating instance has at its disposal a convenient, economical mechanism for doing this: the speech balloon, which mimics direct speech, identifying the person shown in the act of speaking as the emitter of the words.

I have deliberately written: "are supposed to have pronounced." It is clear that (unless the story concerns real, historical characters), the characters have never pronounced any words because they do not exist—they are fictional creatures. However, the narrator pretends to know them and tries to make us take as much interest in them as we would in real people. One of the best ways of securing our adherence is, precisely, to make them speak. The faculty of speech completes their portrayal as supposedly thinking and self-determining beings and tends to make us forget that they are, in the end, just lines on paper.

As the principle enunciating source, then, the fundamental narrator manages the three levels of articulation noted in *System 1*: "The first two, which are homogeneous, concern the chain[37] of images on the one hand and the chain of speech balloons on the other; the third, which is heterogeneous, concerns the articulation of these two sequences—the one iconic, the other linguistic."[38]

5.2 ACTORIALIZED NARRATORS

We now turn to the case of first-person narration by a character involved in the story and represented in graphic form (s/he usually, but not necessarily, has the main role; for example, it is Ezra Winston who recounts his adventures alongside Mort Cinder, to whom he acts as a kind of "Doctor Watson").[39] I will call a character of this type who monopolizes the recitatives, within which s/he says "I," an *actorialized narrator,* on the grounds that s/he appears in the story of which s/he is (or pretends to be) the enunciator.[40] This instance can also be called an explicit narrator in opposition to the fundamental narrator which, as such, always remains masked, manifesting itself only through the delegation of its functions to the reciter or the monstrator.

The actorialized narrator was more or less non-existent in classic comics, which rarely used the first person. In contrast, it has become extremely common in contemporary comics, particularly in works related to the autobiographical genre (where, by definition, the explicit narrator offers us his/her own life story) or in comics reportage (where the narrator is the witness who recounts and contextualizes events). However, characters who say "I" can also be encountered in purely fictional works. For example, Alack Sinner was the longtime narrator of the adventures that Muñoz and Sampayo invented for him (though not in the final ones, collected in the album called *La Fin d'un Voyage* [Journey's End]).[41]

It therefore seems necessary to ask if the status of actorialized narrator needs to be analyzed differently, depending upon whether the work comes under the heading of fiction or whether it belongs to one of the genres governed by what Philippe Lejeune calls the "referential pact," that is to say a relationship to reality founded on a contract of reliability and truth.[42] What is, narratologically speaking, the distinguishing feature of autobiography (and the wider genre of intimate literature)—a category that I will widen by the inclusion of reportage, because this is a genre that guarantees that the narrator "was there" and that s/he took part in the events s/he is recounting as a witness? Lejeune responds: "There must be identity of author, narrator and character." And he specifies that the narrator has, in relation to the story recounted, a "retrospective viewpoint."[43]

5.2.1 The Autobiographical Narrator

On closer examination this identity of the three instances of author, narrator, and character is far from obvious, particularly in a medium split between verbal and visual enunciation. This is because the "character" is a purely conventional representation here, a stylized, arbitrary, and shifting graphic construction. Jean-Christophe Menu is very clear about this:

> If I represent myself, the image that springs from my pen is not one that has a real relationship with "me," it is more often a symbol, a hieroglyphic shorthand (even on the temporal level: it is a kind of synthesis of myself at different ages) [. . .] Normally, what emerges is the *autoarchetype*, which enables the narrative to progress without making an issue of representation.[44]

Moreover, the self-representation undertaken by Menu in his autobiographical album *Livret de Phamille* [Phamily Record Book][45] shows considerable fluctuations in the graphic codes used from one sequence to another: the I-as-character[46] is at some moments highly caricatural, at others rendered with far more surface realism, and a few self-portraits scattered through the work suggest serious introspection.

Lewis Trondheim prefers to draw himself with a bird's head. Moebius likes to multiply his graphic selves; he appears in the guise of different characters, some corresponding to different stages of his life, some to different roles (the child, the serious young man wearing a tie, the hippy sixties artist, the intellectual, the guru, the senior), and takes pleasure in setting up dialogues among them.

To sum up, drawing oneself necessarily involves distancing oneself—which involves the risk, generally accepted, of no longer "delving deep into oneself" and instead "externalizing oneself as a 'hero' who undergoes a series of plot twists."[47] This means that the identity between author and character is very relative. One represents the other, assuredly, but monstration reifies the graphic self as an "actor" (a persona, and so, a mask), endowed with its own identity. The actor is made to play a role and given stage directions.

We should add that the I-as-character can sometimes completely disappear from the image. Three whole chapters of *Livret de Phamille* ("Helsingissa Oleskelu," ten pages; "Saint-Vaast la Hougue," ten pages; and "Mélo mimolette blues," eight pages) employ the mode of "subjective camera," to use the author's own term. Menu does not make an appearance (apart from a brief reflection in a window) and is only present through his narrative voice-over in the caption box.

It is possible, then, in relation to the two expressions of the I-as-character, verbal and graphic, to reiterate the observation that we made about the monstrator and the reciter: they can make their presence felt or remain in the background, and they can intervene together or separately.

The difference between the fundamental narrator and the actorialized narrator in terms of their relationship to the image, is, therefore, clearly marked—the fundamental narrator leaves the task of engendering the images up to the monstrator; the actorialized narrator inhabits the images in which s/he appears as a *shown* element.

Given that, by definition, the I-as-character is graphically incarnated and plays his/her own role before our very eyes, s/he is subject to the same process of enunciation as any other character: s/he too is a paper "puppet" whose strings are pulled by the monstrator.

The narrative founded on a referential pact can often be distinguished from a purely fictional narrative in that it assembles a number of documentary images, such as photographs. The monstrator then has various aesthetic options regarding the treatment of these preexisting images and their mode of insertion into the flow of the sequential graphic narrative. Firstly, the photograph can simply be reproduced as it is, an option that introduces a semiotic break. Secondly, the photograph can be redrawn in a different style from the other images, for example by the use of hatching or a wash, with gray-toned surfaces recalling the texture and grain of the original image.[48] Thirdly, the photo can be redrawn in the same style as the other images, with no break in the graphic code.

An example of this last option can be found on the third page of the first volume of *Persepolis*, by Marjane Satrapi.[49] The narrator of this autobiographical story tells us that "My mother was photographed by a German journalist at one of these demonstrations." The panel beneath this recitative does indeed show the mother of the autobiographical character raising her fist at a demonstration. However, there is no visual clue to signal that the origin of this image is a photograph, given that its graphic presentation does not distinguish it from the rest of the book. There is an obvious dissociation between, on the one hand, the words of the actorialized narrator who affirms the existence of this photograph and therefore the documentary origin of that particular panel (indeed, the following panel shows Marjane holding the published version of this photo in her hands), and, on the other hand, the solution adopted by the monstrator, which does not feel the need to depart in any way from its usual graphic style, taking it for granted that the text will suffice to identify the nature and the origin of this visual element. I have chosen this example to illustrate the fact that the monstrator remains master of its domain, free to offer its own interpretation of the story told by the actorialized narrator.

The question of identity of author, narrator, and character becomes more complicated when, in works that come under the heading of autobiography, the author is a plural entity. Olivier Ka puts his life story into words and his collaborator, the artist Alfred, produces the images;[50] similarly, Loïc Nehou works with Frédéric Poncelet,[51] and Harvey Pekar with the numerous artists who have taken part in the *American Splendor* venture. Emmanuel Guibert takes the appropriation of allobiographical material a step further: after his friends Alan Ingram Cope or Didier Lefèvre have confided in him, he gives narrative form to their words and illustrates them, thereby becoming the mediator and interpreter of lives that are not his own, even though these accounts are written in the first person.[52] In this type of mediated or delegated autobiography, the actorialized narrator is the outcome of a process of creative dialogue, and cannot simply be

Fig. 8. Marjane Satrapi, *Persepolis*, vol. 1 (Paris: L'Association, 2003), p. 3. © L'Association.

collapsed back onto the "author." This does not, though, prevent the "I" of the actorialized narrator from retaining a testimonial validity.[53]

The other precondition for an autobiographical narrative set out by Lejeune, the retrospective viewpoint adopted by the narrator, is not always borne out either. The opening sentence of *Persepolis*, "That's me when I was ten. It was in 1980," by its use of the imperfect tense and by the anchoring of the book's point of departure in a past time frame, does indeed offer evidence of this type of perspective. In contrast, in Lewis Trondheim's *Approximativement* [Approximately],[54] the opening sentence is in the present tense ("As if it wasn't enough to be no good at drawing, I do sloppy work"), and the voice of the I-as-character makes explicit reference, as from page two, to the present of the enunciation ("I'm feeling bad-tempered today"). This slightly expanded present time frame (corresponding roughly to the entire duration of the production of the book) is the starting point for a few time shifts in the form of analepses (the narrator remembers episodes from the past, returning to his childhood for the duration of one sequence) (pp. 37–45) and prolepses (he projects himself into the future, fantasizing about commercial success in Japan for his character from *La Mouche* [The Fly] (pp. 13–14), or making worthy resolutions for the day after his move to the south of France (pp. 142–43).

The purpose of the present work is not to set out a comprehensive theory of the autobiographical genre in comics. My provisional conclusion is as follows: the comics medium makes it imperative to distinguish two levels of production of an autobiographical narrative.

The first level is that of the *structuring* of the narrative, or rather the arrangement of the elements that compose it: the selection of episodes to be recounted, the relative importance to be given to each, the ordering of sequences, the entry and exit points of the story, the narration in the past or present, etc. These are the "strategic" choices, and choices affecting dramatic impact, for which the narrator and author seem to take joint responsibility, or, at least, over which they are not likely to clash (leaving aside the case where there is more than one author, so that one of the collaborators may conceivably insist on carrying through his/her own vision of the artistic transformation of raw material supplied by the other).

The second level is that of narrative *enunciation*. Here it is the actorialized character who comes into the foreground and who appears split between, on the one hand, verbal expression and, on the other, graphic expression. As a voice, s/he takes over the function of the reciter (a function that, as we have established,

is delegated by the fundamental narrator). As a graphic character, s/he is objectiv-
ized by the monstrator.

The I-as-character appears, then, as a special case of a more general phenomenon to which I will return later: the collaboration between an objective regime
(here monstration) and a subjective regime (first-person narration). It will not
take us long to discover that monstration itself can—every time it gives access to
the "inner world" of the character (reverie, fantasy, projection)—tip over into the
subjective regime.

5.2.2. A Few Other Special Cases

Outside the field of autobiography, there exist numerous types of actorialized
narrators, among which we need to distinguish. We will cite a few cases:

A) The actorialized narrator whose function is simply to set the story in motion. This was the case of Uncle Paul whose "belles histories" [ripping yarns] were
one of the cornerstones of the weekly comic *Spirou*. The reassuring sage figure of
the famous pipe-smoking uncle, telling the story of historic deeds or personalities
to his nephews,[55] and, through them, his readers, only appeared in the opening
and closing images of the story. This was sufficient to personalize the voice that
recounted it, that of the uncle-reciter.

Others similarly famous for framing the narrative included, in the horror
comics published by E.C. in the 1950s, the Crypt Keeper, the Vault Keeper, and
the Old Witch.

B) The actorialized narrator who nonetheless remains extradiegetic. In the
cycle of "Les Aventures extraordinaires d'Adèle Blanc-Sec" [The Extraordinary
Adventures of Adèle Blanc-sec], Tardi used, up to and including *Momies en folie*
[Mummy Madness],[56] a non-actorialized narrative voice, that of the reciter. But in
the following album, *Le Secret de la Salamandre* [The Secret of the Salamander],[57]
responsibility for telling the story is laid at the door of a delegated narrator, an
old man in a book-lined room, physically represented in about half of the story
(often in a medallion next to the recitative). This old man remains anonymous,
he is not personally involved in Adèle's adventures, nor does he interact with
any of the characters in the story or tell us the source of the information that he
discloses to us.[58] He disappears from the following albums, Tardi having presum-
ably decided that this personification of the narrator weighed the narrative down
pointlessly, with no significant gain in dramatic effect.

The religious comic *Xavier raconté par le ménéstrel* [Xavier as Told by the Minstrel], by Pierre Defoux, a young Jesuit, for *Spirou* magazine in 1953 (numbers 774 to 815), offers an interesting case. In it, the life of Saint Francis Xavier is recounted by the narrator mentioned in the title, a very young man wearing a red and black Renaissance costume who introduces the work: "Hello, my friends! I'm the minstrel! My profession is story-telling!" This "minstrel" behaves, in general, like an extradiegetic narrator—he most often appears alone, in transitional panels summing up a plot event, signaling a change of location, or an ellipsis. He can also be seen lifting the corner of heavy tapestries giving symbolic access to the next scene. But, on occasion, the young minstrel crosses the statutory boundary that is supposed to cut him off from the world of his missionary hero: he lands as if by teleportation in a new location, where he questions secondary characters and, if necessary, translates their words into French. In short, the author makes very free use of him, and, for the duration of one whole sequence (corresponding to Xavier's stay in Japan), gives him lengthy and tedious recitatives to deliver.[59]

C) The case of the narrator who is a projection of the author, whilst evading the requirements of sincerity and truthfulness upon which the "autobiographical pact" is normally founded. Thus, in *Rubrique-à-brac* [Bric-a-Brac Column], Gotlib intervenes with sufficient regularity as a character for the reader to attribute to the same actorialized Gotlib the voice that acts as reciter for the episodes in which he does not feature pictorially. Furthermore, this Gotlib-character is inherently subject to fluctuation, a caricatural megalomaniac one day, a doting father the next. The point is precisely that the reader should not confuse this character with the real-life Marcel Gotlib, the author of *Rubrique-à-brac*. His voice, in the guise of implied narrator, can say "I" on the mode of make-believe and come out with the wildest assertions, without anyone believing for a moment that they represent the views of Gotlib the author. It goes without saying that this is all just play-acting.

D) The improbable narrator. In the first volume of Joann Sfar's best-selling series, *Le Chat du rabbin* [The Rabbi's Cat],[60] the narrator is revealed in the fifth panel to be the eponymous cat. It is he who will recount, in the first person, the adventures in which he has participated or to which he has had privileged access. The main characters of the action are nonetheless human beings, chief among whom are the rabbi and his daughter. The paradoxical choice made by Sfar is to delegate the narration to a creature that, in theory, does not have access to language. But in fiction anything can happen, and this theoretical impossibility is neatly sidestepped: the cat can talk because it has eaten a parrot.

The narrator of *Asterios Polyp*, by David Mazzucchelli,[61] or more precisely the narrator of some of the chapters, is the hero's dead brother (who had died at birth). He accompanies the hero like a ghost, and his version of events comes to us from some unknown place in the beyond.

These are but a few examples of the range of actorialized narrators in comics. It can be noted that, in every case, the verbal output of the actorialized narrator, unlike the implicit narrator, is not restricted to the role of reciter, and may appear in speech balloons as well as in recitatives. His/her voice accompanies us whether or not s/he appears in the image.

It would be possible to establish another typology, based on the personality of the narrator and the stance that s/he takes towards the events that s/he reports. This raises again, in fact, the issue of emotional involvement, already encountered in relation to the extradiegetic reciter. Being individualized, the actorialized narrator tends, quite logically, to be less neutral than a reciter that is only one of the manifestations of the fundamental narrator. S/he can, for example, get sentimental about childhood memories or take up a critical distance from a former self, go in for self-pity or cynicism, adopt a moralizing tone or stand on a soapbox.

The question of reliability also comes up: again, a point also raised in relation to the anonymous instance of the reciter. Blutch's *Le Petit Christian*[62] is a collection of childhood memories in which reality gets constantly entangled with the fantasies of the actorialized narrator, a small boy with a tendency to embroider the truth who identifies with his heroes of the moment: Steve McQueen, Doctor Justice,[63] and Bruce Lee. So the voice of the reciter makes the claim: "I'm the lonesome guy from Texas," extending the metaphor of the schoolboy who sees himself as a cowboy, while at the same time, the drawing sometimes endorses the fantasy (we do actually see a cowboy), and sometimes refutes it (the "cowboy" is really only a little boy: the monstrator has "given the game away"). The text-image relationship alternates between (spurious) confirmation and invalidation, and this oscillation creates a delicious irony.

The example of Blutch's work encourages me to broaden the notion of "dramatic irony," defined as follows by the German scholar Ansgar Nünning. For him: "Dramatic irony results from the gap between the restricted understanding of the dramatic action by one character at a particular moment, and the understanding that the spectator has at the same time."[64] Comic art is a polysemiotic (or multimodal) medium, and, unlike literature, has a greater range of resources at its disposal and can create dramatic irony by introducing all kinds of gaps and dissonance between a verbal assertion and its corresponding image while offering visual evidence to undermine it.

Moreover, it is clear that, out of all its privileges, there is only one that the fundamental narrator cedes to the actorialized narrator, and that is the power of speech. From the moment a fictional comic lets one of its "actors" be the narrator of his/her own story, the extradiegetic reciter is condemned to silence and the narrative voice is transferred to the narrating character. On the other hand, the fundamental narrator is always in a dominant position over the monstrator, continuing to orchestrate the overall production of narrative discourse, and, in particular, to organize the correlation between verbal and iconic strands. It is the fundamental narrator that decides when and how often Uncle Paul has to be depicted in order to be accredited as the enunciator of the story, and it is to this instance that the irony that characterizes *Le Petit Christian* must be attributed— whereas the eponymous hero, in contrast, maintains the seriousness that befits a child who "tells stories to himself." And it is this instance that chooses, at every moment (that is to say with every new panel) either to represent its "character who speaks in the first person" or to translate his/her thoughts, reveries, memories, fantasies, or feelings into images (and thereby to tip monstration over into a subjective regime). In fact, it is the fundamental narrator that, in all circumstances, has the last word—the final cut.

5.2.3 Haddock as Narrator, or the Eloquence of the Body

We are in 1698. The Unicorn, a proud third-ranking vessel in Louis XIV's fleet, has left the island of Santo Domingo, in the Caribbean, and set sail for Europe with, on board, a cargo of . . . of . . . well, there was mainly rum . . .

Every reader of *Tintin* will recognize the beginning of the stirring tale told by Captain Haddock about the fight between his ancestor Sir Francis Haddock and the pirate Red Rackham.[65] This tale is not just a digression in the plot; on the contrary, it conveys essential information. Haddock summarizes the *Memoirs* left by his ancestor, which he has just read overnight, and it is precisely this manuscript that has revealed the existence of the treasure that he and Tintin will feel duty-bound to recover.

Several aspects of this sequence make it memorable. It takes up some twelve pages of *Le Secret de la Licorne* [*The Secret of the Unicorn*]. It introduces a break in the iconic and thematic continuity of Tintin's adventures that has no equivalent in any other episode: the contemporary fictional world gives way to a historical costume drama. Moreover, it enables Hergé to produce some of his most resonant and spectacular images.

In addition, the episode is based on an unusual mechanism: it constantly goes back and forth between the past (the seventeenth century, the time frame of the events recounted) and the present (the twentieth century, the time frame of the enunciation). The necessity for these temporal shifts, of which there are eighteen, arises out of Hergé's decision not to use a recitative, or narrative voice-over. He lets us experience, "live," the events that the captain recounts, as if we were witnessing them directly—but each time Haddock starts speaking again, since he only expresses himself through speech balloons rather than in the traditional reciter's narrative box, it is the Captain himself who appears in the image and we are brought back to the small flat where his way with words has Tintin listening with baited breath.

This very unusual narrative strategy has one main virtue: it opens up the possibility of greater involvement for the actorialized narrator (the status accorded to Haddock for the duration of this sequence). His emotions are not conveyed by words alone: his verbal eloquence is matched by bodily expressivity. The captain is decked out in his ancestor's feather hat with his cutlass in his hand. He is also drinking rum and reenacts his swordplay, reliving the situations he has conjured up, and identifying with his illustrious ancestor to the point where he bursts through his portrait and substitutes his own face. Haddock is not simply a delegated reciter—his narration also involves miming and theatricality.

Hergé exploits the potential of the medium to the full here. Film would not be able to cope with these continual shifts between past and present—the result would be disjointed and the editing would lose all fluidity. Normally in a film when a character becomes the narrator of an embedded narrative, s/he temporarily disappears from the image and is present only through his/her voice. In a novel, the reification of the actorialized narrator in a body is, by definition, impossible. The capacity to supplement verbal narration with a bodily narration and to weave this double eloquence together is, then, peculiar to comic art (and to theatre).

I insist once more: even if it gets Haddock to take over the narration of Sir Francis Haddock's exploits, the fundamental narrator is still in control, here as elsewhere. It is this instance, sitting in the director's chair, that decides when to switch between past and present, the main narrative and the captain's metanarrative. It is this instance that, along with the monstrator, stage-manages this sensational story. And it is this instance that turns the captain's empathy for his ancestor to irresistibly comic effect—*and* that has the audacity, right in the middle of Haddock's flights of narration, to introduce three images representing the subjectivity of another character. This is, as it happens, Milou [Snowy], who, having tasted the glass of rum put down on the floor by Tintin, starts to see double (p. 23). The monstrator combines in a single panel Milou objectively represented, and the subjective perception the dog has of his surroundings.

5.3 MODALIZATION STRATEGIES

The concept of *modality* can be found, with different usages, in disciplines such as logic, linguistics, law, or music. I will use it here in a very broad sense, as that which colors, qualifies, and particularizes the discourse of the narrator (whether fundamental or delegated), determining how we gain access to the story, how we perceive its content, and how it produces certain effects on us.

I will raise, separately, two questions on the subject of the modalization of narrative discourse, one relating to the verbal aspect of enunciation and the other to its graphic aspect.

5.3.1 The Use of Verb Tenses by the Reciter

We have seen that the comics narrative seems to be characterized by an inherent fluctuation in relation to its temporality: it produces a narration that tends to be in the past by juxtaposing images that tend to be in the present. The choice of verb tense by the reciter will therefore have the potential to tip this unstable equilibrium in one direction or the other—even if, for reasons already explained, the categories of past and present seem less easy to distinguish and contrast in the case of a comic than in a text without illustrations.

The tense that is most often encountered is the past. The reciter goes back in time to recount events that have taken place in the near or distant past. When the prerogatives of the reciter are assumed, not by the fundamental narrator but by an actorialized narrator, this instance takes up a more explicit stance in relation to the events that it recounts. We know "from whence" it speaks. In more technical terms, we can say that the actorialized narrator coincides with what

Karl Bühler calls "a deictic center," which has three components: person ("I"), place ("here"), and time ("now").[66]

The actorialized narrator personalizes the enunciation, which therefore necessarily bears deictic traces. For example, the sentence that opens the first volume of *Persepolis*, "That's me when I was ten," introduces both a narrating "I" and an explicit distance between the period represented and the time of the enunciation (which the reader takes as coinciding with the time of the creation of the book): Marjane Satrapi is no longer ten years old and she is going to tell us about her childhood. (The events recounted in the four volumes of *Persepolis* cover the period 1980–1994 and the whole story is recounted in the past tense.)

Jacques Tardi's work includes manifold examples of the intermingling of past and present. *Griffu*,[67] drawn from a script by Jean-Patrick Manchette, tells the story of a police investigation against a background of property racketeering. The story is recounted by the main character in the past tense; however, certain sentences refer to the enunciative present. For example, on page 5: "What I'm telling you about it is just by way of making conversation." Others establish that the actorialized narrator now knows more than he did at the time that the events took place, and so can make a retrospective judgment; on page 6, for example: "I wasn't thinking about anything. I was wrong. I should have done." But the main peculiarity of the album is that Griffu ends up riddled with bullets and lies dying on the pavement against a row of dustbins. And the last sentence attributed to him operates a shift from narration in the past tense to the present of the enunciation: "That thought, where I am now, makes me laugh" (p. 55). The "where I am now" is obviously ambiguous—it may designate the place where he lies dying (but we would then have to admit the unlikely possibility that Griffu has delivered his entire narration during his dying moments) or the place where souls migrate to after death, whatever name one gives it. In fact, in other slightly earlier works by Tardi, namely *La Véritable Histoire du soldat inconnu* [The True Story of the Unknown Soldier][68] and *La Bascule à Charlot* [The Guillotine], the reciter's voice was already a voice that came from beyond the grave. There is no doubt that Tardi has a certain predilection for this unlikely type of narrator.

In *Brouillard au Pont de Tolbiac* [Fog over the Tolbiac Bridge],[69] based on Léo Malet's book, the investigation is also recounted by the detective, Nestor Burma, in the past tense. But the opening panel does not belong to his narrative, and includes a recitative (which, therefore, serves as the *incipit*) in the present tense: "Paris. At night, on the Tolbiac Bridge, a man is wandering. There is madness in his eyes." The status of this image, which shows the crazed man walking towards the reader, is uncertain; Burma is not present at this scene and has no knowledge of it. The panel can only be attributed to the fundamental narrator. Furthermore, the present tense used by this instance's mouthpiece, the reciter, is intemporal— the scene bears no date, unlike Burma's account, which opens with the caption: "November 10, 1956." I would call this an interpellative present.

On page 27 the same image, still unrelated to the main narrative, appears (although the framing is different), accompanied by an almost identical text: "At the same moment, on the Tolbiac Bridge, a man is wandering. There is madness in his eyes." But this time the "at the same moment" establishes the concomitance between the wanderings of the mysterious man and the scene involving Burma presented on the same page. The two narratives intersect on page 36 when Burma discovers the man's body: he has been stabbed. A press cutting reproduced four pages later will finally establish his identity. This convergence between two narratives that had seemed at first to be unrelated is not unusual in itself. What is unusual is that one of them is attributed to Burma, a delegated and actorialized narrator, and the other to the fundamental narrator—and that one is in the past, the other in the present.

I have already mentioned *Le Secret de la Salamandre*, an adventure in the Adèle Blanc-Sec series narrated by an old man who remains anonymous and outside the action. His narration constantly alternates between past and present, with no obvious justification for these incessant shifts in the time frame. The first sentence reports an event ("Today, at three o'clock in the morning, Lucien Brindavoine died . . .") and the narrative will attempt retrospectively to shed light on what has happened to bring about this event. It should, then, logically be in the past—and this is indeed the case, but it is noticeable that the present tense keeps breaking in. (For example: on page 5, "And where is Adèle Blanc-Sec while all this is going on? [. . .] She's asleep." On page 6: "He is as tired as hell . . . " On page 11: "let us follow this man on horseback who has just entered the city. Where is he going? . . ." On page 24: "Two night watchmen on their round go up the Canebière . . . ," etc.) If this confusion over time frames seems, as one is reading, to arise from a rather anarchic and uninhibited way of conducting the narration, the following lesson can nonetheless be drawn from it: the use of the past tense emphasizes the successive nature of events, the inescapable chain of cause and effect, while the present tends rather to situate a new event or location in a relationship of simultaneity with other events or locations previously introduced. It is as if, every time the omniscient narrator makes us leave one backdrop to go to another, its narrating voice returns, in spite of itself and seemingly intuitively, to the present tense, a fictional present that is not the present of enunciation but that succeeds in giving us "live" access to the scene. After which, the past-tense narration rapidly takes over again and continues its course, because this is the tense that, as we have seen, corresponds to the logic of the narrative situation and to the natural inclination of the medium itself.

5.3.2 The Graphic Personality of the Monstrator

Does the graphic style influence the degree of credit that we accord to the narrator's account? Is it the case that the more "realist" the drawing, the more credible the story? What role does the graphic encoding play in our perception of the facts recounted?

Questions of this type have little point if they are applied to works of fiction. By definition, a fiction does not ask us to believe in the veracity of its claims, but only to play along with them, in the "as if" mode. This is Coleridge's famous "willing suspension of disbelief." It is an attitude that can be likened to that of children in the symbolic world of play, where the categories of true and false are inoperative. In this context, Charlie Brown has no less reality than Flash Gordon, Astro Boy is equivalent to Akira, and I am as much inclined to believe Lapinot as Blueberry.[70] We know that none of these characters exists outside the paper world in which they carve out their careers, but the question must be posed differently when the work belongs to a genre that presupposes faithfulness to reality. This is, by definition, the case of documentary and autobiography in comics format.

Elisabeth El Refaie from the University of Cardiff has looked into this question by comparing two autobiographical comics: *Colin-Maillard* [Blind Man's Buff], by Max Cabanes[71] and Satrapi's *Persepolis*.[72] Drawing on the theoretical framework elaborated by Gunther Kress and Theo van Leeuwen on "multimodal discourse,"[73] El Refaie scrutinizes the albums of Cabanes and Satrapi for the "modality markers" (iconic resemblance, detail, depth, contextualization, color, etc.) that are supposed to suggest that an image is real or truthful. The investigation finds that these markers can readily be found in the work of Cabanes, but are absent, or only mutedly present, in the work of Satrapi. However, it is in fact Satrapi, whose graphic style is highly schematic, who aims to be as faithful as possible to historical facts, while Cabanes, in spite of his considerably more realist style, very freely embroiders episodes from his younger days, and indulges quite openly in fictionalization.

It seems then, that on the part of the enunciator, a claim to truthfulness is not necessarily to be equated with the most realist possible graphic modalization—and that, reciprocally, on the part of the receiver, a "not very realist" graphic encoding is accepted as no less credible and does not give rise to doubts about the accuracy of the narrative in question. The example of Spiegelman's *Maus*, in which the theme of the Holocaust is treated through very schematic characters with animals' heads, comes immediately to mind to corroborate this conclusion.

In any case, the list of "modality markers" seems to apply more to a single image than to a sequential narrative made up of multiple images. This is because it does not take account of the basis of the regime of belief peculiar to comics, namely the persistence of a consistent style throughout the narrative, a style that, because it maintains its identity through repeated appearances of characters and decor, is immediately accepted as a narrative convention, a form of graphic hand-writing as admissible as any other. This was the implication of the remark made by Alain Rey that I have quoted on more than one occasion: "Copi's talkative amoeba-like creature, produced with one deft stroke of the hand, is no lesser a character than one drawn with all the careful detail, shading and finishing touches that the likes of Foster or Giraud can muster," because all of them are endowed with "a stable identity for the duration of the story."[74]

We therefore arrive at the conclusion that, whatever degree of belief in the story the narrator expects from the reader, all the drawing styles that the monstrator can call on will be equally valid; they have no impact on the extent of the reader's willingness to go along with it.

What is highly significant, on the other hand, and highly consequential, is the option that the monstrator has of changing style in the course of the narrative, and the different modalizations that its graphic line may undergo, dictated by impulse or intention.

5.3.3 The End of the Dogma of Homogeneity

I signaled in *The System of Comics 1*[75] that this diversity of graphic handwriting, previously unknown, was becoming apparent in the work of a few artists from the new generation. Ten years down the line, it is patently obvious that the tendency to include breaks in graphic style in mid-narrative has become widespread, and that this is a sign of the progress of the medium in recent years, an expansion of its expressive potential, opening the way to a new artistic language and enabling it in particular to give graphic form to the emotional investment of the monstrator.

Manga, with their frequent recourse to a "multi-faceted style" (a schematic character in a hyperrealist decor, or a normal character who suddenly morphs into burlesque hyperexpressivity) have perhaps hastened this evolution.

It is particularly spectacular in the work of Fabrice Neaud. In the first three volumes of his *Journal* [Diary],[76] the drawing is photorealist in style and only permits itself a minimum of modalization. The fourth volume, in contrast, elevates heterogeneity into a stylistic principle. It suffices to compare the same group of friends from the "Pony Club" represented with realism on page 69 and caricatured on page 90; the artists Aristophane, Menu, and Alagbé turned into Lego figures on page 100; Fabrice's representation of himself as a kind of bendy toy, shown in silhouette (pp. 76–78); or the enormous mouth that he confers on the intrusive female reader, as from page 121, with the sole aim of ridiculing her. Each of these departures is perceived by the reader as a deviation from a graphic norm (the author's habitual style); this could all be merely a gratuitous game, but readers are quite naturally bound to wonder about the motivation of the monstrator and, more often than not, they discover that that these different modalities of expression convey dramatic impact and affective meaning.

Gert Meesters has also taken an interest in authors who no longer respect "a fundamental law of comic art: unity of style." Using the work of Dominique Goblet and Olivier Schrauwen to exemplify his thesis, he has shown how new "semantic possibilities" originate, in both cases, from a "stylistic reference system."[77] Meesters points in particular to the abundance of images or sequences that refer to models internal to the field of comic art (Winsor McCay in Schrauwen's *Mon Fiston* [My Boy]),[78] or, more generally, to the world of "fine art" and to the most varied traditions in the graphic and visual arts (references to icons, to children's drawings, to so-called primitive art, to non-figurative painting, to life drawing, to the "cute" style, etc., in Goblet's *Faire semblant c'est mentir* [Pretending is Lying]).[79]

There is an obvious parallel between these modulations of graphic style and the changes in tone, style, and writing technique practiced by James Joyce in the novel that is emblematic of modernity, *Ulysses*. This aesthetic syncretism cannot be compared to the effects of surprise or semiotic discontinuity deployed in a few previous works of comic art: the inclusion of a photo in a drawn narrative—see for example the epilogue of Tardi and Legrand's *Tueur de cafards* [Cockroach/ Informant Killer][80] or the album *Pourquoi j'ai tué Pierre* [Why I Killed Pierre] by Alfred and Olivier Ka[81]—or the sudden irruption of color into a black and white story—for example, in *La Tour* [The Tower] by Schuiten and Peeters[82] or *La Qu*

. . . [The Qu . . .] by Marc-Antoine Mathieu.[83] What has changed is that an artist's style is no longer perceived as "a signature feature" that must be kept intact, and drawing is now considered as a flexible medium whose expressive potential is infinite.

Henceforth, comic art values the possibility of this kind of rhetorical display more highly than the former imperative of harmony, the classical ideal. As we have noted above, any graphic style tends to make the reader overlook the fact that it is merely an arbitrary code once it is repeated from one image to the next. Its persistence makes it less noticeable, ensures that emphasis will be on the subject matter, and reinforces a reality effect, which gives credibility to the story being recounted. Conversely, any break in the code reminds readers they are looking at a drawing, and so combats or weakens the fictional illusion. When an artist such as Milo Manara decided to have a little fun by drawing his characters in different ways within the same story, it was in the context of an album (*Jour de colère* [Day of Wrath])[84] that explicitly declared itself to be an *exercice de style*, a meta-comic, a reflection on the laws of representation, all of which combined to call into question the principles of the "great adventure" tradition.

Comic art as a patchwork of heterogeneous styles was practiced in a spirit of experimentation by Nicolas Devil, with *Saga de Xam* [The Saga of Xam] [85] and in a spirit of playfulness by Moebius in *Major fatal*[86] and his Italian acolyte Andrea Pazienza in *Le Straordinarie Avventure di Pentothal* [The Amazing Adventures of Pentothal];[87] while another Italian author, Renato Calligaro (Deserto [Desert])[88] saw it as the precondition for a poetical comic art, which "will be saturated with aesthetic and formal information," restraining "the tyranny of plot." This sadly under-recognized artist has written several theoretical texts, from among which I draw the following extract:

> Diversity of styles and techniques is not a gratuitous game, but the inevitable consequence of the effort to reinvent reality. The potential is always polymorphic, and so the author's project is to concretize disparate potentialities. [. . .] And, just as a text can be, in turn, descriptive, allusive, moralistic, stream of consciousness, onomatopoeic, etc., so the image can become, successively, naturalistic, cubist, abstract, graphic or picturesque.[89]

The poetic comics of the Belgian artist Anne Herbauts (particularly *Vague* and *L'Idiot*)[90] are in the same vein as the pioneering work of Calligaro.

Mazzucchelli's *Asterios Polyp* is an example of a work in which the exhibition of a range of styles works in favor of the narrative project instead of counteracting it. In certain sequences, all the characters are drawn in their own graphic style and express themselves in individually shaped speech balloons. This unusual format illustrates a hypothesis formulated by the narrator: "What if reality (as perceived) were simply an extension of the self? Wouldn't that color the way each individual experiences the world?" By modifying the drawing technique according to the character, the monstrator translates into external terms the way that each of them sees the world, their idiosyncrasies. Asterios is an architect and a brilliant conversationalist—his body is represented as a set of hollow forms, decomposable into geometrical shapes, and colored in a cold blue to denote his insensitivity. Conversely, the body of Hana, a young woman who was unloved by her parents and who lacks confidence, is not blessed with a firm outline: she is represented by tiny hatched lines that make her look blurred and her color is an emotive red.

At the faculty party where Asterios and Hana meet and are attracted to each other, the unexpected superimposition of red and blue, of hatching and solid volumes, opens up from the outset the potential for a romantic attachment between these two people whose personalities are so dissimilar.

It is more than likely that Mazzucchelli remembered Saul Steinberg's famous *New Yorker* cover of November 23, 1968, which consisted of a strange group portrait: the eight members of a family and their dog appeared next to each other in the same drawing, each drawn in a different style. *Asterios Polyp* shows that comic art allows for a more consequential use of this graphic fragmentation by exploiting it for narrative purposes.

In the work of some of the best contemporary artists, variations in the graphic line do not spring from a conceptual impulse, but simply a concern to free up graphic technique and allow for spontaneity. José Muñoz is among those who have led the way in this respect. Among French artists, Joann Sfar and David Prudhomme are good examples. In the case of some series, (like *Le Minuscule Mousquetaire*),[91] Sfar draws directly in ink, with no prior penciling, deliberately giving his images an improvised look. In *Le Chat du rabbin*, he frequently changes his drawing implement: most of the album is pen-drawn, but about one panel in four is inked with a brush, producing a more painterly effect. Classical harmony is no longer the ideal—the artist wants to bring a jazz attitude to comics.

Back in 2002, Thierry Smolderen made the observation:
David Prudhomme has long since achieved what astrophysicists call escape velocity (the speed that enables rockets to avoid falling back to earth). In his case, he has succeeded in not falling back into the

Fig. 9. David Mazzucchelli, *Asterios Polyp* (New York: Pantheon Books, 2009), unpaginated.
© David Mazzucchelli.

same style, not falling back on the same solutions, which can easily turn into reflexes for an artist with so much facility and talent. [. . .] When Prudhomme starts juggling with different stylistic universes, it is always in a spirit of risk-taking, always in the moment, at the point where a spontaneous drawing emerges; with each new image, he likes to adopt new constraints, sometimes accidental: changing his drawing instrument, changing the formal protocols, left-handed drawing, drawing without looking at the page, etc. and above all improvising relentlessly, surprising even himself.[92]

Unlike works where clearly differentiated styles cohabit (such as *Ice Haven*, by Daniel Clowes,[93] in which the author tried to recapture the diversity that characterized the weekend comics supplements from American newspapers), albums by artists such as Sfar and Prudhomme display a style that is, from the outset, constitutionally composite. Variations in the graphic line cease to be noticeable, because they are a fundamental characteristic of the artist's graphic hand.

5.3.4 The Intermingling of Voices

Comic art has entered the era of narrative polygraphism and polyphony.

The great contemporary authors have come to realize the dramatic potential opened up to comics by the interplay of narrating instances. Through their scope, which is far beyond the norms of the standard Franco-Belgian album, "graphic novels" lend themselves particularly well to a structuring of the plot based on an alternation between different regimes of enunciation: the intervention of multiple narrative "voices," a reciter that is successively interventionist and mute, narration in the past or present tense, etc. Two examples already alluded to above will suffice to demonstrate this.

The structure of *Asterios Polyp* is built on the interpolation of two narratives, which alternate from one chapter to the next: one—for which, as we have seen, the hero's late brother takes responsibility—recounts, in the past, the salient moments of Asterios's professional and romantic career. The other, in which the images and dialogues speak for themselves, without the intervention of a reciter, allows us to witness, as it is happening, the architect's flight from his former life—he makes this break after a fire ravages his house, goes on the road with a few dollars in his pocket, and even gets himself taken on as a car mechanic in a garage. These two narratives are differentiated by color—in the first blue and pink tones are dominant, and in the second it is yellow and purple. Given that it structures the overall composition of the work, this opposition is attributed by the reader to the fundamental narrator. The ending sees Asterios braving a snowstorm and, more dead than alive, reaching Hana, his ex-partner, and becoming reconciled with her, with himself, and with his past. This final chapter that synthesizes the opposition is the only one to use all the resources of polychromy.[94]

I will not go into detail here about the composition of Chris Ware's *Jimmy Corrigan, the Smartest Kid on Earth*.[95] As readers will know, it is a family chronicle that focuses on the male line of the Corrigans and goes back as far as William, Jimmy's great-grandfather. The book plays on the alternation between sections that can be described roughly as corresponding to the current era and so to the present, in the broadest sense (the five that are centered on Jimmy's life as a child or adult) and others—representing about forty percent of the total—devoted to the life of his grandfather and great-grandfather. The longest of these sections given over to the past amounts to eighty-one pages, during which the eponymous protagonist is completely lost from our view.

Ware adopts three different enunciative strategies in succession. In the story of Jimmy's life, the reciter intervenes very sparingly for brief notes on changes of time or place or to indicate, with one word, in the author's own very particular way, the logical articulations between scenes ("But," "And so," "Thus," etc.). In the other sections, in contrast, the reciter sometimes stays in the background and sometimes becomes very interventionist, punctuating the action with commentaries and narrating in the present tense events situated in a past that is already very distant (the end of the nineteenth century): "Today Mr William Corrigan (age 47) finds himself . . . ," etc. Finally, a long forty-three-page sequence is recounted in the first person by the child that Jimmy's grandfather was at that time, who therefore accedes, for the duration of this sequence only, to the rank of actorialized narrator—the only one of the four generations of Corrigans to be granted this privilege. This retrospective narration, which bears on certain events of his childhood ("At the time, I think I understood little of that afternoon"), seems to have been undertaken in answer to the questions of his granddaughter Amy.

Leaving aside major and complex works such as these, I find it interesting to note the occurrence, here and there, of much shorter, playful interventions of the reciter. These light-hearted instances are based on the idea of permeability between the world in which the characters cavort (the diegesis) and the recitatives that normally sit above the panels. In a regular comic the characters are not supposed to hear the "voice" of the reciter, which is addressed only to the reader—but things can work differently in a parodic or simply ludic context.

Thus, in *Menaces sur L'Empire* [The Empire under Threat], an album by Veys and Barral[96] that parodies the *Blake and Mortimer* series,[97] on page eighteen the

Fig. 10. Art Spiegelman, *One Row, Raw* no. 5, 1982. © *Raw*. Reproduced with kind permission of the author.

character of Olrik suddenly gets annoyed about the content of the recitative above his head, and his furious look reduces the reciter to silence. The authors are making fun of Edgar P. Jacobs's propensity for accompanying his images with redundant description.

A strip by Art Spiegelman that appeared in *Raw* 5 (1982) with the title *One Row* turns upon a comparison between the virtues of dialogue and recitatives.

"There is an *immediacy* in the use of speech balloons," says the reciter above the first panel, in which a man is sitting and reading his newspaper in silence; but in the next panel the man himself speaks and continues the same sentence ("a *directness* that cannot be achieved by a caption floating above the image"), which leads us to suppose that he could hear the beginning at the same time as we were reading it. The reader is amused to see that Spiegelman mentions the speech balloon in a recitative and the recitative in a speech balloon. The third panel opens with another remark by the reciter, which draws the argument to a conclusion: "But captions have a *coolness*, a *distance*, the authority of real prose." The game continues, henceforth on the mode of redundancy. "Screw this self-consciousness!" shouts the character, exasperated. And the reciter reiterates in reported speech: "'*Screw this self-consciousness*,' he said." The fourth panel introduces yet another effect—two pieces of dialogue are exchanged and intercalated into the middle of the reciter's sentence, whose second part is therefore slightly delayed, creating an anti-climactic effect that is comical.

However minor, Spiegelman's fantasy gives us a glimpse of a domain that has hitherto been little explored, a whole potential register of tensions and disjunctions between the dialogue and the narrative voice, which humorists could turn to their advantage.

CHAPTER SIX

The Subjectivity of the Character

We usually describe as "behaviorist" a narrative in which the knowledge that we can have of characters is limited to their actions and their words and in which we are denied access to their thoughts and feelings. As the Finnish researcher Mikkonen has observed, this is still the most common type of narrative in comics—and he cites *Tintin* and *Corto Maltese* as examples.[1] We should not forget, though, that words (in the form of direct speech) emphasized by the expressivity of the body are already, in themselves, a privileged means of access to the subjectivity of a character, be it "Petit Christian" or Captain Haddock, as we have seen above.

However, there are other types of language use to call upon. The "speech records" supplied by the balloons can be supplemented by "records of thought," to adopt the terms of the narratologist Seymour Chatman.[2] In fact, comics can deploy a simple and effective resource to express a character's thoughts, his/her "inner voice": they can be displayed as *direct speech* by "thought balloons" (linked to their source by a chain of smaller balloons). The words conveyed in them take on a special status as the reader knows that they have not been spoken aloud but simply formulated internally by the character. The other characters remain oblivious to these thoughts, which are for the exclusive benefit of the reader, who thereby has direct and highly privileged access to the inner life of the protagonist.

Arguably, the balloon mechanism is used here to carry out a deception—it connotes a false enunciation, one that has not really taken place except in the innermost recesses of a pseudo "consciousness." By availing itself of thought balloons, the narrator explicitly positions itself as omniscient, and capable of penetrating the mind of its paper marionettes.

The narrator has at its disposal two other ways of giving us access to the characters' inner life: by relying on the reciter or the monstrator.

The reciter can intervene by means of *indirect speech*, reporting the thoughts, feelings, conjectures, and other mental activity of the character. In *Jimmy Corrigan*, Chris Ware gives the reciter responsibility for the articulation of what Jimmy's

121

grandfather felt on the day when he realized that his own grandmother was going to die:

> Finally, he decides it's time to go back./But maybe first he'll pick out a rock, and give it a name and he'll keep it with him/for the rest of the night. At least/and it won't matter/what his dad says/ and it won't matter what his dad does /. . . /. . . /And while he might have readied himself for harsh words, rough handling or even a slap nothing prepared this boy/for the unchecked sobs/of a child/anticipating the imminent loss of his mother. (unp.)

However, examples like this are extremely rare.

As a mimetic (or dramatic) art, comics usually favors direct speech, which facilitates the immersion of the reader in the action. Consequently, frequent use is made of the convention whereby thought is transmuted into words. Thus, when Professor Philip Mortimer is exploring the London sewers, it is unlikely that sentences such as "Upon my word, I think this must be the right direction" or "Curses! I'm cornered!"[3] are spoken audibly—unless we imagine that the professor is in the habit of talking to himself. Jacobs, however, puts them in speech balloons rather than thought balloons.

If the reader is not especially surprised, this is because comics is a mono-sensory medium in which all the information is transmitted through the visual channel and words are read instead of being heard (the false orality of the speech balloon corresponds to the false enunciation of the thought balloon). It is also because the character-speech balloon pairing is itself a convention that has become completely naturalized after a century of intensive use; it defines the sphere of action of the graphic persona. As Thierry Smolderen writes, the balloon "makes speech spring from the same source as action, assimilating it to a behavior that persists from one image to the next."[4] Moreover, the solution that Jacobs opts for sets up a more dynamic tension between the professor's soliloquy and the reciter's monologue that provides a parallel commentary on the scene.

It should be noted that, even if the reciter does not report Mortimer's thoughts in indirect speech ("The professor says to himself that . . ."), it still demonstrates, albeit less explicitly, that it has access to his hero's inner life. Proof of this is offered by sentences like "Although he has no illusions about the effectiveness of bullets against his freakish opponent, Blake, who has come to, shoots him twice";[5] or, during the confrontation between Mortimer and Septimus, the moment when the professor "realizes that his opponent is not in his right mind."[6] In

these two examples, the reciter translates the thought processes of both protagonists into words.

The final resource that the narrator has at its disposal to give us access to the
inner life of a character consists of having the feelings or thoughts that occupy
her/him graphically represented by the monstrator. The translation of thought
into images usually works through metaphor, and Dupuy and Berberian's *Journal
d'un album* [Journal of an Album][7] supplies an excellent example of this. Charles
Berberian is in a taxi; the driver asks him:

"What about you? What do you do?"

And the following panel breaks out of the diegetic world: we are no longer in
the taxi, but in front of a flying saucer from which Berberian has just emerged,
dressed as a Martian.[8] The image offers a visual representation of his state of
mind as he replies:

"I'm an artist, I draw comics."

The image conveys to us that Berberian has anticipated the reaction of his interlocutor, in whose eyes anyone who engages in an occupation as trivial as comics might as well be an alien—a view confirmed by the driver's reaction, after a
silence:

"Oh, I see . . . You do that kind of garbage, then . . ."

There are other techniques to be found in comics for the graphic expression of
feelings. Derik Badman has correctly pointed out that:

Comics also make use of various visual effects to make an image show a character's internal thoughts or
feelings. Prominent examples include many of the types of emanata commonly found in comics or the
flowers and stars used in the background of many *shōjo manga.*[9]

(The sun depicted in the middle of the Miwa Ueda page reproduced and discussed above (see page 60 in this book) is an example that belongs to the same
register: cosmic elements or motifs from nature, traditionally associated with
feelings of empathy, well-being, or fascination.)

The term "emanata" was suggested by Mort Walker in his textbook *The Lexicon of Comicana*[10] to designate the dashes, droplets, spirals, stars, and other graphic signs placed near a character's face in order to convey an emotion or physical state. The emanata reinforce the facial expression.

Another code, different from the emanata, is constituted by pictograms (called "symbolia" by Walker) that make up a loosely conventionalized repertoire transmitted from one cartoonist to another. A picture of a heart often suffices to translate romantic feelings into visual language. A heart with a dagger through it means disappointment in love, abandonment, or betrayal. A melting ice cube can materialize a glacial tone, expressing contempt. And so on. Pictograms of this type can, as Walker pointed out, be assimilated to symbols (in the Piercian sense). Moreover, they are usually enclosed within the image, or a balloon, and considered to have been emitted by the character just as words would be. As a general rule, then, they substitute, with some economy, for the words that might otherwise express the same thing.

In the example from *Journal d'un album*, on the other hand, the image of the alien does not substitute for words but complements them, not in order to illustrate them in a literal sense but to register what the speaker feels as he utters them. The character says one thing and simultaneously, but mutely, thinks another. The visual metaphor provides the solution that enables instant grasp of this dichotomy.

There are differences in usage and function between the pictogram and the metaphorical emotion-image, as I have suggested, but they are not intrinsically all that distinct, and the boundary between them is blurred. One could easily imagine in a different context (assuming that the convention had been repeatedly reused by one or two influential artists) that the figure of the alien could have become a conventional pictogram expressing the sense of being an outsider or not belonging.

6.1 SUBJECTIVITY THROUGH THE IMAGE ALONE

When there is no text to anchor them into a subjective regime, certain images can pose problems of interpretation—is what we are seeing to be read as real or imaginary? The American artist Lynd Ward (1905–1985), one of the finest exponents of the *novel in woodcuts*, the genre that appeared around 1920 and died out in the 1950s, made innovative use of color coding to guide the reader. In *Wild*

Pilgrimage (1932), a wordless story of about a hundred pages, Ward introduced a second color—the woodcuts portraying "reality" were printed in black, and those representing the hero's dreams and fantasies were orange.

Among the many silent comics published in the last few years, a certain number can be distinguished (I am thinking in particular about works by Fabio, Guy Delisle, Mahler, François Ayroles—and before them of Avril and Petit-Roulet) by their regular, if not massive, recourse to pictograms. In narratives by definition deprived of "speaking rights," the use of pictograms exemplifies the logic of substitution mentioned above. They introduce a form of interlocution into the narrative discourse of silent comics, which are essentially founded on intergestuality.

Ayroles's short album *Les Penseurs* [The Thinkers] [11] amounts to a comprehensive handbook for using pictograms. Its title is misleading, because the characters featured in it speak as much as they think, through pictograms whose status (verbal production or mental activity) is indicated by the form of the balloon, speech balloon, or thought balloon. Three pictograms in particular are extensively used: a heart, a glass of beer, and a cigarette. They can be objects of desire and different kinds of pleasure, constantly competing with each other in configurations that are renewed from one little playlet to the next.

It quickly becomes evident that pictograms do not necessarily signify the same thing each time they are used; their decoding has to take account of the context and the situation. The cigarette pictogram can mean variously: "I want a cigarette," "I want *another* cigarette," "Do you want a cigarette?" "Would you have a cigarette on you?"; or even "You can't beat a cigarette." The anchoring function performed by the sequence in relation to each of the images that compose it [12] is fully confirmed here. Ayroles's panels do not otherwise pose any problem of understanding: within them, the pictogram is the only element whose polysemy is open to interpretation and needs to be narrowed down. The remaining elements—the characters, the situation—are perfectly transparent.

Even so, the interpretation does not necessarily involve a precise verbal, literal translation of the message symbolized by the pictogram. In one page that shows a man and a woman seated at a table, the woman has a speech balloon with a heart in it on three occasions. The man responds with a glass of beer or a cigarette. An attempt to reconstruct their exact conversation could only lead to the postulation of absurd exchanges like: " I love you," "And I'd love a beer." The most realistic and interesting reading of this page is one that maintains its enigmatic quality and takes the pictograms as indications rather than actual utterances. All we need to understand is this: she talks to him about love and he pretends not to hear,

Fig. 11. François Ayroles, *Les Penseurs* (Paris: L'Association, 2006). © L'Association.

continuing to focus on his banal preoccupations. The interest of the technique resides in its substitution of a certain indeterminacy for the clarity of an ordinary verbal exchange, leaving the way open for the reader's own interpretations and projections.

This is an instance of a highly specific form of access to the subjectivity of a character. The elliptical format of the pictogram is a technique for displaying the thoughts or feelings that preoccupy him/her at a given moment. Depending on the distribution of pictograms across the page (some panels have none), we are granted periodic access to the character's inner life. This access is not gained through verbal enunciation, and neither is it strictly speaking, gained through monstration, but rather through a sort of intermediate code, which introduces a certain fluidity into the narrative discourse of comics.

Another striking example of the silent expression of inner life can be found in the work of Fabrice Neaud in the third volume of his *Journal*.[13] Although the *Journal* is usually fairly talkative, in Chapter 5 of the third volume, the narration is completely silent for some eighteen pages (pp. 40–57). Fabrice, the I-as-character (or autobiographic actorialized narrator) is sitting at a table in a bar called the "François 1er" with the young man with whom he is in love. The first two pages focus on the faces and hands of the two participants in the conversation, who are tightly framed. Changes in bodily posture from one frame to the next indicate that they are each speaking in turn, but the reader has no access to these exchanges: the sound is turned off. These close-ups also express the romantic attachment that leads Fabrice to pay particular attention to the gestures, the facial expressions, and, we presume, the voice of his interlocutor. From the third page onward, the framing widens; the two young men are no longer shown in alternate panels but cohabit within the same panel. This opening up of the field of view continues on the following pages, but the decor of the François 1er fades out to be replaced by scenes graphically conjured up that at first glance seem to have nothing to do with the situation. The two protagonists still sit across from one other at a small bistro table, but are now surrounded by couples whirling around at some Viennese ball, by a string quartet who seem to be serenading them, by a field of sunflowers, by young, joyfully choreographed gymnasts, by a field of freshly harvested wheat, and so on. The meaning of this paradigmatic series is clear—these are all metaphors for the euphoria felt by Fabrice, something approaching ecstasy, arising from this shared moment with his beloved.

What makes this sequence remarkable (apart from its length and its intensity) is the fact that it is completely silent. The narrator's feelings are not verbalized.

Some time ago an article by the linguistics specialist Sylvianne Rémi-Giraud analyzed another sequence from the same book (pp. 334 and 335) in which, conversely, the drawings correspond in various ways to a series of verbal metaphors that appear in first-person recitatives. She noted that the drawing "takes hold of the virtual world of the metaphor and brings it to the foreground" and that "through the drawing, these metaphors gain a spiritual enrichment that goes beyond what words [could] say."[14] Spiritual enrichment or, rather, aesthetic enrichment.

These comments are highly relevant to the sequence that concerns us. Except that, in this case, the visual metaphors do not "translate" verbal utterances into the language of images—they are instances of "thinking in images," where the image demonstrates here its capacity for communicating feelings and emotional states by embodying them without the mediation of language.

But who is speaking to us through these images? The fundamental narrator or the actorialized narrator incarnated here by Fabrice? Unlike the examples discussed above (taken from Berberian and Blutch), the same images can be read as at once objective and subjective. The two characters absorbed in their conversation appear throughout, represented in "realist" style, against a background that undergoes perpetual metamorphosis and that expresses, in a way that is unmistakably lacking in realism and is therefore to be read as phantasmatic, the inner thoughts of one of the two characters, the one who is acting as narrator.

We have seen that as a general rule, the actorialized narrator was above all a reciter. Therein lies the conundrum posed by these pages of Neaud's *Journal*. Because although he may be silent and may have given up his prerogative as a reciter in this chapter, that does not mean that the Fabrice-character renounces the status of narrator. Three elements corroborate this interpretation: first, the title of the work (*Journal*), which marks it as bound by the "autobiographical pact"; second, the fact that this chapter is embedded within a narrative of much greater scope that is carried, before and after, by Fabrice's narrative voice; third, the fact that this chapter gives us access to one subjectivity only—his, while the feelings of the other character remain as opaque for the reader as they were for Fabrice himself in the actual situation.

Fabrice is, then, incontestably, the actorialized narrator of these pages just as he is of the rest of the book. But the objectifying of him as a character must still be imputed to the fundamental narrator (and to its delegated operator, the monstrator) in the same way as the overall organization of the sequence (the framing, layout, rhythm, and space accorded to the conversation). This long silent sequence does not infringe the rule postulated above concerning the autobiographical narrator—this character is always split between an objective and a subjective regime.

6.2 THE EXPRESSION OF AN INNER WORLD

I have so far broached the question of the expression of subjectivity and inner life in relation to one particular instance: the actorialized narrator. Clearly, this issue has wider implications. It very directly concerns narratology, but it is also bound up, more generally, with the poetics of the comics form and the resources that it has to speak to us of the human condition in its private, psychic, and affective dimensions.

When comics was more or less universally regarded as infantile escapism, it was taken for granted that its characters were puppets, inherently lacking in depth, and capable only of generating action, movement, and noise. No one can fail to be aware that the exploration of inner lives has become the key subject matter of contemporary comics. Not only as a result of the significant development of the autobiographical genre in all its varieties, but also as a feature of purely fictional work, from the most self-evidently ambitious graphic novels (like *Cages* by Dave McKean, *Jimmy Corrigan* by Chris Ware, or *Asterios Polyp* by David Mazzucchelli) to more seemingly conventional series (for example, in France, *Monsieur Jean* [Get a Life] by Dupuis and Berberian, or *Le Combat ordinaire* [Ordinary Victories] by Larcenet) or a newspaper strip like Bill Watterson's *Calvin and Hobbes*.

Famously, in this last work, Hobbes is seen as a soft toy by all the characters except Calvin, for whom he is a very real tiger, and the best possible playmate. The author pretends to give credence to the youngster's fantasy and shows Hobbes speaking and enacting this role.

The so-called "gimmick" of my strip—the two versions of Hobbes—is sometimes misunderstood. I don't think Hobbes as a doll that miraculously comes to life when Calvin's around. Neither do I think of Hobbes as the product of Calvin's imagination. The nature of Hobbes's reality doesn't interest me, and each story goes out of its way to avoid resolving the issue. Calvin sees Hobbes one way, and everyone else sees Hobbes another way. I show two versions of reality, and each makes complete sense to the participant who sees it. I think that's how life works. None of us sees the world in exactly the same way, and I just draw that literally in the strip. Hobbes is more about the subjective nature of reality than about dolls coming to life.[15]

The subjectivity of perception was already a pretext for visual gags (or more precisely for graphic experimentation) in the work of some major cartoonists of the 1920s and 1930s. In the *Polly and her Pals* strip that appeared on the Sunday page dated September 26, 1926, Cliff Sterrett plunged the heroine's parents into a visually distorted and threatening world; things were restored back to normal in the final panel, when Paw and Maw, realizing that they had accidentally exchanged glasses, each put their own pair back on. In this example, it was only sensory perception that was at issue. I could cite other comics whose authors find ingenious graphic solutions for portraying drunkenness, fever, and other pathological states, or for exploring the twilight zone between waking and sleeping.

In the *Polly and her Pals* page dated July 29, 1928 (a wordless strip), Samuel Perkins goes to the dentist, sternly encouraged by his wife and daughter. He is petrified, and Sterrett materializes his terror metaphorically, by drawing him in several panels as he must imagine himself to be, in other words, very small. Once he has received the necessary treatment, and has ascertained that his tooth no longer hurts, he goes home filled with a feeling of triumphant euphoria, whereupon Sterrett draws him as a giant.

As in Watterson's work, it is no longer a case, of sensory perception here, but of subjectivity in a wider sense, involving a way of apprehending the world, the power of the imagination, and the credence accorded to psychic representations and projections.[16] It is this wider notion of perception that comes into play in the pages from *Asterios Polyp* referred to above, where Mazzucchelli draws each character in a style that visually translates the way in which s/he "experiences the world."

The example of Mazzucchelli brings together two questions we have encountered. The first concerns the various modalizations of the graphic line, insofar as they form part of a narrative strategy; the second concerns the fusion, within the image, of a regime of objectivity with a regime of subjectivity. We are confronted with a synthesis, which falls within a regime of *subjectivized objectivation*: we see the characters from the outside, but in the way that they themselves see the world and project themselves into it.

In general, the question of the expression of the inner life of a character can only be studied within a narratological theory of comics. This is because one of the objects of narratology is to demonstrate that the narrative is the product of a consciousness, or of more than one consciousness, and because the technique adopted by an author to give access to the subjectivity of his/her characters cannot be described without precise identification of the respective involvement of the reciter and the monstrator—and of their intersecting modes of operation.

The reciter and the monstrator closely collaborate when the latter illustrates quite literally what the words of the former suggest. The magic lantern sequence from *Jimmy Corrigan* provides an example. Jimmy's grandfather, not paying much attention to the slide show, lets his imagination wander:

Thinking about it for a moment,/The boy begins to imagine/The light from the little lamp flame/growing/like hair/through the lantern lens/and flowing indefinitely/out the window./A seamless stream of predictable pictures pointed at the moon.

What the reciter evokes with these words is illustrated by a series of images, spread over two pages, that show the small boy indeed grabbing the contraption, aiming it out of the window and projecting a kind of powerful laser beam through the night sky. What the character imagines is given visual form, a misleading corroboration. The reverie is broken off when the little guy falls asleep.

Comics has the unique capacity to be able to illustrate with the same force of conviction the "real," the imagined, the thought, and the felt—and in the transition from one panel to the next it can glide smoothly from an objective to a subjective register. It is therefore very easy for it to offer equivalents for the free indirect style, to change the point of view and invade the consciousness of its paper denizens. Since storytelling is the natural inclination of the medium, any kind of inner expression (whether thought, reverie, fantasy, or reminiscence) is ipso facto narrativized. This applies even if this narration takes the form of chaos when the mental state of the character is troubled (as in the scenes from Mattotti's *Feux*, where Lieutenant Absinthe is suffering from hallucinations).

Works like *A Small Killing*, by Alan Moore and Oscar Zarate, *Cité de verre* [City of Glass] by David Mazzucchelli and Paul Karasik (based on the book by Paul Auster), or *Cages* by Dave McKean have experimented successfully, by means of the interplay of sequential images (accompanied or not by text), with stream of consciousness, the literary technique that tries to replicate the flow of thought.[17] There is therefore ample evidence that the exploration of consciousness in comics is by no means reserved to the domain of autobiographical narratives and intimate confessions.

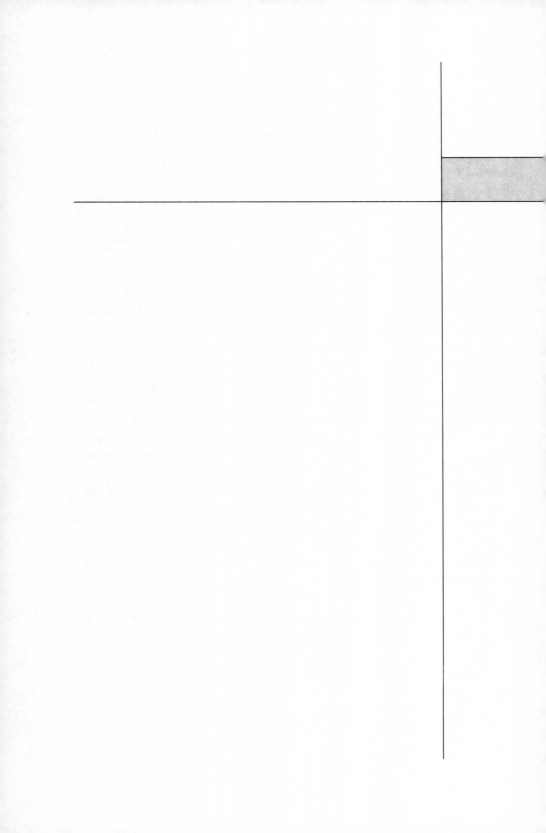

CHAPTER SEVEN

The Rhythms of Comics

Everything that has duration contains music, just as everything that is visible contains graphic design and everything that moves contains dance.

Duration, whether short (a three- or four-panel strip) or long (a 300-page graphic novel), is a natural dimension of comics narrative, as it is of any other narrative.

Consequently, so is "music." And since comic art is distinguished by its capacity for converting time into space,[1] the rhythmic scansion of the narrative necessarily implies certain ways of occupying space.

The importance of rhythm as a structuring element of the narrative discourse of comics was already emphasized in *System 1*, where I wrote:

"The 'text' of comic art obeys a rhythm that is imposed upon it by the succession of frames. This is a basic beat that, as in music, can be developed, nuanced, layered over by more elaborate rhythmic effects emanating from other 'instruments' (other parameters of the medium) . . . ,"[2] and I described the process of reading comic art as a "rhythmic operation of crossing from one frame to the next."[3]

Given the above, one of the six functions that the frame was deemed to fulfill was, precisely, the rhythmic function: "Each new panel propels the narrative forward and, simultaneously, contains it. The frame is the agent of this double maneuver of progression/retention."[4]

But if a general theory of the language of comics aims to lead on to a poetics, it cannot be satisfied with such lapidary observations. It needs to develop a more comprehensive theory of rhythm.

It is, indeed, remarkable that this issue is never raised by theorists,[5] whereas artists, in contrast, frequently refer to it as one of their major preoccupations. As I write this chapter, I have just read these words of Christophe Blain:

Comic art is like singing. Rhythm is part of the challenge. [. . .] When I start writing a story, before getting to the stage of the storyboard, I tell it to myself, giving it a rhythm that has to include moments of intensity.

133

The story has to move along, but the rhythm must not be jerky. It needs subtleness, changes of tempo, accelerations of pace. Every story has an underlying musical score . . . .[6]

Unsurprisingly, musical terms come spontaneously to mind when the question of rhythm is raised.

Will Eisner devoted the third part of his textbook *Comics and Sequential Art*[7] to the question of timing. The creator of *The Spirit* observed that the number, size, and shape of panels help create a rhythmic effect, and that modifying one of these parameters in the middle of a page is equivalent to speeding up or slowing down the narration. Without much more theoretical elaboration, Eisner illustrated his point by commenting on a *Spirit* episode first published on March 27, 1949, entitled "Foul Play."

In the anthology *Abstract Comics* (2009), the short shrift given to the story and, almost always, to mimesis and representationalism, has the effect of increasing the salience of rhythm as one of the inherent characteristics of the multiframe, the sequential apparatus peculiar to comic art. Indeed, the text on the back cover emphasizes this:

Panel rhythm, page layout, the sequential potential of color and the panel-to-panel play of abstract shapes have all been exploited to create potent formal dramas and narrative arcs, bringing the art of *comics* the closest that it, or any other visual art, has yet come to the condition of instrumental music.

And most reviewers of the volume put together by Molotiu have also pointed to the musical dimension of the formal dynamic at work on the page, whether this is a matter of harmony, dissonance, or progressive transformation. Charles Hatfield has gone so far as to suggest that the entire book could be thought of as a long musical piece, with each artist's contribution representing a movement.[8]

It is easy, then, to acknowledge that abstract comics have the power to bring out the rhythmic and musical dimension intrinsic to the formal resources of the medium, an observation that comes as no surprise to anyone who remembers that as far back as the 1920s, "art cinema," sometimes referred to as "abstract cinema" or "cinema without a screenplay," was already giving priority to the exploration of its own potential for "rhythmic actions." I am referring here to films by artists such as Fernand Léger, Viking Eggeling, Hans Richter, or Luigi Veronesi. Were the first abstract films by Richter not called *Rhythm 21*, *Rhythm 23* and *Rhythm 25*?

Rhythm 21 is a play on shapes (squares, rectangles) and on color contrasts (gray, black, white), conceived as dynamic elements in themselves, and the film transmits a beat that seems to give these "elementary shapes" a life of their own; the style becomes still clearer with *Rhythm 23*, where lines whose thickness, segmentation and direction (sometimes diagonal) introduce new rhythmic variations.[9]

All in all, we have to concede that comics trails way behind cinema: its belated discovery of the rhythmic and formal potential of abstraction seems like a replay of a long-outdated avant-garde.[10] We will return to the problematic of "belatedness" in the final chapter.

The rhythmic aspect of "classic" (figurative and narrative) comics may seem less immediately obvious than that of abstract comics. This is, first, because it does not have as a priority the organization of a melodic dialogue among formal elements; it does not always aspire to the creation of a visual rhythm. Second, even if it does set up, deliberately or not, rhythmic effects, these are probably not salient for the reader, whose attention is primarily captured by the plot and consequently focused on the content of each panel, which, in its capacity as an "utterable" and an "interpretable," demands his/her co-operation.[11]

In narrative comic art, rhythm is no longer part of the content in itself (as it may be on some pages of abstract comic art) but merely a mode of narration. To summarize, we can, with Isabelle Guaïtella, say that we are most often confronted with an "intersecting play of iconicity and rhythm," which can be analyzed in aesthetic terms but also in terms of meaning production.[12]

This "intersecting play" opens up several possibilities. Classic comics may go no further than using the apparatus itself by following the rhythm intrinsic to the preconfigured multiframe (a rhythm that will be more or less marked depending on the organization of the page layout, as we will see below); alternatively it can mobilize other parameters to produce "more elaborate rhythmic effects," either at the level of the page as a whole, or over a smaller area. In the first case, the narration can be described as *smooth*, and in the second as *accentuated*.

7.1 THE MULTIFRAME AS BEAT

The emblematic apparatus of the medium, the multiframe, that is to say the page divided up into a certain number of framed subspaces, is a very powerful *solidarity operator*—within it, successive images do not just make up a string, they comprise, from the outset, a totality. Readers approach the page both as a fraction of a story and as a visual unit. They notice immediately that the page they are about to read is composed of numerous panels, and thus has moments of stasis, pauses programmed into the narrative.

The number of panels comprising the whole-page multiframe determines the density of the page. Experienced readers take this in at a glance, just as they can see whether the images are high or low in information. This instantaneous perception enables them to calculate two things: the (approximate) reading time (they see whether it is a page that can be skimmed or whether it needs to be lingered over) and the rhythm that will govern the phased, disjointed reading process.

The first rhythm that we encounter, the underlying rhythm, which provides the background for all the others, i.e., the beat, is precisely indicated by the number of panels, and, as a function of this, their size. On a page consisting of two large images one above the other, the beat is slow and steady (the first two albums by Anthony Pastor, *Ice Cream* and *Hotel Koral*, for example, use this duple time); in a page containing numerous rows of small panels, it is faster.

Once the reading process is under way, the multiframe displays another of its powers, the power of attraction that entices the reader forward. Reading could be said to deconstruct the page, in the sense that it gives direction to the succession of panels, unfurls them, and arranges them in single file (each one will have its moment) within the "imaginary ribbon" that I evoked in *System 1*.[13] The multiframe lures the reader ever onwards, it designates in advance the images still to come; the reader therefore feels summoned by them and rushes headlong after the forthcoming narrative segments, as if running down a flight of stairs. Eager to discover the surprises in store, but also, in some way, to exhaust the apparatus itself, to get to the end of it, to miss nothing.

In fact, this force of attraction is even stronger at the creative stage. A string of empty frames drawn on a piece of paper provides a matrix whose content cannot be other than sequential. As Henri Van Lier noted, frames are not just filled with images, they actively call them into being. I have used the term "gridding" for this first appropriation of the space, this initial occupation of the page, which calls forth a drawing.[14] Chris Ware's notebooks, in particular, reveal a whole series of little squares representing a preliminary multiframe, where the artist has begun to improvise without always filling the entire grid.[15]

The act of filling in one little square, then another, then another, obviously recalls the way in which children tell a story, using the "and then . . . and then

. . . and then . . ." method. But the process of reading a comic also follows this cumulative logic: readers extricate themselves from one panel only to plunge into the next one, and so on. It is this discontinuous and rhythmic operation that sets up a beat at the heart of the reading process.

In *Naissances de la bande dessinée*, Thierry Smolderen quotes an essay written by the film editor Walter Murch, who worked with Coppola, among others. According to Murch:

> We are permanently "editing" the film of our lives, and the blinks that so often punctuate our utterances and our thoughts represent one of the most obvious symptoms of this editing process."[16]

And Smolderen goes on to suggest:

> If Murch is right, if these micro-cuts really do explain our readiness to accept the discontinuities in an edited film, then that also means that reading a comic comes much closer to the experience of watching a film than we had thought, because in this case, our brain certainly works in the same way—through brief cuts—in order to move from one panel to the next.[17]

I do not know how it would be possible to provide scientific proof of this daring hypothesis, according to which crossing between frames would coincide with a micro-blackout, equivalent to a blink. If it could be proven, it would confirm the view that the reading process is fundamentally disjointed and jerky.

At all events, there is no need to refer to the blinking of the eyes to remind us that human beings are entirely possessed by rhythm: the biological rhythm of breathing and of the beating heart, the muscular rhythm of walking, the back-and-forth movement of intercourse, and so on.[18]

Paul Fraisse, a specialist on rhythm,[19] has shown that a subject who listened to musical extracts was able to isolate the regularities of tempo, that is to say, to identify the beats occurring at equal intervals beneath the melody. In the same way, the comics reader is aware of the underlying beat engendered by the multi-frame, which gives rhythmic pattern to the narrative that s/he is embarking on, even if an irregular arrangement of frames and a profusion of content seem to screen out and disrupt it.

Of all the different human rhythms mentioned above, the one that most closely approximates the comics apparatus is walking. A character who is repre-sented walking from left to right over several consecutive panels, a character who peregrinates from panel to panel, travels across the space of the page along the same pathway as the one tracked by the reader's eye. The character's movement is segmented, just like the reading process. Each panel does not correspond to a single step, but there is nonetheless a correspondence between the rhythm of walking and the movement of our zone of vision as we progress across the page. This is why a character just walking along is a perfect way of engaging the reader in the narrative—from the outset, we are in sync with his/her perambulation.[20]

The multiframe is, then, an instrument for converting space into time, into duration. It is entirely appropriate to describe it in terms of rhythm.

Émile Benveniste has shown that in Greek 'rhuthmos' originally means "characteristic arrangement of parts within a whole." The spatial connotation becomes temporal in Plato, who extends the notion of rhythm to the movements of the body in gymnastics and dance.[21]

For the Greeks, rhythm is, in Pierre Sauvanet's formula, a kind of "temporalized spatial form."[22] It is precisely at the intersection of these two dimensions, space and time, that comic art has developed its own rhythmic practice.

7.2 THE CADENCE OF THE WAFFLE-IRON GRID

The beat emitted by the multiframe is closely dependent on page layout, that is to say the arrangement of the panel frames. In *The System of Comics*, I devoted three pages to a "defense and illustration of regular layout," the pattern that has become known as the "waffle-iron," in which all the panels are identical in size and shape. I argued the opposing case to theoreticians who have criticized its "mechanical aspect" or who consider it a constraint on creativity.[23] I could see several advantages in it (the slightest variation from one image to the next becomes significant, any braiding effects can more easily be positioned on the page . . .) and most notably "the potential for setting up spectacular and violent breaks with the norm initially established." This particular quality is highly important in relation to rhythm.

When the layout is regular, so is the beat. The progression from one panel to the next is smoothed out in compliance with an immutable cadence. The "waffle-iron" is remarkably well suited to any narrative (or section of a narrative) that itself relies on the stability of some element, or in which a phased process unfolds. It is also ideal for materializing the inexorable flow of time. More generally, and with reference to the work of Fraisse, Isabelle Guaïtella argues that a regular page layout and, hence, a regular rhythm, have the effect of "inducing a state of receptiveness in the reader" and so promote "a more immediate integration of meaning."

In order to illustrate all these properties, we will take as an example a three-page story by Robert Crumb, *Mr Natural's 719th meditation* (1970).[24] Mr Natural, the famous guru, rolls out his mat in the middle of the desert and sits on it to meditate. Only the first image of page one occupies a full-width panel, and so is well suited to the evocation of "desolate solitude." The rest of the story is made up of thirty-three rectangular panels of identical format. Mr Natural remains almost completely still for the entire duration of the story until the last three images, when he finally stands up, stretches, rolls up his mat, and leaves, saying: "Wow, that was a pretty good session, boy . . ." In fact, while he was absorbed in this "pretty good session," a road had been built under his nose, a town had grown up around him, and when a traffic cop finally ordered him to move on, Mr Natural had resisted by emitting thought waves so powerful that everything had collapsed around him and reverted to its desert state. So he "wakes up" as if nothing had happened, nothing having been registered by his conscious mind.

The regularity of the layout is echoed here by the regularity of the composition. All the images are organized around the same focal point: Mr Natural is systematically at the center facing the reader in an identical position (apart from the way that his hands are crossed). The cadence is all the more strongly marked by the correspondence between the repetition of the frame and the reiteration of the motif (a point to which I shall return). The combination of these two factors confers a very expressive *ostinato* rhythm on the reading process.

It is also clear from this short tale that the rhythm overlaid onto the narration is autonomous, that is to say that it bears no relationship to the time that has elapsed within the diegesis. It is impossible to make a precise estimate of the "real" duration of the events represented. The information supplied by the author, or rather the reciter (see above 5.1.4)—"Days pass into weeks . . ."—remains deliberately vague, and aims only to suggest a protracted time span. We are thereby warned that two images juxtaposed in space, even with more or less identical content, correspond not to immediately consecutive moments, but to moments that are chronologically spaced out.

How widely are they spaced out? One clue would be the alternation of days and nights. But, throughout the story (at least each time that the sky is visible) the sun is always shining. Until the end, that is, where an image of the setting sun followed by a single nocturnal view immediately precedes the "awakening"

Fig. 12. Robert Crumb, *Mr Natural's 719th meditation*, in *The Book of Mr. Natural* (Seattle: Fantagraphics, 1995), pp. 34–36. © Robert Crumb 1970.

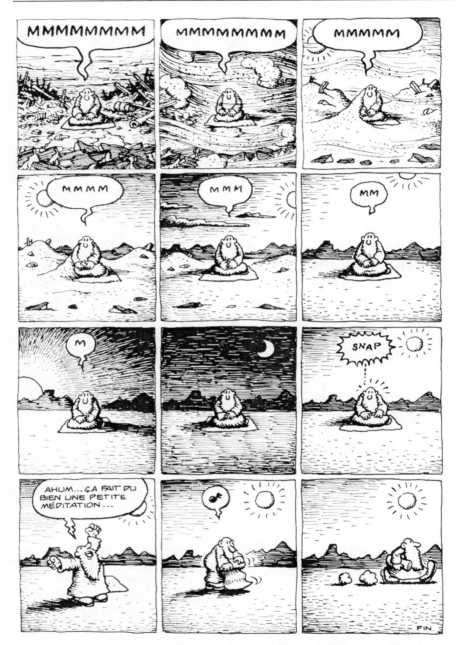

Fig. 12. Robert Crumb, *Mr Natural's 719th meditation*, in *The Book of Mr. Natural* (Seattle: Fantagraphics, 1995), pp. 34–36. © Robert Crumb 1970.

of Mr Natural. If we rely on this clue alone, it would seem that all the preceding events have taken place on one day, a conclusion contradicted both by the words of the narrative voiceover and by the logic of the images. It follows that the sun acts here as a signifier of heat (Mr Natural has not been afraid to sit out under the burning heat of the desert) and not of daylight.

We are, then, faced with an extended diegetic time frame conveyed by a narrative tempo that gives the impression of a brisk rhythm. By opting for marked regularity of the panel frame and the motif, Crumb has compressed the passage of time, producing an accelerated scrolling effect.

If we cannot precisely measure the speed at which the narrative unfolds, we can at least observe the variations that it undergoes. We can see, for example, that the second and third strips of the second page deploy six panels in order to subdivide a very brief moment, that of the confrontation between Mr Natural and the traffic cop, up to the point where the cop backs off. The dialogue and the breakdown make it clear that it takes no more than a few seconds to enact the scene. Six images to cover a few seconds, when something of the order of days or weeks elapses between the others. This remarkable change in the pace of events is expressed visually by a break in the scale of the images, a zoom in on Mr Natural who, for the duration of these six images, is blown up to three times the size of his previous and subsequent manifestations. Thus, within the temporal progression of the story, a brief fragment has been dilated and scrutinized in more detail, as if under a magnifying glass. And this effect, even as it slows down the action, enlarges the central motif.

Even though it was already competing with other types of organization,[25] the regular layout had been massively used as a default format in classic Épinal prints [popular illustrated broadsheets], just as it was in the early days of the funnies. Comic art tended subsequently to move away from it and to explore other possibilities in order to accentuate its difference from cinema, which was restricted to a screen of fixed dimensions. This led to the dominance of the rhetorical model.[26] But the merits of regularity—not least in relation to rhythm—have been rediscovered and amply demonstrated in recent years, most notably by North American comic artists. A regular layout is the preferred format not only of artists who specialize in highly personal subject matter (such as Julie Doucet, Joe Matt, Jeffrey Brown, or Ivan Brunetti) and of personalities as diverse as Ron Regé Jr and Sammy Harkham, it is also a feature of major graphic novels such as Chester Brown's *Louis Riel: A Comic-Strip Biography*, or the two most acclaimed works of scriptwriter Alan Moore, *Watchmen* and *From Hell*.

Depending on the type and subject matter of the narrative, the regularity of the page layout can take on different tonalities. In autobiographical comics, it connotes the rooting of the story in daily life (the regularity of passing days and hours) and the relative insignificance of the events recounted. A succession of small panels seems to be the most modest and most neutral solution, and the rhythm produced is that of existence itself, the clock of life as it ticks by. Whereas, in the three graphic novels cited above, this regularity takes on another meaning, that of the inexorable march of destiny.

The rebellion of the mixed-race Louis Riel results in a death sentence, the countdown of the masked crime fighters ends in a massacre, and Jack the Ripper executes, one by one, all the women implicated in the conspiracy against the royal household. All three stories are inescapably drawn towards a tragic ending, and the regularity of the cadence fixed by the waffle-iron grid makes the reader feel that every step (every panel) brings them nearer to this ineluctable ending. The magnetic attraction of the apparatus (the series of multiframes) is heightened by the metronomic regularity with which the action unfolds.

7.3 THREE TYPES OF EMPHASIS

Every page of *Louis Riel* is made up of six square panels surrounded by a thick line.[27] A first reading makes it clear that the cadence is felt as stronger or weaker depending on the sequence where it occurs. The reader encounters two types of effects which both reinforce this perception: those that arise out of repetition and those that play on periodic alternation.

Repetition: this is the effect of the "static shot" of a character, a group, part of the decor (this borrowing from film vocabulary indicates that the whole scene is perceived from a single spatially determined point). I will also refer to this as a "seriality effect." By repeating the same framing over and over again, the artist emphasizes a key moment within the narrative and prolongs it not on the mode of "and then" but rather of "and still . . . and still . . . ." On page 23, five panels offer a high-angled viewpoint over a stockade. A man is nailing a proclamation to the fence, and people are stopping to read it—first a single passer-by, then two more, then some others. On pages 70–72, the final seconds before the execution of Thomas Scott, found guilty of treason, are cruelly dragged out, as the question as to whether he should stand or kneel before the firing squad is posed three times. The same framing is used eleven times before the white panel used by Chester Brown to render the actual moment when the condemned man is shot. Throughout the sequence, time seems to stand still, and the sight of Scott becomes more and more unbearable each time it is reiterated. The repetition creates a particular kind of dramatic tension—it is as if the reader can hear the reverberation of the drum that beats out, unflinchingly, these solemn and dreadful moments.[28]

Alternation: Brown makes skilful use of the three colors in his palette, black, white, and gray. The hierarchy of values can be overturned at any point. So black, heavily present in one scene, can disappear altogether in the next. These contrasts may emphasize the general structure of the narrative, its division into scenes, whose respective length is in itself a rhythmic element; they may also set consecutive panels on the same page against each other and create a checkerboard or stroboscopic effect.

Alternation can also concern the actual iconic content or the angle of vision. To take the example of *Louis Riel* again, the long final scene of the trial which led, in July 1885, to the sentencing of Riel, takes up thirty pages (pp. 203–32). The witnesses, the judge, the accused, and the counsels are represented in turn—almost always alone in their respective panels—with each one systematically shown in profile from the same side. It thereby follows that the 178 panels that make up this sequence can actually be reduced to about ten types, interwoven and all repeated with slight variations[29] The rhythmic effect is very powerful, especially in the passages corresponding to the questioning of the witnesses, which have the pace of a verbal and visual ping-pong match.

(There is a famous example of a comic that bases its narrative project on the repetition of a small number of images. This is the Alberto Breccia adaptation of Edgar Allan Poe's short story, *The Tell-Tale Heart*.[30] I have written elsewhere that the "stroboscopic effect" produced by Breccia proves to be a "remarkable graphic transposition of the heartbeats of the victim" that the murderer believes he can hear in his room.[31] It is, of course, this auditory hallucination that induces him to confess his crime and to lead police to the body buried under the floorboards.)

Periodic alternation is one of the eight characteristics of rhythm enumerated by the Belgian philosopher and semiotician Henri Van Lier after an investigation of the properties of human walking. Another of his examples is "stanza formation," or the combining of several elementary units (in this case, strides) into larger ones.[32] The notion of the stanza, used in poetry to designate a section of the poem made up of several lines, can easily be transposed to comic art. It designates a group made up of several panels that stand out in relation to the page, the sequence, or the book as being particularly salient, because the panels in question produce a seriality effect through the repetition or alternation of content or formal features. The panels in the same stanza echo each other and display one or other of these types of cohesion to a remarkable extent. The stanza is therefore a key component of rhythm, not only in the case of the "waffle-iron" but also, if not more, as we shall soon see, in irregular layouts.

There is yet another type of effect that also reinforces the perception of rhythmical patterning prompted by a consecutive group of regular frames. This third type (of which there are few significant instances in *Louis Riel*) is progressivity. We need to distinguish between two kinds of progressivity: on the one hand, the cinematic decomposition of the action represented, and, on the other, the equivalent of the zoom in or out, which gradually brings us closer to or further away from a given subject. I will term these instances, respectively, cinematic progressivity and optical progressivity.

Cinematic progressivity usually goes hand in hand with the insistent repetition of the same framing. Historically, it emerges out of the chronophotographic experiments of Muybridge into the breaking down of movement, as Thierry Smolderen has demonstrated.[33] It was with the artist Arthur B. Frost, an ardent admirer of Muybridge, that comics became interested in movement, arising out of its specificity as an art form composed of intervals. Smolderen shows how Frost's "chronophotographic waffle-iron grid" rapidly became adopted as standard in the Sunday newspaper comics.

One of the cartoonists who exploited it to most spectacular effect was certainly Cliff Sterrett.[34] Among the *Polly and her Pals* Sunday strips, there are remarkable examples of "static shots" (for example, the pages from August 8, 1926, and July 13, 1930, which both have an underwater setting and frame only the legs of the characters), and others, just as striking, of the cinematic decomposition of an action (we can cite the occasions when Samuel Perkins falls into the water on August 25, 1926, and August 24, 1927, collides with a passing woman during a storm [March 3, 1929], or attempts to close and secure a trunk [July 21, 1929]). Sometimes the two effects come together, as on the page which sees the same Sam trying to swallow a pill with the help of water from a fountain (January 16, 1927).

On the last-quoted page above, the twenty images that decompose Sam's fruitless efforts are, in addition, silent. They fall into the category of sheer slapstick

and pantomime art, of which Sterrett was a master. I will return to the importance of rhythm in wordless comic art shortly.

Thus, the three main ways of activating (and reinforcing) rhythm—repetition,
periodic alternation, and progressivity—can extend their effects and operate at
the level of whole pages. This capacity arises out of a conception of the page, and
especially of the "waffle-iron," as a panoptic field, where all the images enter into
dialogue with each other *in praesentia*. The cadence is thereby underlined, and
not only informs the reading of the page but also makes its presence felt, from
the first glance, as a formal structuring principle.

The author of *Polly* did not, of course, have a monopoly on this procedure. As
Smolderen notes, "This deliberate visual play on repetition would become one of
the major distinctive features of 20th century comic art."

Among comic books that conform to a regular layout, some observe the rule
strictly (this is the case of *Louis Riel*, a work of deliberate austerity), while others
are more flexible in their adherence to it. In *Watchmen* and *From Hell*, famously,
the nine-panel grid works on a modular system, with some images double or
triple the size of a standard panel.[35] Although any infringement of the regular pattern is significant, it is obvious that the more it departs from the norm, the more
it will stand out. In this respect, the first six pages of the twelfth and last chapter
of *Watchmen*, the only splash pages of the whole work, have a remarkable impact.
The rhythm of the narration freezes, and time is suspended over these images
of devastation, an effect underlined by the title of the film being shown at the
Utopia Cinema: *The Day the Earth Stood Still*.[36] Douglas Wolk has made the valid
comment that the reader perceives these six outsize images like "six consecutive
unexpected gongs of a clock."[37]

A final parameter that should be linked to the notion of cadence is that of
fixed metric form. Some artists have, in fact, specialized in short-format strips,
subdivided into an invariant number of regular panels. For decades, day after
day, Schulz's *Peanuts* strips were made up of four panels. In France, series like
Le Retour à la terre [Back to the Land], by Ferri and Larcenet, or *Victor Lalouz*,
by Diego Aranega, opted for a particular format, the half-page, which corresponds to six panels. This standard template can be used in a flexible way but, for
Aranega, it corresponds to an ideal form:

> I find the rhythm of six images ideal for a gag. Over a page, the gag would be diluted, there would be
> redundant panels. I am confident that I can tell a good funny story in six panels. [. . .] My gag machine
> runs on six panels.[38]

It is indeed a question of metric structures (in the same way that the term "meter" is used to designate the number of syllables in a line of poetry) within which artists develop a narrative mechanism that meets their needs. In relation to *Peanuts* in particular, I will take the liberty of reproducing an analysis that I wrote some time ago:

> Schulz is completely at ease in the confines of the daily strip. There is a kind of spontaneous fit between this "stretch" and his narrative technique. His respect for the constraints imposed by the four-panel format means that he never extends his dialogue more than necessary. The quaternary schema [today I would have written: "the quaternary rhythm"] proves to be the most apt at rendering the natural progression of the anecdote—in the same way that, for most seventeenth-century writers, the alexandrine became the natural vehicle of thought. Far from avoiding the pitfall of monotony, Schulz positively seeks out this consistency, very often repeating, from one panel to the next, an almost identical visual image. [. . .] [So] the very stability of forms and composition within the strip works to accentuate the slightest variations in posture or facial expression, and confers on them the status of graphic events that are information- and often emotion-bearing. Schulz knows that, by its nature, the gag strip is a static and repetitive form, and that there is no getting away from that.[39]

7.4 THE AWARENESS OF RHYTHM

As we know,[40] it is not, however, the regular page layout that is most prevalent in modern comics, but rather the rhetorical layout, where the size (and sometimes the shape) of each frame is adapted to the content, to the subject matter of the panel. When a layout is of the irregular type, there is no evenly divided, rhythmic grid and no basic structure on which to hang other more or less elaborate rhythms. In this case, the beat inherent to the multiframe, whatever its configuration, is still operative, but no longer in the marked form of a cadence.

When irregularity becomes the rule, it is localized incidences of regularity that stand out. The reader notices immediately if a series of three or four consecutive panels have identically shaped frames in common, particularly if the shape is unusual, either longer or wider than the norm for the other images. These panels work together: they constitute a stanza.

A simple and striking example is provided by Jason, on page 18 of his album *Je vais te montrer quelque chose* [I'm going to show you something].[41] Unusually for him, the Norwegian artist uses a rhetorical layout in this book, but he returns to his more accustomed regular layout for the duration of a bout of verbal ping-pong between Alex, the fugitive, and Sandra, the little girl. If they had been spread over just two strips, the eight panels that make up this stanza would be perceived as a more homogeneous visual group, one corresponding to half of the page. Instead, they are distributed over three strips in a 2-4-2 pattern. They nonetheless stand out against the rest of the sequence and are conspicuous as a stanza at first glance. Eight panels is more than enough for a cadence to emerge, and here it is reinforced by two of the seriality effects that we have already noted: repetition (each of the eight panels is a close-up on a face, whereas in the other images the characters are framed at half or full length) and an effect of periodic alternation (Sandra and Alex speak in turn; moreover, they are represented in three-quarter profile along symmetrical axes).

Although it is impossible to assign a precise duration to the four wordless images that are also included on this page (we do not know how long the meal preparation takes, nor how long Alex and Sandra stare at each other before breaking the silence, nor how long their meal lasts), this is not the case for the dialogue, which consists of short responses, conferring a rapid tempo on this stanza. We can reasonably assume that the time taken up by the reading of these eight images corresponds more or less to the actual duration of this verbal exchange.

It is of course important to make a distinction between the time of the action and the time of reading, which have an inverse relationship to each other. Our eight panels containing dialogue recount a very short scene, but, because they include text, they possibly take a little longer to read than the wordless images that occur before and after them, even though the latter represent more story time.

Rhythm, in comic art, is never a matter of time intervals that can be measured but of time intervals that are felt, through an impression that is built up in stages. This begins with an instant visual fix on the configuration of the multiframe, which will be perceived as regular or not, composed of a greater or smaller number of panels and featuring or not featuring seriality effects (all factors that can be taken in at first glance). It is then activated by the reading process, which is subject to variation in speed, now faster, now slower.[42] We must refrain, here again, from an over-mechanistic or simplistic description, because not only does the reader's awareness of rhythm depend on his/her own alertness and sensitivity, it is also something other than a simple matter of correlation with the time of the action or the time of the reading. It is, precisely, forged in the gap, the tension between these two dimensions: the reader's engagement with what is being

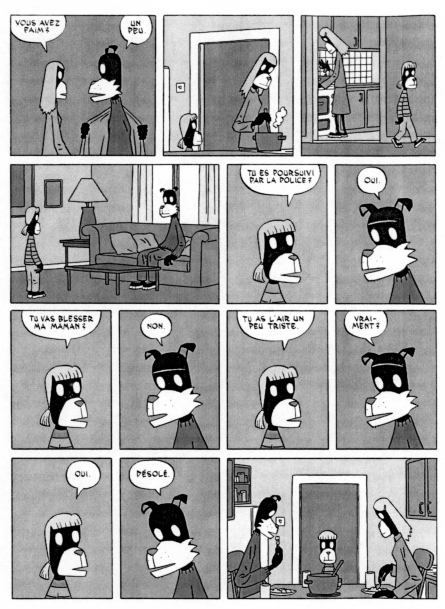

Fig. 13. Jason, *Je vais te montrer quelque chose* (Paris: Éditions Carabas, 2004), p. 18. © Éditions Tournon-Carabas, Jason.

recounted, and, correspondingly, the decoding of a greater or lesser amount of visual and verbal information.

The configuration of the multiframe and the density of the information are objective criteria. However, nothing is more subjective than our involvement in the *fabula* that is being recounted or shown, the narrative discourse that is addressed to us. It is all the more subjective for having a double motivation, emotional and aesthetic. Let us take the example of a wordless panel representing a (silent) character in close-up. Reader A will skim over it: s/he has noticed that this is a lull in the action and so (in his/her opinion) the panel is not worth tarrying over. Reader B (especially if she is a female reader?) will be moved by the expression on this mute face and will linger over it, intuiting a sentiment that arouses empathy (the importance of close-ups in shōjo mangas is well known). Reader C will be held up by his/her interest in the drawing style of the close-up: it may be striking on account of the intensity, the accuracy,—and sometimes the comic effect—of the facial expression (as in the theatre, we can speak of a powerful *presence*), or it may simply be worthy of admiration for its graphic virtuosity, as a particularly felicitous portrait, a face that is etched and detailed, a remarkable "phizog" (think, for example, of certain close-ups by Giraud or Goossens).

In the final analysis, the author proposes but the reader disposes. It is the latter who animates, identifies with, punctuates, and brings to life the story in his/her own way. The reader therefore contributes to the rhythm of the narration, which, ultimately, coincides with the pulsating flow of the reading process.

Let us now consider page 16 of the album *La Marque du condor* [The Mark of the Condor], the seventh and final volume of the series *Les 7 Vies de l'Épervier* [The Seven Lives of the Sparrowhawk] drawn by André Juillard and scripted by Patrick Cothias.[43] This page is characterized by seriality effects, even if they are not as marked as in the work of Jason. The geometrical arrangement of the page, as the reader first apprehends it, however vaguely, is as follows: vertically the page is divided in two across the middle. Horizontally it is also divided in two, but the parts are of unequal size. This structure (an off-center cross shifted towards the left) dictates the rhythm of the page: one large image followed by a stanza of three horizontal images "bracketed together," then two more classically shaped images one above the other, then again a group of three images, this time vertically elongated.

The operation of reading this part of the narrative is not regular or cadenced; it is more syncopated, as the sequence is processed in successive chunks. The

Fig. 14. Juillard and Cothias, *Les 7 Vies de l'Épervier*, vol. 7, *La Marque du condor* (Paris: Glénat, 1991), p. 16. © Éditions Glénat.

most expressive element is of course the vertical juxtaposition of these two tercets (three-panel stanzas) oriented along opposing axes.

Over and above the arrangement of the frames, other structuring parameters are involved in the production of rhythm, the two main ones in our example being the distribution of colors and the spacing out of speech balloons. As regards the colors, red stands out strikingly, very prominent in the first panel, and then punctuating the lower part of each half of the page. But the pale blue of the sky creates an effect of continuity among the last three images and contributes to their perception as three components of a single group. As regards the text, it is noteworthy that every panel of this page contains one speech balloon, with the exception of the three horizontal panels of the top stanza, which each contain two. There again, we have a factor that, by introducing a variation into the tempo of reading, singles out the stanza and designates it as homogeneous in its difference.

7.5 ACCENTUATION AND POLYRHYTHM

The localized occurrences noted above are specific examples of the accentuation of rhythm (in this context, *differentiation* and *accentuation* are synonymous). There now emerges a general rule, which is as follows. In the case of a comic with the smoothest possible beat (regular layout, reiteration of very similar iconic content, standard distribution of balloons over the page), many resources are available for accentuation, whether at the level of the stanza or at that of a single panel. Some of these resources come under the heading of the spatio-topical system, and have, for that reason, been signaled in *System 1*: a panel can be accentuated by its siting (especially when it occupies the central or the final position), by its shape or by its size. Others concern the content represented. These are: a break in the scale of images, in the continuity of a phased process (cinematic or optical progressivity), or in the chromatic range (through contrast in color). The final parameter that can be brought into play is, as we have seen, the amount of information offered to the reader, and, notably, the amount of text. These different kinds of accentuation can be used at the same time. The more of them the author brings together to make an image or a stanza stand out, the more remarkable the cumulative effect of scansion will be.

In my essay on *La Cage* [The Cage] written in 2002, I referred to the super-imposition of a number of structuring rhythmic procedures in Martin Vaughn James's famous experimental "visual novel":

> Like any published work that is inherently visual, *La Cage* consists of a sequence of double pages that are immediately perceived as a succession of diptychs. To this basic binary beat are added, in this instance, all kinds of rhythmic and even melodic effects. The reader only has to leaf through the book to make them visible: there are sequences which, like musical phrases, are sustained over several diptychs and are then suddenly broken off as another tune comes in; effects of rhyme, repetition, always with [. . .] some variation; alternation between large images split into two halves set out on facing pages and diptychs that juxtapose unrelated, self-sufficient images; and, finally, variations in the framing of the image that affect two of its parameters: size and position on the page. All these procedures, working together, stamp a particular rhythm onto Vaughn James's visual novel, a rhythm made up of accelerations and pauses, moments of intensity and glissandos. The text intervenes on two levels. Considered in its simple physical materiality, it is, variously, absent altogether, reduced to a single line or expanded into a block of type, and may be positioned above or below the image. Considered as reading matter, it holds the attention for longer or shorter periods.[44]

The interweaving of different rhythms is also in evidence on certain remarkable pages of *Watchmen*, characterized by the alternation of two narrative sequences that intersect within the waffle-iron grid, overlaying onto the page an X-shape, which is reinforced by the distinctions in color tone between the two sequences in question.[45] Moore's skill lies in not disrupting the continuity of the text—the same dialogue goes on throughout the entire page, sometimes "on" (the speakers are shown: we will call this scene A) and sometimes "off" (the "image track" is uncoupled from the "soundtrack" and we see another scene in another place: scene B). The result is that on top of the cadence set up by the waffle-iron grid, the A-B-A/B-A-B/A-B-A structure actually interweaves several different rhythms: the ternary rhythm of the strip, the binary rhythm of the A-B alternation, and the rhythm of the text, at once regular in that it sits atop two series of images with no interruption—and irregular, in view of the varying length of the lines of dialogue.

The discontinuity that is the basis of the language of comics ensures that rhythm is a central element of its discursive resources. It has been important to establish the following points here: that the rhythm peculiar to each work is enriched by multiple effects and strategies, that this rhythm is unceasingly

modulated throughout the work as a function of multiple parameters, that almost all the great authors are past masters at interweaving rhythms (emphatic
and muted), and, finally, that readers have a role to play in the actualization of
these combined processes—it is they who must interpret the score.

The latter expression originates from Chris Ware ("When you read a comic
strip, it's like reading a musical score. It's up to us as readers to bring the music from the score alive");[46] and if there is one artist who has established , if
not rhythm, then at least duration, as one of the essential dimensions of his
own poetic art, it is without doubt the author of *Jimmy Corrigan*, whom we
meet again here. When his work first began to attract attention, readers were all
struck by his management of time, characterized by the stretching out of certain
sequences, sometimes to an almost unbearable extent, further exacerbated by
the nature of the sequences in question, which were marked by the immobility
and indecisiveness of their protagonists, by non-communication and aphasia. As
Jacques Samson writes, in Ware's work, "time moves sluggishly, and displays its
sluggishness."[47]

The visual translation of the miring of the action—which amounts to an anti-
rhythm—is achieved by a constant recourse to seriality effects: avoiding shot-
counter shot sequences and pointless changes in framing, Ware cultivates instead
the systematic, reiterating the same angles of vision over and over again. To which
is added a very personal conception of layout, analyzed above (p. 49) as "a combination of quadrangular blocks." In fact, the eye perceives at first glance that
these blocks are not all equivalent: one large image means a pause, another series
of small images represents the unfolding of a process, or is a figurative expression
of emphasis. To the different formats configured by the artist there correspond
different rhythms of apprehending the material, time spans mentally calculated
by the reader. Ware likes to quote Goethe's definition of architecture as "frozen
music." This metaphor applies perfectly to the architecture of his comics pages.

The question of rhythm is, nonetheless, all-pervasive in his work. It is transmitted, as we have seen, by the insistent repetition of certain iconic contents,
but also by the mathematical principles on which the compartmentalizing of the
space on the page is based. To the "nested regularities" that we have observed (the
fact that the panels correspond to three or four standard formats, perfect multiples of each other), there correspond different beats, so that the page (and the
narrative as a whole) is made up of interwoven rhythms—even when, within this
rhythmic mechanism, the author manages to suspend the flow of time.

7.6 RHYTHMS IN SILENCE

It goes without saying that the importance of rhythm varies considerably from one comic to another. Without even going into the individual take that each author has on the medium, by focusing on some parameters rather than others, one can make the claim that, in general, in the American context, it is newspaper strips on the one hand and graphic novels on the other that have made rhythm such a predominant factor, whereas rhythmic effects are far less salient in mainstream comic books.

There is another comics form in which rhythm is determinant: wordless comics, which have undergone, on every continent, a resurgence of interest over the last quarter century (even if they can lay claim to a tradition that goes back to the nineteenth century).[48] Or more precisely, some of the variants of this form, which we will call, case by case, satirical, choreographic, or minimalist.

The stories that I am thinking about here, notably those of Sempé, François Ayroles, Guy Delisle, Lewis Trondheim, or Marion Fayolle (to restrict myself to French-language authors—but we have already encountered above some of Sterrett's Sunday strips), are characterized firstly by a very detailed sequentiality, a highly analytical breakdown. They also have in common the elimination of decor or its reduction to its starkest expression in order to concentrate on the deeds and gestures of one or several characters. This focus on the actants of the story, who are followed step by step, implies a third characteristic: a high level of redundancy. If the character is considered as a graphic motif, it can be said that in the works in question the narrative is essentially based on the reiteration of this motif. Because of the consistency of the content, these authors logically opt for a regular page layout. We find again here the repetition effect analyzed above in relation to *Louis Riel*, with the sole difference that, in wordless stories, the text does not intervene to modulate the tempo to accentuate one image rather than another.

This repeated graphic motif (which, of course, does undergo certain alterations or transformations, without which there would be no story to tell) corresponds exactly, then, to the English term "pattern," which has the advantage of designating not only a distinct and repeated shape in the visual domain but also, in music, a basic rhythmic motif. The Americans have, indeed, coined the expression "pantomime strip" to designate picture stories where the characters remain mute.

The stronger the redundancy, the more one has the impression of seeing the storyboard of an animated film, or something like a flip book whose leaves, instead of being one on top of another, are spread out in space.

It was, precisely, a silent page by François Ayroles that featured on the cover of the French edition of *System 1*.[49] But the term "silent" is not appropriate here, given that the characters do emit utterances, but their words are materialized by illegible marks. The interest of this page, like all those in the same collection, is that it foregrounds the importance of the speech balloon itself, by signaling the fact that there is speech, and that the balloons work as an apparatus for generating rhythm. Even if they contain nothing that can be deciphered, and so there is no point in pausing over them, the balloons still provide the page with a metrical structure, and when "silent" images, where no one "speaks" come along, they puncture the flow of speech very effectively. The rhythm of the page inheres in the way that panels with and without balloons are distributed. A binary rhythm is superimposed on the beat of the waffle-iron grid: a mouth has to be either open or closed.[50]

In another book from the same collection, *Les Penseurs* [The Thinkers],[51] Ayroles renders his characters' words through pictograms. (As we have shown in our analysis above (6.1), the three most frequent represent a glass of beer, a cigarette and a heart—crossed through when the propositions made by the characters are turned down or their hopes dashed). A similar iconization of speech also features in *Aline et les autres* [Aline and the Others] and *Albert et les autres* [Albert and the Others] by Delisle.[52] In these works, the balloon isolates within one drawing a space containing another drawing, which does not have the same status as the first; while the principal drawing represents a scene, the enclosed drawing consists of speech translated into another semiotic system. The alternation *panel with balloon/panel without balloon* is still operational, but the content of the balloons has to be decoded, as the meaning of the pictogram fluctuates from one example to the next and has to be worked out from the context.[53] The rhythm of reading becomes less predictable, even staccato, as the reader has to make pauses of varying lengths in order to make the correct inferences.

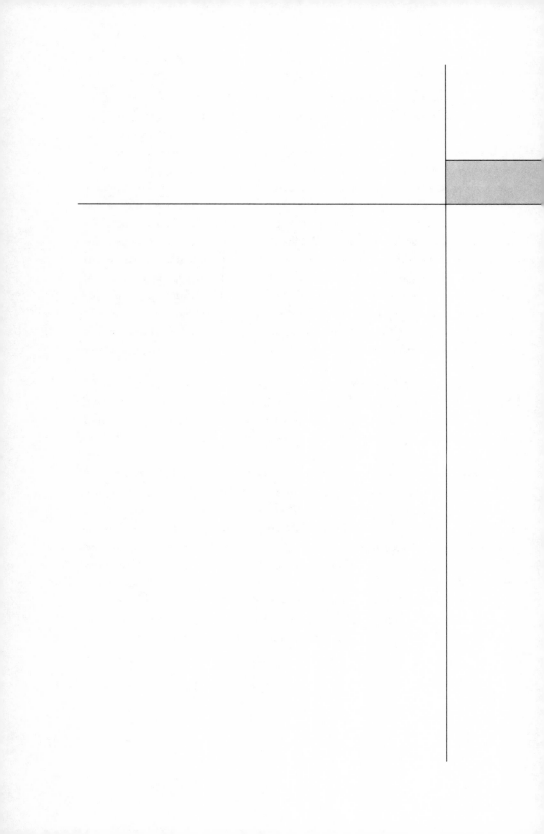

CHAPTER EIGHT

Is Comics a Branch of Contemporary Art?

In this final chapter, we are going to leave the domain of semiotic or narratological analysis and move onto the terrain of sociology of art, art history, and cultural history. It would undoubtedly be worth developing the following reflections into a full-length essay. However, it seems appropriate to include them in the present volume, since, as we shall see, they will ultimately lead us back, by another route, to the question of narration.

In general terms, the art world and the comics world have long kept their distance from each other, to the point of seeming irreconcilable. And in high-cultural circles, comics has often been reproached for not keeping in step with the history of other arts in the twentieth century, for not being, in other words, contemporaneous with contemporary art.

The historian Pierre Couperie took an opposing view. In his concern to promote the legitimacy of comics, he set out to demonstrate that the medium had not remained untouched by the evolution of other art forms. In 1972 he wrote: "It is possible to distinguish within the development of comics, successive (or concurrent) tendencies that have marked the history of art from 1880 to the present day." He supported this assertion by pointing to elements taken from Art Nouveau by McCay or Rubino, from Art Déco by McManus or Saint-Ogan, from Expressionism by Caniff and his followers (including Breccia), and so on, right up to the most recent artists, among whom could be found echoes of Psychedelic Art, Surrealism, Pop and Op art (from Peellaert and Steranko to . . . Carlos Gimenez).[1]

Most of these examples are pertinent, but, in fact, they amount to little more than pastiche, quotation, or unconscious borrowing, which are an insufficient basis on which to base a claim that comics participated in any real sense in "the great formal rebellion that characterized avant-gardes, successive episodes in the upheavals of *modern art*." It is safe to say that comics "was not (or not to a significant degree) directly concerned with the breaks introduced by Fauvism, Cubism, Suprematism or Abstraction, at the time when these movements were happening . . ."[2]

8.1 THE HYPOTHESIS OF HISTORICAL BELATEDNESS

Jean-Christophe Menu maintains that comics now has its own avant-garde movement, albeit with a historical time lag in relation to "official" art. This avant-garde is, he claims, embodied by works produced in the decades since 1990, a period during which independent (or alternative) publishing houses have been a moving force, none more so than the Association, the publishing collective that Menu co-founded, and of which he ultimately became the sole director between 2006 and 2010.

Between January 2006 and January 2007, the Association published three issues of a theoretical journal called *L'Éprouvette* [The Test Tube], before "scuppering" it; the three issues nonetheless add up to 1,284 pages. The first issue included, in its preliminary pages (pp. 7–8), a kind of manifesto proclaiming: "Comics is an art form whose arrival was overdue. It's a bit goddamn stupid. But, unlike some, it's not dead. It might be full of shit, but at least it's not full of postmodernism."

In a text that appeared as a conclusion to the third issue (p. 569), Menu challenges the idea that this self-proclaimed avant-garde status was just a pose.

> In this journal, we have published abstract painting, automatic drawing, body painting, comics embroidered on fabric, sixteenth century engravings, forerunners of graphic narratives . . . And all that has caused consternation in the small world of mainstream comics, in just the same way as Art Nègre or the art of the insane asylum, invited to trespass on the terrain of official art by Apollinaire, Picasso or the Surrealists, filled the bourgeois of the early twentieth century with consternation.

One could of course retort that the fact that an artwork causes shock or indignation does not in itself deliver a certificate of avant-gardism, nor does it guarantee the quality or significance of the work. And that, moreover, the reaction of the "small world of mainstream comics" to *L'Éprouvette* consisted mainly of complete indifference. And, finally, that the concept of avant-garde may simply no longer be very meaningful, either in the context of the period in which we now live, or in the field of comic art.

A few years earlier, Menu had already written in *Plates-Bandes* [Flower Beds/ Flat Strips] that the Association had been set up "as an avant-garde." And had specified that "some of (its) ideas were deliberately and historically linked to the literary avant-gardes of the twentieth century, beginning with Surrealism. One could even say that the Association was, among other things, an attempt to extrapolate a few basic principles of Surrealism to comics."[3] These included, in particular, the recounting of dreams and the "exquisite corpses" technique.[4]

I note that the examples offered in *L'Éprouvette* in support of the avant-gardist claim belong clearly to the field (and history) of visual art, whereas *Plates-Bandes* had positioned the intervention of the Association as a continuation of earlier literary avant-gardes. This apparent contradiction must doubtless be read as a further sign of the irreducible doubleness of comics (Menu refers to its *equivocation*), of the fact that it is ultimately and inseparably both a form of literature and a visual art.

But it is the verb "extrapolate" that holds the key to Menu's argument, and that shows the limits of the lineage that he lays claim to. His project may be resumed as the importation of literary techniques and the testing and verification of their applicability to comics. The creation of Oubapo [The Workshop for Potential Comics] in 1992 effectively demonstrated the same logic: it consisted of the extrapolation to comics of the aims and methods of Oulipo [The Workshop for Potential Literature], founded in 1960.

The Surrealists themselves had not been slow to extend the technique of automatic writing to drawing and painting. The first literary text produced by this method, *Les Champs magnétiques* [Magnetic Fields], by Breton and Soupault, dates from 1919, and the first artist to apply it to drawing was André Masson, from 1923 to 1927.[5] And, in 1924, the first Manifesto defined Surrealism itself as a "psychic automatism in its pure state, by which one proposes to express—verbally, by means of the written word, *or in any other manner*—the actual functioning of thought" (my italics). This means that, when Menu drew an "automatic comics page" in 1993,[6] he was essentially doing nothing more than perpetuating a long-standing and duly documented practice.

His innovation lies in the way that he respects the comics apparatus: his "automatic" drawings are contained within a space that is divided up. It is an automatic comics page, then, not an automatic drawing. However, Steinberg (with two sheets called *Comic Strip* in 1958) and Crumb (*Abstract Expressionist Ultra Super Modernistic Comics*, three pages dating from 1967 reprinted on the opening pages of Molotiu's anthology) got there first. And the result inevitably falls into the category of infranarrative comics.[7] It is indeed doubtful whether a series of drawings really can be completely and authentically produced "in the absence of any control exercised by reason," according to Breton's definition, when the drawings in question are framed and juxtaposed. We will leave this point aside. As an exercise for warming up or warming down, the production of an automatic comics page is by no means without interest. But does it constitute, of itself, an imperishable creative gesture that secures entry to the avant-garde? Is the "automatic comics page" not on its way to becoming a genre, rather like single-color canvasses in contemporary art?

We have seen, in the previous chapter, that some experimental work with abstract comics consisted mainly of "extrapolation," along directions already explored by art films of the 1920s.

Not content with having "extrapolated" literary or graphic techniques into comics, Menu is now advocating the "extrapolation of comics into three-dimensional space"[8] and urging comics artists to escape the confines of paper.

It seems clear, then, that for the author of *Livret de Phamille* [Family Record Book],[9] the only way in which comics can catch up with historically more advanced art forms is to get involved in the import-export business, to absorb techniques from other media, and to become transposable onto non-paper formats.

One of the slogans of *L'Éprouvette* was the "gradual erosion of frontiers." This was the title of one of the sections of the second issue (which was reproduced in *La Bande dessinée et son double*, p. 365), but by the third issue it had turned into the "gradual explosion of frontiers." Eclecticism, recycling, hybridization, decontextualization—unless I am mistaken, this program fits right into the aesthetic paradigm of postmodernism, even if, as we have seen, Menu professes to abominate the word, if not the thing it designates.

8.2 HIGH & LOW: THE LICHTENSTEIN SYNDROME

Comics was for a long time a medium that had scant legitimacy, and was considered to be an impure mode of expression, a childish form of literature with no claim to any artistic dignity.

The 1960s, the decade in which its rehabilitation began, also happened to be the decade in which, in spite of its almost complete lack of symbolic prestige, comics became a major source of inspiration for certain artistic movements: Pop

Art in the United States, New Figuration in France. Roy Lichtenstein was the most emblematic artist of this period, and his case is symptomatic.

This "recuperation" of comics by official art has not been unanimously understood or appreciated. The art critic Pierre Sterckx believes that it was beneficial: "In my view, from 1960, the exposure given to comics by Lichtenstein was exceptionally valuable: he revealed the visual qualities, up until then a closely guarded secret, of comic art and juxtaposed it to works by Picasso, Léger and Mondrian."[10] The American critic Adam Gopnik went so far as to write that "Pop art saved the comics."[11] He argues that the comic book industry, which had been declining since the end of the 1940s, had been completely reenergized after integrating elements of Lichtenstein's style, such as irony or the rejection of realist details. He claimed that this applied particularly to the series produced by Stan Lee for Marvel Comics at the beginning of the 1960s.

So should Lichtenstein be credited with having simultaneously magnified comics panels and reinvigorated comic art?

The historian Pierre Couperie took the opposite view. In a reference to the 1967 exhibition *Bande dessinée et figuration narrative*, of which he was one of the curators, he declared: "We were reacting against Pop Art in general and Roy Lichtenstein in particular. At that period, comics was perceived only through the lens of his painting, he had shown up its vapidity and inanity . . . by taking the worst images and blowing them up to an excessive degree."[12]

Two of the greatest American artists, Will Eisner and Art Spiegelman, have also expressed their low opinion of Lichtenstein's work. Eisner is reported to have said that he was upset by Roy Lichtenstein's work and by the arrogant snobbishness of his paintings.[13] Without making specific reference to Eisner, the critic Bart Beaty offers an explanation for the hostility of part of the profession: "By reducing comic books to source material, Lichtenstein is accused of having made the legitimatization of comic books—already a difficult task—that much more challenging." A grievance that he extends, in fact, to the whole of the *High & Low* exhibition (to which I will return shortly): "Nowhere in the exhibit was there an acknowledgement of comics as an art in and of themselves. Like a kind of mutely passive muse, they can only inspire art, not create it."[14]

Spiegelman's criticism of Lichtenstein is, though, somewhat different. A comics page that he drew for *Artforum* in December 1990 addresses Lichtenstein thus: "Oh Roy, your dead high art is built on dead low art! . . . The real political, sexual and formal energy in living popular culture passes you by. Maybe that's—sob—

Fig. 15. Art Spiegelman, *High Art Lowdown*, in *ArtForum*, 1990. Reproduced with kind permission of the author.

why you're championed by museums!" The author of *Maus* is also reported to have declared in October 2010 at the Cartoon Art Festival in Columbus, Ohio, "Lichtenstein did no more for comics than Warhol did for soup."[15]

In order to understand, not the "truth" of his art, but at least what Lichtenstein's attitude really was towards comics, it is perhaps best to seek a first-hand account from the artist himself (something both his admirers and denigrators usually disdain to do). In an interview recorded in January 1966 for the *BBC Third Programme*, David Sylvester asked him what he liked about comics images. He does, to say the least, express reservations:

Well, I think that it was the startling quality of the visual shorthand and the sense of cliché—the fact that an eye would be drawn a certain way . . . . [. . .] There is a kind of order in the cartoons, there's a sort of composition, but it's a kind of a learned composition. It's a composition more to make it clear, to make it read and communicate, rather than a composition for the sake of unifying the elements. In other words, the normal aesthetic sensibility is usually lacking. . . . [. . .] I don't care whether they're good or bad or anything else. But they are subject matter, and I'm only using them and I am re-interpreting them. [. . .] I both like and dislike the cartoons. I enjoy them, they're probably amusing in some way, and I get a genuine kick out of them, though usually only a few frames will be really interesting to me.[16]

What clearly emerges from these words is less any real regard for comics than a self-interested strategy of appropriation.

High & Low, Modern Art and Popular Culture, presented at MoMA in New York in 1990, was the first important exhibition to bring together comics—but also graffiti art, caricature, advertising images—and recognized artists representing official culture. In the introduction to the catalogue, Kirk Varnedoe and Adam Gopnik, the two curators, explain the title of the exhibition:

We call all these areas of representation "low," not to denigrate them out of hand [. . .] but to recognize that they have traditionally been considered irrelevant to, or outside, any consideration of achievement in the fine arts of our time—and in fact have commonly been accepted as opposite to the "high" arts in their intentions, audiences, and nature of endeavor. [. . .] Our goal is to examine the transformations through which modern painters and sculptors have made new poetic languages by reimagining the possibilities in forms of popular culture; and, as a corollary, to acknowledge the way those adaptations in modern art have often found their way back into the common currency of public visual prose.

The reader will have noticed the terms that are defined oppositionally by this quotation: painting and sculpture are regarded as poetry, while popular cultural forms, like comics, are classed as prose.

The exhibition demonstrated, among other things, that comics acted as a resource for official art in two different ways: on the one hand, by supplying it with themes, myths, characters, an imagery, and, on the other hand, by inspiring it on a formal level through its apparatus (seriality, the multiframe, the coexistence of text and image) and by the panels, speech balloons, and onomatopoeia designated by Gopnik as the "secondary machinery" of comics.[17]

The Spiegelman comics page quoted above was intended as a response to the exhibition (which had given rise to indignant reactions way beyond the milieu of professional comics artists). He drew attention to the omission of numerous artists, who in his view, should rightfully have been there, the most glaring of which was the omission of Spiegelman himself along with all the artists whose work he had been publishing for a decade in *Raw*, the main "avant-garde" comics journal of the time. But the most conclusive objection to the preconceptions of the curators was put by Spiegelman into the mouth of Ignatz Mouse (a character from George Herriman's *Krazy Kat* series):[18] in the view attributed to Ignatz, the question of high and low art is not a matter of aesthetics but of social class and economics. Instead, the exhibition reinforced the notion of an aesthetic hierarchy between high art and low art, the latter quite clearly treated as mass culture and entertainment, and, therefore, as alienating its consumers.[19]

During the two decades since the exhibition in New York, a dual tendency has been apparent: comics (or more precisely, *a certain branch* of comics) has moved closer to the preoccupations of "official" contemporary art; at the same time, painters (or *certain* painters) have moved back towards drawing and figurative art. There are now three annual exhibitions in Paris devoted to drawing. The art critic of *Le Monde*, Philippe Dagen, emphasizes that "ten years ago, it would have been hard to imagine this vogue for a mode of expression that the contemporary art milieu saw as being dated." And he does not fail to note "the key importance and influence of press cartoons, caricature, comics and manga in this development."[20]

Comics has undergone a process of rehabilitation, and its cultural legitimacy is now more securely established—while the very notions of high art and low art have become diluted by the rise of entertainment culture (in France, this has taken the form of the ideology of "le tout culturel"[21] that has been dominant since Jack Lang's reforms of the 1980s).

Thus, it seems that for the first time we have reached a conjuncture where a certain number of necessary, if not sufficient, conditions have come together to allow for the emergence of a real dialogue between comics and other forms of contemporary artistic expression.

8.3 CONVERGENCES

Something new has happened: for the last fifteen years or so, some comics authors seem to be driven by the same ambitions as their colleagues in the fine arts,[22] and have begun, consciously or not, to adopt the language of contemporary art.

The editors of *Art Press* duly noted this in the editorial to their special issue entitled *Bande d'auteurs* [Auteurist Gang/Strip] (2005):

> The formal preoccupations [of comics authors and critics] coincide with our own (where to go with abstraction, sequencing, exiting the frame, etc.) as do their avenues for thematic exploration (autofiction, documentary fiction). Even our long-standing interest in pornography, or our more recent discovery of the virtues of acting the fool, find a certain echo . . .

Some current comics artists' work has hung in galleries, e.g., Jochen Gerner and Killoffer (represented by the Anne Barrault Gallery), Frédéric Coché (La Ferronnerie Gallery), and Frédéric Poincelet (Catherine Putman Gallery). We could add another name to the list: Pierre la Police, who (like others) is no longer producing comics for publication, but whose paintings have been shown in the Kamel Mennour Gallery, highly prestigious in Parisian art circles. We should also mention Stéphane Blanquet, for his installations and body paintings, or Benoît Jacques, who exhibits comics made of unusual materials: embroidery (done by Harizo Rakotomala, a Madagascan embroiderer), wood, metal, etc.

The Association's list now includes, outside any regular collection, books of drawings that go beyond the comics field, for example Killoffer's *Recapitation* [Re-capitation]("pure drawing, neither illustrative nor narrative"), Jochen Gerner's *Branchages* [Cut Branches] ("a book of sketches done by telephone"), Kiki and Loulou Picasso's *Engin explosif improvisé* [Improvised Explosive Device] ("diptychs brightened up with texts and slogans"), or Thomas Ott and Gila's *La Grande Famiglia* [The Big Family (Italian spelling)] (photos and pinholes by Gila based on a graphic and narrative installation by Ott"; a "hybrid book, part drawing, part photographs, part thriller").[23]

This "contemporary art" tendency appears even more pronounced in Belgium, as was amply demonstrated by the *Génération spontanée* [Spontaneous Generation] exhibition presented at the Angoulême Festival in January 2011. The *Tintin* and *Spirou* traditions have long been so preponderant in Belgium that the country seemed destined only to produce descendants of Hergé or Franquin. However, following in the footsteps of Joe Pinelli, Louis Joos, and Alain Corbel—all pioneers of independent Belgian comics—a whole generation of authors has begun to approach the medium in a spirit of experimentation, research, and openness to hybridization. Three publishers are particularly involved in this development: Frémok, which prioritizes the poetic and visual but also the social dimensions of comics, La 5ᵉ couche, and L'Employé du moi, more focused on autofiction and reflexive play on the codes of the medium. As Thierry Bellefroid, the curator of the exhibition, wrote, this new Franco-Belgian comics scene "is spreading through art galleries, onto stages where contemporary dance is performed, and into the streets." And Thierry Van Hasselt, one of the founders of Frémok, spells the message out: "We're often put into the comics box. But we define ourselves as poets and visual artists who use the comics form."[24]

With regard to the American context, I will confine myself here to the work of Jerry Moriarty. Moriarty was born in 1938 and began exhibiting his paintings in 1974, but was an active participant over the following decade in *Raw*, the comics journal founded by Spiegelman and his wife Françoise Mouly. His highly distinctive comics were brought out in book format in 1984 under the title *Jack Survives*. This book describes the daily round of the artist's father, who constantly tries to keep up with a new era that he understands less and less. This comic, which stages everyday life at its most derisory, is impressive not only on account of its cruelty, but also because of a certain strangeness that arises out of silence and out of the often very tight framing that imprisons the protagonist in a world of material objects whose peaceful order seems to be disrupted by his presence.

Moriarty's recent work achieves a synthesis between his practice as a comics artist and as a painter. The canvas (whose format is generally 130 x 180 cm) is divided into three sections that segment a scene from daily life into separate instants. A silent action is thus broken down into a sequence. Moriarty now chooses to describe himself as a "paintoonist": part painter, part cartoonist.

8.4 INSIDE/OUTSIDE

Twenty years after *High & Low*, other exhibitions, particularly in France, have set out to bring comics pages into contact with the work of fine artists. I will restrict myself here to the *Vraoum!* [Vroom!} Exhibition held in Paris at the Maison Rouge during the summer of 2009, and the biennial exhibition of contemporary art in Le Havre, held for the third time in October 2010, taking as its title on that occasion *Bande dessinée et art contemporain, la nouvelle scène de l'égalité* [Comics and Contemporary Art, a Newly Equal Scene]. The thinking behind these events deserves closer examination.

David Rosenberg and Pierre Sterckx, the curators of the *Vraoum!* exhibition, state in the catalogue that they want to "show together, and on the same level, works from spheres that traditionally remain separated: on one side, low art with its origins in popular culture, produced by 'authors', and on the other, contemporary art produced by 'artists'." They wish to acknowledge the fact that there is now "complete permeability" to outside influences in the practice of certain comics artists, and, correspondingly, the fact that for contemporary artists like Hervé Di Rosa, Gilles Barbier, or Bertrand Lavier, comics "is no longer deprecated as an inferior form of culture, but is perceived as the source of a reference system common to their whole generation." And the two curators conclude that there is "on one side, comics, an art that is unaware of its own status as art, and on the other, artists mocking solemnity by using comics as a source of inspiration for work that will ultimately make it possible to see comics differently."

These quotations are taken from the free visitor's guide given out at the entrance to the exhibition. In the catalogue proper on sale in the bookshop, there is the further affirmation that the exhibition "celebrates the encounter of paintings, sculptures and drawings *with no hierarchy or divide*" (my italics). And Pierre Sterckx insists: the point is to "disrupt the categorization that separates these media and keeps them apart, and hierarchizes them at the same time." He deplores the fact that comics has not until now been sufficiently "viewed as a major part of culture, with its own classic artists, schools and masterpieces."[25]

The sincerity of Sterckx's interest in comics (and in particular, in a few masters such as McCay, Hergé, Moebius, Reiser, and Swarte) is not to be doubted. But good intentions are not enough. In spite of the declared wish to exhibit comics and contemporary art *on the same level, with no hierarchy or divide*, the conditions under which the two fields were brought into contact were neither convincing nor equitable. For one thing, why not allow *contemporary* art to dialogue solely with *contemporary* comics? Why were five or six successive generations of comics artists exhibited alongside just one or two generations of fine artists? In their desire to show that comics constitutes a major part of culture, the curators rounded up old masters like Outcault, McCay, and Saint-Ogan, thereby effectively skewing the comparison. Comics was insidiously portrayed as an undifferentiated whole, lacking any history. Furthermore, the exhibition layout was organized around *genre*: "Rascals and Scoundrels," "Far West," "Science Fiction," "Superheroes," or "Creepy-Crawlies and Creatures," reinforcing, without acknowledging it, the idea that comics is simply *genre literature*. And among the different thematic sections, only one, called "Pictorial," seemed to have the potential to open up a fruitful comparison with certain currents in contemporary art.

Moreover, it emerges very clearly from the quotations included above that comics requires the mediation of the fine artists whose eyes need to alight upon it in order to magnify it, reveal it to itself, and allow it to claim its rightful place as art. In the end, this attitude is not very far away from that already evinced by *High & Low* (and is coherent with Sterckx's judgement on Lichtenstein, referred to above): "low art is not all that inferior, because it has been revalorized by high art, which has used it as a source of inspiration."[26]

We will now examine in equal detail the introductory texts from the catalogue to the Le Havre biennial exhibition.[27] According to Linda Morren, the artistic director of the event, a dialogue with contemporary art has only become possible because of the profound evolution of comics, not only in terms of its formal qualities and artistic ambition, but also its status. She writes (on p. 5):

> Authors like Robert Crumb, Moebius, Philippe Druillet or Enki Bilal succeeded in freeing themselves from traditional criteria, and initiated an important transition: *comics cast off its status as a "genre" and became a "format,"*[28] *like painting or sculpture.*

The latter part of this sentence (italicized by me) needs to be discussed at some length. It raises firstly questions of vocabulary: are painting and sculpture "formats"? What meaning can we give to this term? And has comics ever been a "genre"?[29] Why should this term be preferred to "medium," "language," "art form," or "literature"? There are three possible answers. Morren may consider comics to be a literary genre (but then why compare it to contemporary art?) or as a genre of visual art (like portrait, still life, etc.). Or she may see it, more precisely, as the *genre* literature that we referred to above. This third possible answer uses the term in the most pejorative sense. It corresponds to the definition given by Menu, for whom any artistic field that becomes inward-looking gets fossilized into a "genre," unable to evolve or renew itself.[30] On this reading, there was a historical phase when comics production retreated back to basics, and then a "modern" phase, characterized by opening up and hybridization.

We will let Morren's sentence remain ambiguous. What is really interesting about her affirmation is the alternatives it offers: are we to understand that comics, henceforth equal in dignity with contemporary art, can be exhibited alongside it on an equal basis, or rather, as the sentence seems to imply, that comics has itself become one of the forms of contemporary art?

Which alternative one chooses, in this dialectic between the same and the other, has important consequences. We must maintain either that artists can, henceforth, legitimately and *on an equal footing*, express themselves through painting, sculpture, comics, or any other "format" (video, installation, performance . . .), or that comics and contemporary art, while remaining separate, can be mutual sources of inspiration. Unfortunately, the subsequent texts from the Le Havre catalogue fail to come to come down clearly on either side.[31]

This ambiguity of status is perfectly illustrated by the situation of comics in art education. For a long time, comics authors were autodidacts, but for just over two decades they have increasingly emerged from art schools offering specialized courses.[32] In these colleges, "the students have the opportunity to come into contact with different techniques, like engraving, to encounter different areas of research, to develop, in other words, a wider artistic culture. [. . .] it is certain that many of the most innovative comics of the last twenty years would have been inconceivable if their creators had not attended art school."[33]

But, at the same time, an art school can too often also be the place where the watertight separation between the culture of comics and that of contemporary art is forcefully reasserted. Many comics artists who have emerged from the top French art schools, like Joann Sfar in Paris or Ruppert and Mulot in Dijon, have testified to the fact that comics are nowhere to be found, are banished from the programme of study, and that they had never been able to find a professor who was willing to engage in dialogue with them on the subject. As for art schools that do offer specialized comics courses, judging from my own experience of teaching the history and theory of comics at the École européenne supérieure de l'image (Angoulême campus), I can only reiterate the painful conclusion that I drew in 2006 in my book *Un objet culturel non identifié* [An Unidentified Cultural Object].[34] The graft of comics onto an institution previously dedicated only to the teaching of traditional disciplines (painting, sculpture, engraving) and various contemporary art forms (video, installations, digital art . . .) has not taken. Two cultures are cohabiting without ever meeting—in a climate that, too often, veers between hostility and indifference.

8.5 THREE ART WORLDS

The thesis I am defending here is that comics and contemporary art differ in their *essence*.

The works of visual artists, hung on walls, generally produce an effect of monumentality. Even serial or multiple works are offered to the eye as a visual totality.

Viewed solely in terms of their physicality, their objective characteristics, comics look very different: they are presented as a series of small-format, printed images. And the reader's attention is dispersed among the too-numerous and fragmented attractions of the page; the eye glides over the surface of a continuum, already enticed onwards by the next image, never stopping or lingering.

There is, of course, a further difference: in comics, the drawing never reigns supreme and does not pursue its own ends; since it serves a higher *design*, it is bound by a narrative project, by some kind of story.

I would like to refer here to the illuminating perspective of Chris Ware, as expressed in his preface to the catalogue of the *UNinked* exhibition at the Phoenix Museum in 2007. Here are the words of the author of the graphic novel *Jimmy Corrigan, the Smartest Kid on Earth*:

> Comics, with rare exception, are a visual language, one composed of pictures intended to be read and distributed as mass-produced objects, not scrutinized individually as one might carefully peruse a painting or a drawing. (. . .) they have more to do with the mechanisms of reading than of looking. (. . .) Comics are at base an art of visual storytelling, and as such, are resistant to the sort of emotional distance and reserve that characterizes so much of 20th and now 21st century art. (. . .) storytelling is simply 'not what artists do anymore'.[35]

On film, the theorist Youssef Ishaghpour has written that "as a world of myths, images, passion, violence, stars and romance—of which *Gone with the Wind* was perhaps the chef d'oeuvre—[it] has little in common with the modern idea of art."[36] When I quoted these words for the first time in *Un objet culturel non identifié* (page 51), I added that the same thing could be said of comics "as a world of dreams, comedy, epic, visual poetry" that sets out to narrate, entertain, move, bear witness, to stir the imagination. With the consequence that "to disqualify comics on the grounds that it has not conformed to movements in [modern and] contemporary art is quite simply to judge it according to criteria that are foreign to it."

Comics is descended from a long tradition of caricature and cartoon drawing. Even if Töpffer and his early imitators published their first works in book format, it was in the press—and as a result of three developments—that the medium evolved. These developments were the liberalization of censorship, the professionalization of illustrators, and the progress of printing techniques. Before long, comics were mainly appearing in the form of serials published daily or weekly.

In France the "illustrés" were for many years intended for children; in America, comic books were aimed at a teenage readership. Even if they did not always achieve it, both aspired to a mass circulation.

Whether from the material, cultural, economic, or sociological point of view, the history of comics has little to do with that of modern art and contemporary art. That has not, of course, prevented a certain contamination *in the margins*; from the earliest days, for example, in the work of Lionel Feininger, whose series drawn in 1906–1907 for the *Chicago Tribune* abounded in graphic effects among which it is easy to discern traces of Art Nouveau, the influence of Expressionism, or even affinities with Cubism, then in its embryonic phase.[37] Sometimes comics has actually been in a position to anticipate artistic ventures still to come: thus, the extravagant productions of Gustave Doré, particularly in *Histoire pittoresque, dramatique et caricaturale de la Sainte Russie* [Picturesque, Dramatic and Caricatural History of Holy Russia] (1854), was many decades ahead of The Incoherents, an art movement that seems to have been inspired by it. But none of the innovatory artists whose names we could evoke here has ever changed the course of comics history.

Contemporary art and comics have to be considered as two different "art worlds" in the meaning given to this expression by the sociologist Howard S. Becker,[38] that is to say two different economic, cultural, and sociological systems. Two quite distinct art worlds, in terms of the conditions of production of the work, the networks that link the artist and other individuals involved in marketing the work, the criteria for reception, the way that value is added, and, ultimately, the aesthetic reference systems. These are all crucial factors that interact with each other and influence the form and content of works, as well as the way in which they get into circulation and become integrated into the cultural landscape of an era—and that, ultimately, perhaps, define the "essence" and the mission peculiar to each art world.

Several commentators have insisted on the fact that contemporary art has its own identity; it is not a simple continuation of Modern Art (from which it took over in the 1960s), but, in many ways, a different "art world."

In the view of Nathalie Heinich, "a large proportion of the works produced after 1945 or 1960 are de facto excluded from what is catalogued as 'contemporary art', which itself must be recognized as a aesthetic category, analogous to what used to be called, in the days of figurative art, a 'genre'." In fact, she argues, just as was once the case for history painting, the contemporary art "genre" [. . .] "is supported more by public institutions than by the private market, is at the summit of the hierarchy in terms of prestige and awards, and enjoys close links with academic and text-based culture."[39]

Contemporary art is too heterogeneous to fit easily into a "genre." But it seems appropriate to see it as an "art world" in itself, in the sense that it is associated with a conception of artistic creation radically different from the one that held sway not only in the nineteenth but also in the first half of the twentieth century.

At the end of the 1950s, Yves Klein declared "long live the immaterial!" Since then, art has been characterized by "artificialization and the increasing dematerialization of the artist's material." Florence de Méredieu has offered a remarkable description and analysis of this tendency toward "factitiousness," this novel situation in which "the proliferating world of forms seems more and more like a mental world." Indeed, contemporary art has, in its most radical manifestations, replaced the work of the artist's hand by the concept (the role played by conceptualization is so great that works and artists often seem to be a mere pretext for the theoretical ruminations of critics, philosophers, and other thinkers). Moreover, multiple techniques and modes of expression have gradually been integrated into the domain of the visual arts. The artist is no longer a painter or sculptor but a *plasticien* [visual artist], that is to say someone who works in any or all of these areas: performance art, video art, set design, photography, installation. In fact, "the artist is no longer expected to produce works, but art. That is to say to produce and exhibit the signifiers of art."[40] In other words, any production, any object that a self-proclaimed artist declares to be art is by that token recognized as art.

Having followed on from Modern Art, contemporary art operates according to a logic different from that of previous avant-garde painters, but, as Chris Ware has convincingly argued, this logic is even less applicable to the world of comics.

8.6 MUST NARRATIVE BE RENOUNCED?

So, what does the "progressive erosion of frontiers" called for by the Association, amount to?

We have ascertained that it is under way in the world of galleries, and that it has inspired a small number of comics creators. However, no such erosion has affected commercial ("genre," if you like, or "mass-market") comics, a sector that has never renounced its own conventions and practices, and that has never ceased to exist. But, fortunately, another kind of comics has become possible, and now co-exists with the mainstream. We can agree to call it "auteurist comics"—even though I am aware of the reductive nature of a polarizing vision of the comics world, and I do not believe it to be divided into two watertight sectors. Within what, for want of a better term, I am, then, calling auteurist comics, several tendencies cohabit. One of these is inclined towards formal experimentation and flirts with the categories and procedures of contemporary art, inciting the artists to leave the book behind and seek out other materials and other ways of disseminating their work.

It is important to distinguish, in this respect, research that seeks a redefinition of the methods, the aims, and the aesthetic of comics as such, and the ad hoc techniques that may be invented as a creative response to a request from a private or public gallery, in order to respond to the challenge posed by display on a wall to enable comics to "be hangable."[41] A reminder is called for here. Adventure comics have already had their "becoming cinema" moment back in the 1930s, when artists took their inspiration from the visual codes and the glamour of Hollywood. For the last quarter century, comics have been undergoing a "becoming literature," with what is now termed the *graphic novel*. There is no reason why certain auteurist comics should not embark upon a process of "becoming contemporary art," and, in so doing, revitalize the tradition of the artist's book. Like other forms of expression, comics are enriched by a wide range of heterogeneous outside influences (one need only think about the importance of video games as part of the culture of the new generation of comics creators). And so I do not believe that comics is destined to become one of the "formats" of contemporary art. On the contrary, I can foresee the fatal, in both senses of the word—inevitable and lethal—outcome of any such evolution.

Alain Berland, the artistic advisor to the Le Havre biennial exhibition, maintains that a comics author "has a duty, if s/he wants to move with the times, to mistreat the medium by engaging in multiple hybridizations with other artistic disciplines.[42] What comes through in this declaration is the idea that comics can only accede to the status of "contemporary" (and so, we understand, artistic value) on condition of being "mistreated," in other words by being made to run counter to its natural bent, and expelled from its own domain. How can it achieve this? Berland implies that it must "emancipate itself from narrative." And it is in just this direction that the recent work of artists like Jochen Gerner[43] or Andrei Molotiu[44] has led.

It is entirely legitimate for certain artists to pursue this ambition. At the periphery of the comics field, there is room for experiment, for going off the beaten track in a direction that may lead to mutations of the medium. Nonetheless, I am certain that, from Chris Ware to Joann Sfar, many of the most exciting current comics authors would fiercely disagree with the injunction requiring comics to enter a post-narrative era. This is because, for comics, liberation from narrative and liberation from its own self would be one and the same thing. The curators of the *Vraoum!* exhibition were quite right to contrast fine *artists* with comics *authors*. In his day, Töpffer referred to "literature in prints"; and history has proved him right: it is indeed a literature that has come into being, that is to say a vast corpus of narrative works, structured according to genres, schools, collections, readerships. Harry Morgan, writing in our day, also recognizes this history and this artistic predisposition when he uses the term "graphic literature."[45] If comics were to free itself from literature, this would be less a liberation than a disavowal.

The closing statement of *System 1* argues that in modern comics, it had been possible for form to become freer because narrative content had itself evolved, demonstrating the protean nature of the medium. In this new book I have aimed to offer an account of new kinds of expressive narrative devices in their rhythmic and poetic dimensions\ and stylistic variability. Far from deconstructing narration, or rendering it outmoded, these advances enrich it, and so fulfill the potential of comics as an art form that is both visual and narrative.

TRANSLATOR'S FOREWORD

1. Henceforth *Système 2*.

2. Thierry Groensteen, *Système de la bande dessinée* (Paris: Presses Universitaires de France, 1999). Henceforth *Système 1*. English version translated by Bart Beaty and Nick Nguyen, under title of *The System of Comics* (Jackson: University Press of Mississippi, 2006). Henceforth *System 1*.

INTRODUCTION

1. Thierry Smolderen, "Of Labels, Loops and Bubbles: Solving the Historical Puzzle of the Speech Balloon," *Comic Art*, no. 8, Summer 2006, 90–112.

2. Thierry Smolderen, "Trois forms de pages" [Three types of page], *Neuvième Art*, no. 13, January 2007, 20–31.

3. Thierry Smolderen, *Naissances de la bande dessinée* (Brussels: Les Impressions nouvelles, 2009). To be published in English translation under the title *The Birth of Comics, from William Hogarth to Winsor McCay*, trans. Bart Beaty and Nick Nguyen (Jackson: University of Mississippi Press, 2013 forthcoming).

4. Jean-Christophe Menu, *La Bande dessinée et son double* [Comic Art and its Double] (Paris: L'Association, 2010), p. 447.

5. Harry Morgan, *Formes et mythopoeia dans les littératures dessinées* [Forms and Mythopoeia in Graphic Literature], unpublished doctoral thesis, in the History and Semiology of the Text and Image, Paris 7, 2008.

6. Translator's note: Morgan's actual term is "littératures dessinées," or "drawn literatures."

7. For an initial evaluation of the activities of Oubapo, I refer readers to the dossier that appeared in *Neuvième Art* no. 10, April 2004, 72–99, and in particular to my article "Ce que l'Oubapo révèle de la bande dessinée" [What Oubapo reveals about comics], 72–75.

8. For more details about this evolution, see my article "La conquête du silence" [The Conquest of Silence], *Art Press* special edition no. 26, *Bande d'auteurs* [Band of Authors], 2005, 68–73.

9. See 3.2 below.

CHAPTER ONE

1. Ann Miller, *Reading Bande Dessinée* (Bristol: Intellect, 2007), p. 75.

2. I offer a perspective on the whole debate ensuing from the question of a definition of comics in my text "Définitions," forthcoming in 2012 in *L'Art de la bande dessinée* [The Art of Comics], to be published by Citadelles & Mazenod.

3. *La Bande Dessinée et son double*, op. cit., p. 414.

4. Ibid. p. 413.

5. Kirk Varnedoe and Adam Gopnik, *High & Low: Modern Art and Popular Culture* (New York: The Museum of Modern Art, 1990), p. 189. My italics.

6. Notably at the Maison rouge in Paris, in 2009, at MoMA in 2007 (at the *Comic Abstraction: Image-Breaking, Image-Making* exhibition) and, again in New York, at the New Museum in 2010.

7. Alex Baladi, *Petit trait* (Paris: L'Association, 2008).

8. In a sense close to that proposed by Harry Morgan, but narrower. For him, "the apparatus encompasses the actual form in which the graphic narrative is presented (strip, single page, booklet, album, etc.), as well as the means of dividing it up and the inscription of texts." *Forms and Mythopoeia*, op. cit., p. 16. Translator's note: the term used by Groensteen is "dispositif," which might be translated as "mechanism," "apparatus," or "operation," none of which is entirely satisfactory. Until this point we have used "formal apparatus." Henceforth we will simply refer to the "apparatus."

9. Groupe Mu, *Traité du signe visuel* (Paris: Seuil, 1992), p. 189.

10. But also of vocabulary and conceptual categories that vary from one cultural sphere to another. For example, in Korea (and perhaps in other countries?) one does not say "to read a comic" but "to look at a comic." The emphasis is on visual perception, not on cognitive processes. It follows logically that the idea of abstract comics should be more readily accepted.

11. These pages have been reprinted in his album *Nautilus* (Copenhagen: Fahrenheit, 2009).

12. See http://diplomes.etapes.com/profiles/2227-thomas-higashiyama?locale=en, accessed March 16, 2011.

13. Translator's note: *in Système 1*, pp. 173–74, *System 1*, p. 146, Groensteen makes a distinction between the "sequence" (images linked by a narrative project), the "série" (images with some iconic, visual, or semantic element in common), and the "suite" (a random succession of images). I will translate "suite" by "string."

14. See "La narration comme supplément" [Narration as a Supplement], *Bande dessinée, récit et modernité* (Paris: Futuropolis, 1988), pp. 45–69. As I recall, an *amalgam* was defined as a "simple juxtaposition of disparate images."

15. See *Système 1*, p. 124, *System 1*, p. 106.

16. Scott McCloud, *Understanding Comics: The Invisible Art* (New York: Harper Collins, 1993), pp. 70–72.

17. Ibid. pp. 74–80.

18. Ibid. p. 72.

19. Art Spiegelman, *Breakdowns: Portrait of the Artist as a Young %@§*!* (New York: Pantheon, 2008).

20. A recurrent characteristic of the Samuel Lipinski strips is, precisely, the deployment of extreme close-ups, very tightly framed, on details that seem to be part of a much larger image that has been withheld from us in its complete version.

21. *Système 1*, p. 133, *System 1*, p. 113.

CHAPTER TWO

1. *Système 1*, p. 125, *System 1*, p. 106.

2. Ibid. p. 130, p. 111.

3. Harry Morgan, *Principes des littératures dessinées* (Paris: L'An 2, 2003).

4. Ibid. p. 40.

5. Ibid. p. 41.

6. Ibid. my italics.

7. Aron Kibedi Varga, *Discours, récit, image* [Discourse, Narrative, Image] (Liège: Pierre Mardaga, 1989), p. 96 and following.

8. Ibid. p. 98.

9. François Garnier, *Le Langage de l'image au Moyen Âge* [The Language of the Image in the Middle Ages], vol. 1 (Paris: Le Léopard d'Or, 1982), p. 40.

10. Wendy Steiner, "Pictorial Narrativity," in *Narrative across Media. The Language of Storytelling*, ed. Marie-Louise Ryan (Lincoln and London: University of Nebraska Press, 2004), pp. 145–77. There also exist works that condense into one image distinct moments in a story, without having recourse to the repetition of the same figures. In *Telling Time* (London: National Gallery Company, 2000), Alexander Sturgis gives the example of *Saint George and the Dragon* by Paolo Uccello (c. 1470) in which the Saint can be seen cleaving the dragon with his lance, while the creature is already held on a leash by the Princess who is going to take it back, tamed, to the city that it had terrorized. But it is obvious that this condensation is somewhat unintelligible. The image seems to offer a contradiction in terms (why attack an animal that has already been tamed?) and only prior knowledge of the legend makes it possible to rearticulate the elements of the image into a coherent chronology.

11. "Pictorial Narrativity," op. cit., p. 154.

12. Ibid. pp. 155–56.

13. Gotthold Ephraim Lessing, *Laocoon: An Essay upon the Limits of Poetry and Painting*, trans. Ellen Frothingham (Boston: Roberts Brothers, 1887), p. 91.

14. Ibid. p. 109.

15. Ibid. p. 92. My italics.

16. Louis Marin, "Représentation narrative" [Narrative Representation], consulted on the *Encyclopaedia Universalis* site, February 14, 2002.

17. The concept of narrative painting is sufficiently fuzzy to accommodate the whole of history and genre painting, paintings belonging to a cycle (like Rubens' paintings of Marie de Medici (1622–1624) or Mucha's *Slav Epic* [1910–1928]), Victorian painting, certain canvasses by Vallotton, or Norman Rockwell's *Sunday Evening Post* covers.

18. Julia Thomas (ed.), *Victorian Narrative Painting* (London: Tate Publishing, 2000).

19. Ibid. p. 19.

20. Harry Morgan, "Narrativité et réflexivité: Les couvertures de Norman Rockwell pour le *Saturday Evening Post*" [Narrative potential and reflexivity: Norman Rockwell's covers for the *Saturday Evening Post*] http://theadamantine.free.fr/rockwell.htm Accessed February 12, 2010.

21. *The Flirts* appeared on the cover of the *Saturday Evening Post* on July 26, 1941. Rockwell's image is reproduced in *Norman Rockwell* by Karal Ann Marling (Cologne: Taschen, 2006), p. 29. It is the framing of the image, not its pseudo-narrative qualities, that I find striking.

22. Christian Moncelet, "*L'Angélus* de Millet" [Millet's *The Angelus*], *Ridiculosa* no. 3: *Pastiches et parodies de tableaux de maîtres* [Pastiches and parodies of masterpieces], Université de Bretagne Occidentale, 1996, pp. 13–26.

23. Hergé, *Les Bijoux de la Castafiore* (Tournai: Casterman, 1963). English version trans. Leslie Lonsdale-Cooper and Michael Turner (London: Methuen, 1963).

24. Translator's note: the play on words is lost here as the French term includes the word "grâce," meaning "grace."

25. Here Groensteen uses the abbreviation "BD," a term that tends to be reserved to mainstream, commercial comics production.

26. See below, Chapter 7.

27. See *Système 1*, pp. 107–19, *System 1*, pp. 91–92.

28. Jodorowsky and Moebius, *Les Yeux du chat* (Paris: Les Humanoïdes associés, 1978).

29. Martin-Vaughn-James, *The Cage* (Toronto: The Coach House Press, 1975).

30. Vincent Perriot, *Entre Deux* (Bordeaux: Les Éditions de la cerise, 2007).

31. *Système 1*, p. 135, *System 1*, p. 115.

32. In *La Bande dessinée et son double*, Menu enumerates (section 9.4, p. 463 onwards) various examples of "comics made up of one panel per page." He too maintains that "if a story is narrative (sic), sequential and graphic, but is made up of only one panel per page, there is no reason to exclude it from the domain of comics. And author-publisher-theoretician Menu concludes that "if there is one level in comics that is predominant, it is the level of the book as foliated space."

33. *Laocoon* op. cit., pp. 91–92.

34. See *Système 1*, p. 190, *System 1*, pp. 161–62.

35. Henri Van Lier, *Anthropogénie* [Anthropogenics] (Brussels: Les Impressions nouvelles, 2010), p. 230. "Talking" comics adds interlocution to intergestuality.

36. Translator's note: Groensteen's terms are: "le montré, l'advenu, le signifié." These past participles do not happily turn into nouns in English, and the translation inevitably sounds more awkward than the original.

37. See below, 5.1.2.

38. Translator's note: it is obviously to Groensteen's own term "advenu" that his explanation applies. The closest English translation, "intervened," includes the idea of "between," absent from Groensteen's original but not inappropriate in the context in which the term is used here.

39. Chris Ware, *Jimmy Corrigan, The Smartest Kid on Earth* (New York: Pantheon Books, 2000).

40. See below, Chapter 6.

41. Benoît Peeters and Jacques Samson, *Chris Ware: la bande dessinée réinventée* [Chris Ware: Comics Reinvented] (Brussels: Les Impressions nouvelles, 2010), p. 125.

42. Any more than he takes account of the page as a visual unit as well as a unit of narration. Nor does he consider the relationships that can operate among distant images, whether through retroactive determination at the more encompassing plane of meaning constituted by the sequence, or by braiding. For McCloud, the dialog among images is always conducted with immediate neighbors, isolated from any wider context: it concerns only panels that are next to each other, and they are never considered in relation to their siting on the surface of the page or within the flow of a sequence.

CHAPTER THREE

1. See below, Chapter 7.

2. Christophe Blain, *Isaac le Pirate*, vol. 4, *La Capitale* (Paris: Dargaud, 2004).

3. The "varying height of strips" is a parameter identified and commented on by Renaud Chavanne in his treatise *Composition de la bande dessinée* [The Composition of Comics] (Montrouge: PLG, 2010), p. 63. The author has decided to use the term "composition" for what is commonly known as "page layout," a solution that has the drawback of making the term "composition" unavailable to designate the arrangement of motifs within panels, the opposition of color or monochrome masses, the play of lines of force, etc.

4. Translator's note: I have not used the term "splash panel" here, sometimes applied to a panel that stands out because of its large size (and which can become a "splash page" if it covers the entire page), because "splash panel" does not imply the height conformity that is a feature of the panels discussed by Groensteen in this section.

5. I am aware that the criterion of density is primarily a matter of breakdown, which prescribes how much information and how many images the page will contain. But the effect of this on the visual aspect of the page will incline the reader to see it as a matter of page layout. Clearly, any page layout is the spatial translation of the "contractual conditions" imposed by the breakdown.

6. Nicolas Dumontheuil, *Le Roi cassé* (Tournai: Casterman, 2010).

7. Régis Loisel and Jean-Louis Tripp, *Magasin général*, 7 volumes (Tournai: Casterman, 2006–2011).

8. François Boucq and Alexandro Jodorowsky, *Face de lune*, 5 volumes, (Tournai: Casterman, 1997–2004).

9. Enki Bilal, *Le Sommeil du monstre*, (Geneva: Les Humanoïdes associés, 1998).

10. Enki Bilal, *32 Décembre* (Geneva: Les Humanoïdes associés, 2003).

11. Translator's note: again, I have avoided the term "splash panel"—on this occasion because, although the term implies an oversized panel, it does not necessarily imply one whose width coincides with that of the whole strip.

12. In *L'Oeuf de l'âme* [The Egg of the Soul], the fifth volume of the *Face de lune* series by Boucq and Jodorowsky, I calculate that there are seven pages in which all the panels are full-width. The page therefore coincides with a single, maximum-length column.

13. Joann Sfar, *Le Minuscule Mousquetaire*, vol. 3 *On ne patine pas avec l'amour* [No Skating with Love (a play on words alluding to an 1834 play by Alfred de Musset)] (Paris: Dargaud: 2006).

14. Nicolas de Crécy, *Prosopopus* (Paris: Dargaud, 2003).

15. See Benoît Peeters, *Lire la bande dessinée* [Reading Comics] (Paris: Casterman, 1998 and Paris: Flammarion, 2010), pp. 48–53.

16. Chavanne categorizes the Jacobs/Ceppi practice as "fragmentation" of the strip and/or the panel. Out of the four conceptions of page layout identified by Peeters, he retains only two: "regular" and "rhetorical." But this leads him (*The Composition of Comics*, op. cit., p. 163) to separate out the variation in the size of images from their iconic and semantic content, thereby making the adjective "rhetorical" into a mere synonym of "irregular."

17. See my article "Tendances contemporaines de la mise en page" [Contemporary tendencies in page layout], *Neuvième Art*, no. 13 (January 2007), 43–51, of which this chapter is a revised version. Apart from manga, another source of the "neo-baroque" can be found in some American comic books of the 1980s.

18. See below, Chapter 7.

19. See *Système 1*, p. 28, *System 1*, p. 23.

CHAPTER FOUR

1. Translator's note: in French-speaking countries illustrated children's books are known as "albums."

2. For example, *Bonhommes de neige* [Snowmen] by Samivel (1948), who openly acknowledges the influence of Töpffer, several albums by the British artist Raymond Briggs, or *Désordre au paradis* [Trouble in Paradise] by Gabrielle Vincent (Duculot: Pars, 1989; reprinted Tournai: Casterman, 2008).

3. We should include contemporary French-language authors such as Nicole Claveloux, Anne Herbauts, Nadja, Yvan Pommaux, Marcelino Truong, José Parrondo, Bruno Heitz, and Benoît Jacques.

4. Sophie Van der Linden, *Lire l'Album* (Paris: L'Atelier du poisson soluble, 2006).

5. Ibid. p. 157.

6. Ibid. p. 29.

7. Ibid. p. 87.

8. See above, 3.1.

9. See *Système 1*, p. 171, *System 1*, p. 144.

10. *Lire l'Album* op. cit., p. 65.

11. Ibid. pp. 44–45.

12. Ibid. p. 46.

13. See above, 2.4.

14. *Lire l'Album* op. cit., p. 122.

15. Ibid. pp. 68–70.

16. Serge Tisseron, *Psychanalyse de la bande dessinée* [The Psychoanalysis of Comics] (Paris: Presses Universitaires de France, 1987), p. 90.

17. See "L'interview graphique" [The Graphic Interview] with Claude Lapointe on the site http://www.ricochet-jeunes.org/magazine/article/45-claude-lapointe Accessed March 5, 2010.

18. Claude Lapointe, "Tête-à-tête," interview with Catherine Germain and André Leblanc, *La Revue du livre pour enfants* [The Journal of Children's Books], no. 113 (Spring 1987), 38–40.

19. Anne Herbauts, *Vague* [Wave] (Asnières: L'Association Grandir, 1999); *Autoportrait* [Self Portrait] (Noville-sur-Mehaigne: L'Esperluète, 2001); *Cardiogramme* [Cardiogram], *Par-delà les nuages* [Beyond the Clouds], *L'Idiot* [The Idiot] (Angoulême: Éditions de l'An 2, 2002, 2004, 2005).

20. See above, 2.2.

21. I have described the aesthetic resources of comics of this type in terms of *narrative drawing* (*Système 1* pp. 190–92; *System 1*, pp. 161–63), appropriatenes,s and "dependent beauty." See *La Bande dessinée, son histoire et ses maîtres* [Comics: History and Masters of Comic Art] (Paris: Skira Flammarion, 2009), chapter entitled "Les Maîtres du trait" [Masters of the Graphic Line].

22. Thierry Groensteen, *L'Univers des manga. Une introduction à la bande dessinée japonaise* [The World of Manga. An Introduction to Japanese Comics] (Tournai: Casterman, 1991, revised and enlarged edition 1996).

23. Other works by the same artist are distinctive, in contrast, for their radical experimentation with the codes of the comics medium.

24. A technique analyzed in *Système 1*, pp. 100–106, *System 1*, pp. 85–91.

25. Henri Van Lier "La Bande dessinée, une cosmogonie dure" [Comics, a hard cosmogony], *Bande dessinée, récit et modernité* [Comics, Narrative and Modernity] (ed.) Thierry Groensteen (Paris: Futuropolis and Angoulême: CNBDI, 1988), pp. 5–24; 5.

26. A more detailed study would necessitate a chronology of the stages of their introduction and frequent or dominant use, but that is beyond the scope of this essay. I hope that I may be forgiven for referring to *shōjo* in rather general terms; the point here is simply to contrast their most salient characteristics with the canonical features of Western comics.

27. See *Système* 1, p. 107, *System 1*, p. 91.

28. See above, 3.2.

29. *Système 1*, pp. 49–68, *System 1* pp. 39–57.

30. Manabu Inoue (ed.) *Manga no yomikata* (Tokyo: Takarimasha, 1995), p. 181.

31. Jacqueline Berndt "Considering Manga Discourse: Location, Ambiguity, Historicity," in Mark W. MacWilliams (ed.), *Japanese Visual Culture* (New York and London: M.E, Sharpe, 2008), pp. 295–333 (p. 302). This point is also addressed in an essay by Gō Itō, *Tezuka is deddo. Hirakareta manga hyogenron* [Tezuka is Dead. Towards a Theory of Manga] (Tokyo: NTT Shuppan, 2005).

32. Translator's note: "montage" in the original.

33. *Système 1*, pp. 118–19, *System 1*, pp. 101–2.

34. Ibid. pp. 118–19, p. 101.

35. Respectively, *Le Monstre* [The Monster], vol. 1 *Le Sommeil du monstre* [The Sleep of the Monster] (Paris: Casterman, 2006) and *Mémoires du XXᵉ Ciel 98* [Memories of the twentieth Sky 98] (Paris: Delcourt, 1999).

36. See my article "L'ère du montage" [The Era of Editing], *Neuvième Art* no. 4 (January 1999), 128–29.

37. François Schuiten and Benoît Peeters, *L'Aventure des images: de la bande dessinée au multimédia* [The Adventure of Images: from Comics to Multimedia (Paris : Autrement, 1996), p. 148.

38. Ibid. p. 161.

39. See *Système 1*, pp. 36–37 and 175, *System 1*, pp. 28–29 and 148.

40. Scott McCloud enumerates other advantages of print comics over digital comics in *Reinventing Comics* (New York: Paradox Press, 2000), p. 175. I would add, as a personal view, that the book satisfies the acquisitive instinct, and we know the importance—for better or worse—of the phenomenon of collection mania among comics readers.

41. Comics published by DC and Marvel now come out on the same day in print format and in an electronic downloadable version.

42. I am aware that the works cited here were all originally published in installments, in the form of comics, or chapters in magazines. These fragments could all equally well have been published online. But once completed, they do indeed become "graphic novels" noteworthy for their narrative scope, presented to readers as coherent wholes, and henceforth only circulated in the form of thick volumes.

43. We are forced to admit that this is incontestable: according to an article in *Le Monde* of July 23, 2010, 80 percent of the content downloaded onto their cell phones by Japanese users consists of manga. In France, it is too soon to tell, as the comics market was not available to cell phones until 2009.

44. Translator's note: Rageul's original term is "lectacteur."

45. Anthony Rageul, *Bande dessinée interactive: comment raconter une histoire* [Interactive Comics: How to Tell a Story], dissertation presented for the degree of Master of Arts and Digital Technologies, Université Rennes 2, Haute Bretagne (2008–2009), p. 67. This dissertation can be downloaded from the site www.prisedetete.net, which also presents an interactive comic by the author (under the pseudonym of Tony), *Prise de tête* [Pain in the Neck], first uploaded in 2009, and for which a "textual analysis" is given in the dissertation.

46. *Principes des littératures dessinées*, op. cit. p. 151.

47. *Reinventing Comics*, op. cit., p. 210.

48. Magali Boudissa, *La Bande dessinée entre la page et l'écran: étude critique des enjeux théoriques liés au renouvellement du langage bédéique sous influence numérique* [Comics Between Page and Screen : a Critical Study of Theoretical Considerations Linked to the Renewal of the Language of Comics under the Influence of Digital Comics], unpublished doctoral thesis, Paris VIII Vincennes at Saint-Denis, 2010, p. 359.

49. Ibid. pp. 353 and 360.

50. *Reinventing Comics*, op. cit., p. 210.

51. Translator's note: the French translation of McCloud's term "tricked-up" is "customisée" [customized].

52. *La Bande dessinée entre la page et l'écran* op. cit., pp. 152, 269, and 359.

53. Anthony Rageul, "Pour une bande dessinée interactive" [Towards Interactive Comics], February 2009 on www.du9.org. Link to the article : http://www.du9.org/Pour-une-bande-dessinee.

54. To use a term from Boudissa, who analyzes in particular a story called *L'Oreille coupée* [The Severed Ear] by Jean-François Bergeron and André-Philippe Côté, that can be found on: http://www.youtube.com/watch?v=F5UELmOzhwQ.

55. This series was originated by Edward Packard (Waitsfield, VT: Vermont Crossroads Press, from 1976).

56. See *Système 1*, pp. 27, 107–8 and 167–69, *System 1*, pp. 22, 91–92, 142–43.

57. *Reinventing Comics* op. cit., p. 223.

58. *Ibid.* p. 220.

59. *Système 1*, p. 71, *System 1*, p. 59.

60. *Bande dessinée interactive* op. cit., pp. 58–59.

61. Jean-Louis Boissier, "Jouable" [Playable], in *Jouable: Art, jeu et interactivité* [Playable : Art, Games and Interactivity], Catalogue of exhibition and collected papers from conference of same name (HEAA Geneva, ENSAD Paris, Ciren/University of Paris 8, Geneva, Paris, Kyoto, 2004), p. 17.

62. The terms "schizophrénie" [schizophrenia], "décrochage" [disconnect], and "distanciation" [distancing] are taken from Rageul himself, pp. 71, 87, and 89.

63. See *Système 1*, p. 9, *System 1*, p. 8.

CHAPTER FIVE

1. Postface to Gaétan Soucy, *L'Angoisse du héron* (Chauvigny: L'Escampette, 2009).

2. *Système 1*, p. 187, *System 1*, p. 159.

3. *Le Narrateur. Introduction à la théorie narrative* [The Narrator: Introduction to Narrative Theory], Paris: Armand Colin, 2009.

4. In my discussion of Schaeffer's position on this point in *Système 1*, pp. 11–12, *System 1*, pp. 9–10, I went so far as to describe it as "counter-intuitive," given that it is obvious that a film, a comic—or even a pantomime or a ballet—normally tells a story. Even if I still disagree with detailed elements of his exposition of this point, I was wrong to attack him for what was only, in reality, methodological caution on his part. The absence of a narrator, or narration, in the "technical" sense, does not necessarily mean absence of a story.

5. *Système 1*, p. 124, *System 1*, p. 106.

6. *Cinéma et production de sens* [Cinema and the Production of Meaning], (Paris: Armand Colin, 1990), p. 5.

7. *Système 1*, p. 14, *System 1*, p. 12.

8. See for example *Reading Bande Dessinée* op. cit., chapter 6.

9. *Le Récit filmique* [The Cinematic Narrative], (Paris: Hachette, 1993) pp. 109–10.

10. See, in particular, *L'Œil-caméra, entre film et roman* [The Camera Eye, Between Film and Novel], (Lyon: Presses Universitaires de Lyon, 1987).

11. See Henri Van Lier, *Philosophie de la photographie* [The Philosophy of Photography] (Brussels: Les Impressions nouvelles, 2004 [1983]), chapter 2.

12. *Reading Bande Dessinée*, op. cit., p. 110. Ann Miller examines in particular André Juillard's *Le Cahier bleu* (Tournai: Casterman, 1994), which is marked, famously, by a complex

play on intersecting narrative perspectives. She concludes that the album demonstrates that, in this area, comic art shows "considerable flexibility." The same album is studied from a similar perspective by Éric Lavanchy in his *Étude du* Cahier bleu *de Juillard: Une approche narratologique de la bande dessinée* [A Study of Juillard's *Le Cahier bleu*: A Narratological Approach to Comic Art] (Louvain-la-Neuve: Academia-Bruylant, 2007).

13. Kai Mikkonen, "Presenting Minds in Graphic Narratives," *Partial Answers: Journal of Literature and the History of Ideas*, vol. 6., no. 2 (June 2008), 301–21 (p. 312).

14. André Gaudreault, *Du littéraire au filmique. Système du récit* [From the Literary to the Filmic: The Narrative System] (Paris: Méridiens Klincksieck, 1988), p. 91.

15. Ibid. p. 42.

16. *Traces en cases* [Traces in Frames], Doctoral thesis, Université catholique de Louvain, Département de Communication sociale, March 1991. (Published version: Louvain-la-Neuve: Académia, 1993.) I will not go into the more psychoanalytical section of Marion's theory, concerning the construction of empathy and affective involvement of the reader.

17. Douglas Wolk, *Reading Comics: How Graphic Novels Work and What they Mean* (Cambridge, MA: Da Capo Press, 2007), p. 21.

18. Translator's note: the original is *mise en dessin*, by analogy with *mise en scène*.

19. *Le Récit filmique*, op. cit., p. 103.

20. I analyzed the characteristics of the narrative drawing in *Système 1*, 190–91, *System 1*, 161–62.

21. Paper given at the conference entitled "Academic Perspectives on Comics, Manga & Graphic Novels as Intercultural & Intermedial Phenomena," University of Växjö, Sweden, 16–18 April 2009. Conference proceedings are forthcoming.

22. Gilles Deleuze, *Cinéma 2: L'image-temps* [Cinema 2: The Time-Image] (Paris: Minuit, 1985), p. 54.

23. Gérard Genette, *Figures III* (Paris: Seuil, 1972), p. 230.

24. In France the term *voice-over* is more commonly used in audiovisual media, in the case, for example, of a foreign program adapted for a French audience, when the voice of the actor reading the translation is superimposed on the voice of the original speaker. It can also refer to the technology used to transfer voice to the Internet.

25. Franquin, Jidéhem and Greg, *L'Ombre du Z* (Marcinelle: Dupuis, 1962).

26. *Système 1*, p. 156, *System 1*, p. 131.

27. Translator's note: the term in French is "postures."

28. To be precise, it should be noted that this sequence also includes three frames in which the narrator remains silent. But they are not essential to the understanding of the scene.

29. See below, 5.3.3.

30. Edmond Baudoin, *Salade niçoise* (Paris: L'Association, 1999).

31. Fabrice Neaud, *Journal 4* (Angoulême: ego comme x, 2002).

32. The caption reads as follows: "And it is with this disbelieving and proud smile, dear reader, that I encourage you to embrace what only mad erudition or blind hatred of Russia could have inspired."

33. *Système 1*, pp. 128–29, *System 1*, pp. 108–10.

34. Translator's note: Gaudreault, in a discussion of written texts, uses the English spelling of the word "narrator" to refer to this fundamental instance (the equivalent of the instance that, in relation to film, he refers to as a "mega-narrateur" [mega-narrator]). I have quoted Groensteen's original French term here, in order to make it clear that, unlike Gaudreault, he sees no need to adopt the English spelling.

35. *Système 1*, p. 107, *System 1*, p. 92.

36. Ibid. p. 152, p. 128.

37. With the reservations that I have outlined above concerning this term, which I now prefer not to use.

38. *Système 1*, p. 152, *System 1*, pp. 128–29.

39. *Mort Cinder* is a work written by Hector Œsterheld and drawn by Alberto Breccia, published in the Argentinian magazine *Misterix* nos. 718–798 (1962 to 1964).

40. This corresponds to Genette's "homodiegetic narrator," which has also been called a "personalized" or "implied" narrator by other critics.

41. José Muñoz and Carlos Sampayo, *La Fin d'un voyage* (Tournai: Casterman, 1999).

42. In the case of autobiography, the referential, pact is in general co-extensive with the autobiographical pact . . . [. . . .] The formula would no longer be "I the undersigned," but "I swear to tell the truth, the whole truth and nothing but the truth." Philippe Lejeune, *Le Pacte autobiographique* (Paris: Seuil, 1975), p. 36.

43. Ibid. pp. 14–15.

44. Jean-Christophe Menu and Christian Rosset, *Corr&spondance* (Paris: L'Association, 2009), p. 10.

45. Jean-Christophe Menu, *Livret de Phamille* (Paris: L'Association, 1995).

46. Translator's note: the original French expression is "le moi-personnage."

47. A risk pinpointed by Fabrice Neaud, in his responses to a questionnaire on autobiography, *Neuvième Art* no. 1 (January 1996), p. 73.

48. Alison Bechdel adopts this procedure in *Fun Home*. The drawings at the head of each chapter are presented as Polaroids, but their drawn status is obvious.

49. Marjane Satrapi, *Persepolis* (Paris: L'Association, 2000).

50. Olivier Ka and Alfred, *Pourquoi j'ai tué Pierre* [Why I Killed Pierre] (Paris: Delcourt, 2006).

51. Loïc Nehou and Frédéric Poincelet, *Essai de sentimentalisme* [On Sentimentality] (Angoulême: ego comme X, 2001).

52. Emmanuel Guibert, *La Guerre d'Alan, d'après les souvenirs d'Alan Ingram Cope* [Alan's War, as told by Alan Ingram Cope], 3 volumes, (Paris: L'Association, 2000–2008); Emmanuel Guibert, Didier Lefèvre, Frédéric Lemercier, *Le Photographe* [The Photographer] (Marcinelle: Dupuis, 2003–2006). In the case of *Le Photographe*, it is detailed in the album that we are reading "a true story, lived, photographed, and recounted by Didier Lefèvre, written and drawn by Emmanuel Guibert, with layout and color by Frédéric Lemercier" (p. 6).

53. Jan Baetens comments as follows on this unusual mode of collaboration:

In a mixed medium like comics, when the roles of scriptwriter and artist are often split, the doubling of the narrative function can often lead to very peculiar situations in works that are in autobiographical mode. It is reasonable to wonder whether it is possible to entrust an autobiographical narrative produced by an author-scriptwriter to someone else who would draw it, without the narrative in question ceasing to be autobiographical and so losing its authenticity.

However, Baetens concludes:

By rejecting as inauthentic the collaboration between two different narrators, one in charge of the story and the other the drawing, we underestimate, I believe, the potential for "fusion" that can arise out of a successful collaboration.

"Autobiographie et bandes dessinées" [Autobiography and Comics], Belphegor vol. 4. no. 1 (November 2004) http://etc.dal.ca/belphegor/vol4_no1/articles/04_01_Baeten_autobd_fr.html.

54. Lewis Trondheim, *Approximativement* (Paris: Cornélius, 1995).

55. Uncle Paul calls them "boys" or "my little friends." The nephews are obviously the representatives of the young readers that he is addressing. It is significant that the uncle has no nieces.

56. Tardi, *Momies en folie* (Tournai: Casterman, 1978).

57. Tardi, *Le Secret de la salamandre* (Tournai: Casterman, 1981).

58. This narrating character had been introduced for a re-edition of *Adieu Brindavoine* [Farewell Brindavoine] (Tournai: Casterman, 1979), for the duration of two pages intended to create a transition between this episode, originally published by Dargaud, and *La Fleur au fusil* [The Flower in a Gun Barrel], a short story that was not in the first edition, but which featured the same protagonist, Lucien Brindavoine.

59. This story was published in album format by Hélyode in 1990 and re-serialized in the newspaper *La Libre Belgique*, and then brought out in a new edition by Coccinelle BD in 2002 in full and in color for the first time.

60. Joann Sfar, *Le Chat du Rabbin*, vol. 1, *La Bar-Mitsva* (Paris: Dargaud, 2002).

61. David Mazzucchelli, *Asterios Polyp* (New York: Pantheon Books, 2009).

62. Blutch, *Le Petit Christian* (Paris: L'Association, 2002).

63. The hero of a popular comics series from the 1970s by Jean Ollivier and Raphaël Marcello that appeared in the weekly magazine *Pif Gadget*.

64. I am quoting Nünning as paraphrased by Sylvie Patron, *Le Narrateur: Introduction à la théorie narrative* [The Narrator: Introduction to Narrative Theory] (Paris: Armand Colin, 2009), p. 145.

65. Hergé: *Le Secret de la Licorne* (Tournai: Casterman, 1943), p. 14. Translator's note: I have not used the published translation here, as it transposes the events to the reign of Charles II in England, rather than simply translating the original.

66. Karl Bühler (1879–1963) is one of the great theoreticians of language of the twentieth century. On the concept of "deictic center" see *Le Narrateur* op. cit., p. 238.

67. Tardi and Jean-Patrick Manchette, *Griffu* (Tournai: Casterman, 1978).

68. Tardi, *La Véritable Histoire du soldat inconnu / La Bascule à Charlot* (Paris: Pepperland, 1974).

69. Tardi and Léo Malet, *Brouillard au Pont de Tolbiac* (Tournai: Casterman, 1982).

70. Translator's note: Lapinot is a very sketchy rabbit-like creature, albeit a sophisticated conversationalist, invented by Trondheim. Blueberry is Jean Giraud's cowboy character, drawn in careful detail against highly realist backgrounds.

71. Max Cabanes, *Colin-Maillard* (Tournai: Casterman, 1989).

72. I am referring to her conference presentation: "Autobiographical comics and the concept of 'visual modality'," given at the conference entitled: "Academic Perspectives on Comics, Manga and Graphic Novels as intercultural and intermedial phenomena," op. cit.

73. Gunther Kress and Theo van Leeuwen, *Multimodal Discourse: the Modes and Media of Contemporary Communications* (London: Arnold, 2001). The authors themselves borrow the concept of modality from the linguist Michael A. K. Halliday.

74. Alain Rey, *Les Spectres de la bande* [The Ghosts in the Strip] (Paris: Minuit, 1978), p. 45.

75. *Système 1*, p. 146, *System 1*, p. 123.

76. Fabrice Neaud, *Journal* (4 volumes) (Angoulême: ego comme X, 1996–2002).

77. Gert Meesters, "Les significations du style graphique" [The Meanings of Graphic Style], *Textyles*, Revue des Lettres belges de langue française, nos. 36–37: *La bande dessinée contemporaine* (2010), 215–33.

78. Olivier Schrauwen, *Mon Fiston* (Angoulême: Editions de l'an 2, 2006).

79. Dominique Goblet, *Faire semblant c'est mentir* (Paris: L'Association, 2007).

80. Tardi and Benjamin Legrand, *Tueur de Cafards* (Tournai: Casterman, 1984).

81. Alfred and Olivier Ka, *Pourquoi j'ai tué Pierre* (Paris: Delcourt, 2006).

82. François Schuiten and Benoît Peeters, *La Tour* (Tournai: Casterman, 1987).

83. Marc-Antoine Mathieu, *La Qu . . .* (Paris: Delcourt, 1991).

84. Milo Manara, *Jour de colère* (Tournai: Casterman, 1983).

85. Nicolas Devil, *Saga de Xam* (Paris: Losfeld, 1967).

86. Moebius, *Major fatal* (Paris: Les Humanoïdes Associés, 1979).

87. Andrea Pazienza, *Le Straordinarie Avventure di Pentothal* (Rome: Fandango Libri, 1982).

88. Renato Calligaro, *Deserto* (Cosenza: Edizioni della Periferia, 1982).

89. Translated from the original Spanish. "De la poesía en el cómic de vanguardia" [On poetry in avant-garde comics], *Taka de Tinta*, University of Barcelona (May 1989), unpaginated. From the same author, see also: "Les aventures de la forme" [The Adventures of Form], *Les Cahiers de la bande dessinée*, no. 71 (Sept.–Oct. 1986), 62–64.

90. *Vague* and *L'Idiot*, op. cit.

91. *Le Minuscule Mousquetaire*, op. cit.

92. Taken from the site www.coconino-world.com, currently withdrawn from the site, published by permission of the author.

93. Daniel Clowes, *Ice Haven* (New York: Pantheon, 2005).

94. The reader will have noticed that the movement that brings together the two color ranges that are initially kept apart, and finally mixes them, is analogous to that, commented

on above, that brings together two different graphic codes (those used to characterize the respective personalities of Asterios and Hana), until they are finally superimposed and merged.

95. Chris Ware, *Jimmy Corrigan, The Smartest Kid on Earth* (New York: Pantheon Books, 2000).

96. Pierre Veys and Nicolas Barral, *Menaces sur l'Empire* (Paris: Dargaud, 2005).

97. Translator's note: a famous series of the 1940s and 1950s by Edgar P. Jacobs, whose two eponymous heroes were both British. Olrik, of indeterminate middle-European origin, was their implacable enemy.

CHAPTER SIX

1. "Presenting Minds in Graphic Novels," op. cit., 308.

2. Seymour Chatman, *Story and Discourse: Narrative Structure in Fiction and Film* (Ithaca: Cornell University Press, 1978), quoted in *Le Narrateur*, op. cit., p. 62.

3. E. P. Jacobs, *La Marque jaune* [The Yellow "M"] (Brussels: Le Lombard, 1956), p. 45.

4. *Naissances de la bande dessinée*, op. cit., p. 127.

5. Ibid. p. 35.

6. Ibid. p. 52.

7. Dupuy and Berberian, *Journal d'un album* (Paris: L'Association, 1994). An English translation was published by Drawn and Quarterly in 2006 under the title of *Maybe Later*.

8. This is in fact the image that was chosen for the cover of the book.

9. Derik Badman, "Talking, Thinking and Seeing in Pictures: Narration, Focalization and Ocularization in Comics Narratives," *International Journal of Comic Art*, vol. 12. nos. 2/3 (Autumn 2010). Available online at http://madinkbeard.com/archives/talking-thinking-and-seeing-in-pictures-narration-focalization-and-ocularization-in-comics-narratives.

10. Mort Walker, *The Lexicon of Comicana* (Bloomington: iUniverse, 2000, first published 1980).

11. François Ayroles, *Les Penseurs* (Paris: L'Association, 2006).

12. *Système 1*, p. 154, *System 1*, p. 130.

13. Fabrice Neaud, *Journal III* (Angoulême: ego comme x, 1999).

14. Sylvianne Rémi-Giraud, "Métaphore et métonomie dans le *Journal* de Fabrice Neaud" [Metaphor and Metonomy in Fabrice Neaud's *Journal*], *Neuvième Art* no. 9 (October 2003), 85–89.

15. Bill Watterson, *The Calvin and Hobbes Tenth Anniversary Book* (Kansas City: Andrews and McMeel, 1995), p. 22.

16. An analogous principle is at work in *Reine beauté* [Beauty Queen], a story written by Hubert and drawn by Kerascoët, prepublished in *Spirou* in 2010 (and published in album format by Dupuis in 2011). The heroine, an ugly duckling mocked and mistreated by those around her, is granted a wish by a fairy; other people will henceforth perceive her as the "personification of ideal beauty," the incarnation of absolute beauty, but when she looks in her mirror she will continue to see herself as she really looks. The young woman is drawn alternately as ugly and as ravishingly beautiful.

17. See Jean-Baptiste Bazin, *Le Flux de conscience en bande dessinée* [Stream of Consciousness in Comics], unpublished Masters dissertation, ÉESI, Angoulême, academic year 2009–2010.

CHAPTER SEVEN

1. Cf. *Understanding Comics* op. cit., pp. 99–100.

2. *Système 1*, p. 55, *System 1*, p. 45.

3. Ibid.

4. Ibid.

5. With the notable exception of the book by Jan Baetens and Pascal Lefèvre, *Pour une lecture moderne de la bande dessinée* [Towards a Modern Reading of Comic Art] (Brussels: CBBD, 1993), which devotes several pages to the question (pp. 52–57).

6. In connection with the album *Quai d'Orsay*. See *Casemate* 25 (April 2010), p. 15.

7. Will Eisner, *Comics and Sequential Art* (Northampton, MA: Poorhouse Press, 1985).

8. See his comments on the blog http://www.thoughtballoonists.com/2010/02/abstract comics.html. Consulted 11 March 2010.

9. François Genton, "L'image libérée ou le cinéma selon Hans Richter" [The Liberated Image or the Cinema According to Hans Richter], *Ligeia*, 97–98–99–100, (January–June 2010), qtd in *Peintres cineastes* [Painter Film Directors], pp. 49–61, 54.

10. Even if the tradition of abstract cinema lives on in animated film, in the work of artists like Lazlo Moholy-Nagy, Len Lye, or Takashi Ishida, to name but a few.

11. *Système 1*, p. 125, *System 1*, p. 107.

12. See Isabelle Guaïtella, "Au rythme des images: multimodalité et multilinéarité de la bande dessinée" [In rhythm with images: the multimodality and multilinearity of comic art] *Semiotica* vol. 146 nos. 1/4 (2003), 519–26.

13. *Système 1*, pp. 70–71, *System 1*, pp. 58–59.

14. Ibid. pp. 171–72, p. 144.

15. *Acme Novelty Date Book*, vol. 1, pp. 155 and 189; vol. 2, pp. 131, 143, 152, and 188.

16. Walter Murch, *In the Blink of an Eye* (New York: Silman-James Press, 2001).

17. *Naissances de la bande dessinée*, op. cit., pp. 132–33.

18. Gaston Bachelard once called for a reconciliation of human consciousness with the natural rhythms of the body. He took up the concept of "rhythmanalysis," put forward in 1931 by the Brazilian Pinheiro Dos Santos. See *La Dialectique de la durée* [The Dialectics of Duration] (Paris: PUF, 1950).

19. Paul Fraisse, *Psychologie du rythme* (Paris: Presses Universitaires de France, 1974).

20. It has often been pointed out that more than one Hergé album begins with Tintin simply out for a walk.

21. Claude Lévi-Strauss, *Regarder écouter lire* [Look, Listen, Read], (Paris: Plon, 1993) p. 157. Lévi-Strauss is referring to Émile Benveniste's article "Le rythme dans son acception linguistique" [Rhythm in the Linguistic Sense], reprinted in *Problèmes de linguistique générale* [Problems in General Linguistics] vol. 1, (Paris: Gallimard, 1966) pp. 327–35.

22. *Le Rythme grec, d'Héraclite à Aristote* [Greek Rhythm, from Heraclitus to Aristotle], (Paris: PUF, 1999).

23. *Système 1*, pp. 112–14, *System 1*, pp. 96–97.

24. Robert Crumb, "Mr Natural's 719th Meditation," first published 1970, reprinted in *The Book of Mr Natural* (Seattle: Fantagraphics, 1995).

25. See Thierry Smolderen, "Trois formes de pages" [Three kinds of page design], *Neuvième Art*, no. 13 (January 2007), 20–31.

26. *Système 1*, pp. 110–11, *System 1*, pp. 94–95.

27. Page references are to the paperback edition of *Louis Riel: A Comic-Strip Biography* (Montreal: Drawn and Quarterly, 2006).

28. Similarly, in *From Hell*, the almost unbearable scene from chapter 10, which details every step of the murder committed by William Gull on November 9, 1888, and particularly pages 4 to 9, where the victim is savagely disfigured and ripped apart, draws its power from the regularity of the layout and the continuity of the angle of vision. It is noteworthy that *From Hell* makes frequent use of the static shot, which is not the case for *Watchmen*. Alan Moore and Eddie Campbell, *From Hell* (Marietta: Top Shelf Productions, 1999).

29. In this respect, the narrative exercise that Chester Brown undertakes is not dissimilar to the Oubapian album of Jean-Christophe Menu and Lewis Trondheim, *Moins d'un quart de seconde pour vivre* [Less than a Quarter of a Second Left to Live] (Paris: L'Association, 1991), whose hundred strips result from the combination of just eight panels.

30. First published in French in *Charlie mensuel*, no. 88, (May 1976).

31. See my article: "Le cadavre tombé de rien ou la troisième qualité du scénariste" [The corpse that fell for no reason, or the scriptwriter's third quality], *Revue de l'Université de Bruxelles*, nos. 1–2 (1986), *Autour du scénario*, pp. 111–18.

32. See Henri Van Lier, *Anthropogénie* [Anthropogenics], Brussels: Les Impressions nouvelles, 2010) pp. 18–21. (Translator's note: Van Lier's original term is "strophisme.") The other characteristics of rhythm noted by the author are: interstability, accentuation (which I will include in my own analysis below), tempo, autoengendering, suspense, convection, and distribution through nodes, envelopes, resonances, and interfaces.

33. *Naissances de la bande dessinée*, op. cit., pp. 104–17.

34. The work of Frost and Sterrett was published in France in the twenty-first century by the L'An 2 publishing house.

35. This flexible approach to the "waffle-iron" is not new. Burne Hogarth had made it his own in the Sunday *Tarzan* pages. In the work of Milton Caniff, it can be seen that during the first few weeks that *Terry and the Pirates* appeared in 1934, the layout was rhetorical. Caniff's conversion to a regular layout was sudden: it took place as from the twenty-first Sunday page. Subsequently, Caniff remained faithful to the waffle-iron for the rest of his career. Even so, in his post-war masterpiece, *Steve Canyon*, he gradually got into the habit of introducing the page with a full-width panel (a triple panel, including the title) and, still more interestingly in relation to rhythm, ending it with a double panel.

36. A famous 1951 film by Robert Wise.

37. See Douglas Wolk, *Reading Comics* (Cambridge, Ma: Da Capo Press, 2007), p. 239. Other critics have noted that this point about *Watchmen* also applies to the rest of Alan

Moore's work: images taking up a whole page almost always coincide with some kind of apocalypse.

38. Interview on the Actuabd.com website, posted March 1, 2008.

39. "Le système Schulz" [The Schulz System], *Les Cahiers de la bande dessinée*, no. 81 (June 1988), pp. 88–113; 91. An English translation of this article by Dwight R. Decker has been published under the title "The Schultz System. Why Peanuts Work," *Nemo: The Classic Comics Library* nos. 31–32 (January–Winter 1992), pp. 26–41.

40. *Système 1*, pp. 110–11, *System 1*, pp. 94–95.

41. Jason, *Je vais te montrer quelque chose* (Paris: Carabas, 2004).

42. When Baetens and Lefèvre write: "The rhythm of narration of a comic can be measured by a comparison between the probable duration of the action and the number of panels covering it in the album" (*Pour une lecture moderne*, op. cit., p. 53), they are confusing rhythm with speed. Although the speed of the narration can indeed be measured by this relationship, it will by now be clear that rhythm is a considerably more complex matter.

43. André Juillard and Patrick Cothias, *La Marque du condor* (Grenoble: Glénat, 1991).

44. "La Construction de *La Cage*" [The Construction of *La Cage*], afterword to Martin Vaughn-James, *La Cage* (Brussels: Les Impressions nouvelles, new edition 2010) p. XLVI.

45. See, for example, the second, third, and fourth pages of Chapter 1, the first pages of Chapter 2, or pages 9 and 10 of Chapter 3.

46. Unpublished comment, during round table with author.

47. Jacques Samson et Benoît Peeters, *Chris Ware, la bande dessinée réinventée* [Chris Ware, Comic Art Reinvented] (Brussels, Les Impressions nouvelles, 2010), p. 150. See also Georgiana Banita, "Chris Ware and the Pursuit of Slowness," David M. Ball and Martha B. Kuhlman (eds), *The Comics of Chris Ware* (Jackson, U P of Mississippi, 2010) pp. 177–90.

48. See my article "Histoire de la bande dessinée muette" [The History of Wordless Comic Art], *Neuvième Art* no. 2, (January 1997), pp. 60–75, and no. 3, (January 1998), pp. 92–105.

49. He has since included this in his album *Les Parleurs* [The Talkers] (Paris: L'Association, 2003).

50. Translator's note: this is a reference to an 1845 play by Alfred de Musset, *Il faut qu'une porte soit ouverte ou fermée* [A Door has to be Either Open or Closed].

51. François Ayroles, *Les Penseurs* (Paris: L'Association, 2006).

52. Guy Delisle, *Aline et les autres* (Paris, L'Association, 1999 and 2001).

53. For a more detailed commentary on this point, see Mai-Li Bernard, *Problématique du texte et de l'image dans la bande dessinée muette: Le motif dans le processus de lecture* [The Problematic of Text and Image in Silent Comic Art: The Motif in the Reading Process], unpublished Masters dissertation, Angoulême, École européenne supérieure de l'image, June 2010.

CHAPTER EIGHT

1. Pierre Couperie, "Reflets de l'art moderne dans la bande dessinée" [Reflections of Modern Art in Comics], in *Comics: l'art de la bande dessinée* {US Comics and Comic Art] (Zurich: The Graphic Press, 1972), pp. 15–25.

2. I take the liberty of quoting my essay *La Bande dessinée, son histoire et ses maîtres* [Comics: History and Major Artists] (Paris : Skira Flammarion, 2009), p. 324.

3. Jean-Christophe Menu, *Plates-bandes* (Paris: L'Association, 2005), p. 12.

4. In order the better to follow in the "spirit" of the "most radical" literary and artistic journals of the twentieth century, *L'Éprouvette* was not averse to engaging in "polemics and old-fashioned ad hominem attacks . . . ." See *La Bande dessinée et son double*, op. cit., p. 365.

5. The method of drawing beyond conscious control is originally derived from Spiritualism: hypnotic trances induced by a medium were used to obtain drawings.

6. Reproduced in *La Bande dessinée et son double*, op. cit., p. 412.

7. See 1.1. above.

8. *La bande dessinée et son double*, op. cit., p. 496. The third chapter is given over to this issue.

9. Jean-Christophe Menu, *Livret de Phamille* (Paris : L'Association, 1995).

10. Pierre Couperie, *VRAOUM!*, exhibition catalogue (Lyon: Fage editions and La Maison rouge, 2009), unp.

11. See *High & Low: Modern Art and Popular Culture*, op. cit., p. 208.

12. Nicole Gaillard, "Autour du mouvement bédéphile: entretien avec Pierre Couperie" [Concerning the Comics Appreciation Movement : Interview with Pierre Couperie], *Contrechamp*, no. 1 (1997), pp. 131–46; pp. 137–38. Couperie's reaction can largely be explained by his hostility towards the comic books that inspired Lichtenstein, attested by his articles in *Giff-Wiff* and by the catalogue for the exhibition *Bande dessinée et figuration narrative* [Comics and Narrative Figuration]. See Pierre Couperie ed., *Bande dessinée et figuration narrative* (Paris: Musée des arts décoratifs/Palais du Louvre, 1967), p. 69.

13. Quoted by Erwin Dejasse in *Flux News* no. 37 (April–May–June 2005), p. 5.

14. Bart Beaty, "Roy Lichtenstein's Tears: Art vs. Pop in American Culture," *Canadian Review of American Studies*, vol. 34 no. 3 (2004), pp. 249–68; pp. 251–52.

15. The page is featured in the catalogue: Art Spiegelman, *Comix, Essays, Graphics & Scraps* (Palermo: Sellerio edotore/Centrale dell'Arte (1999), p. 64.

16. The transcription of the entire interview appears on the website http://www.lichten steinfoundation.org/frames.htm.

17. See above, 1.2.

18. *Krazy Kat* is celebrated in the catalogue (on p. 168) for its "deep affinity to the spirit and form of vanguard art." In general, only two comics authors are recognized as outstanding figures: George Herriman and Robert Crumb.

19. For a discussion of these issues, and specifically the MoMA exhibition, French readers can refer to Georges Roque ed., *Majeur ou mineur? Les hierarchies en art* [High or Low? Hierarchies in Art] (Nîmes: Jacqueline Chambon, 2000).

20. Philippe Dagen, "Pourquoi les jeunes artistes font à nouveau du dessin" [Why young artists have turned back to drawing], *Le Monde* (29 March 2011), p. 30.

21. Translator's note: a (usually pejorative) expression roughly meaning "everything counts as culture," referring to the policy pursued by Jack Lang (Minister of Culture under François Mitterrand, as from 1981) of encouraging cultural diversity at the expense of a monolithic notion of high art as national culture.

22. Translator's note: the original term is "plasticiens," which denotes those who practice the "arts plastiques." These include sculpture and painting but also installation art, video art, performance art, etc.

23. The descriptions are taken from the 2010 Association catalogue.

24. "Ce paradoxe qu'est le Frémok" [The paradox that is Frémok], interview with Thierry Van Hasselt, *Book by Brussels* 1 (2010), p. 23.

25. *Vraoum!* catalogue, unp.

26. *Majeur ou mineur?* Op. cit., p. 11.

27. *Bande dessinée et art contemporain, la nouvelle scène de l'égalité* [Comics and Contemporary Art: a Newly Equal Scene] (Blou: Monografik, 2010).

28. Translator's note: this is the term used in French by Linda Morren.

29. Not, in any case, in the sense that heroic fantasy, thriller, satire, or autobiography can be called genres, since—and I am stating the obvious here—all of these genres (and quite a few more) coexist within the field of comics.

30. *La Bande dessinée et son double*, op. cit., p. 11.

31. Jean-Marc Thévenet, the curator of the Biennial Exhibition, writes "Yes, comics belongs to the domain of Art," while the artistic advisor, Alain Berland attributes to the event the aim of "identifying instances of hybridization" between comic art and art other than comics.

32. In France, the Arts décoratifs in Strasbourg, the École Émile Cohl in Lyon, the ÉESI in Angoulême. In Belgium, ESA and ERG in Brussels, the Académie des Beaux-Arts in Tournai and in Liège, to list only the main art schools.

33. I take the liberty of quoting my own words here, from the introduction to Thierry Groensteen and Gilles Ciment (eds.), *100 Cases de maîtres. Un art graphique, la bande dessinée* [100 Panels by Masters. Comics, a Graphic Art] (Paris : La Martinière, 2010), p. 26.

34. Thierry Groensteen, *Un objet culturel non identifié* (Angoulême : L'An 2, 2006), pp. 135–38.

35. Nathalie Heinich makes the point that some erudite detractors of contemporary art have called for the return of "an existential art, close to experience, close to emotion," and that it is this re-emergence of emotion and affect that "motivates demands for a return to figurative painting." *See Le Triple jeu de l'art contemporain* [The Triple Game of Contemporary Art] (Paris: Minuit, 1998), p. 233.

36. Quoted by Suzanne Liandrat-Guigues and Jean-Louis Lieutrat, *Penser le cinema* [Thinking Cinema] (Paris: Klinksieck, 2001), p. 24.

37. See the articles on Feininger by Thierry Smolderen and Jean-Claude Glasser in *Neuvième Art* no. 10 (April 2004),pp. 8–19 and pp. 20–25.

38. Howard S. Backer, *Art Worlds* (Berkeley: University of California Press, 1982).

39. *Le Triple jeu de l'art contemporain*, op. cit., p. 11.

40. See Florence de Méredieu, *Histoire matérielle et immatérielle de l'art moderne et contemporain* [Material and Immaterial History of Modern and Contemporary Art], (Paris : Larousse, 2008),pp. 479 and 483. For an enlightening complementary approach, see Aude de Kerros, *L'Art caché. Les dissidents de l'art contemporain* [Hidden Art. The Dissidents of Contemporary Art], (Paris: Eyrolles, 2007).

41. See Christian Rosset, "Tenir le mur" [literally "hold the wall"], *Neuvième Art* no. 15 (January 2009), pp. 166–75. See also the other articles in this dossier called "Loin de la planche à dessin" [Far from the Drawing Board].

42. See *Bande dessinée et art contemporain*, ed. Jean-Marc Thévenet (Blou : Monografik, 1999), p. 9. Shall I admit this? Something in me bridles and instinctively resists every time someone thunders dogmatically that an artist *must* do this or that; it seems to me that the recognition that is owed to art is, on the contrary, conditional on the freedom accorded to artists to follow their own path—and to take the risk of being resolutely out of step with the times.

43. In a workshop at the École nationale supérieure d'Art in Nancy in 2006, Gerner got students to use Hergé's album *L'Oreille cassée* (Tournai: Casterman, 1937) as a starting point. The instruction was to use comics as a "take-off point," "raw material to be kneaded and transformed." See his own account of this experiment: "Caramba!," *L'Éprouvette* no. 3 (January 2007), pp. 413–17.

44. Molotiu's website, http://blot*comics*.blogspot.com, shows that one variation of his art takes the form of large-format backlit panels, and is more convincing as gallery art than in the pages of a book.

45. See his essay *Principes des littératures dessinées*, op. cit.

INDEX OF THEMES

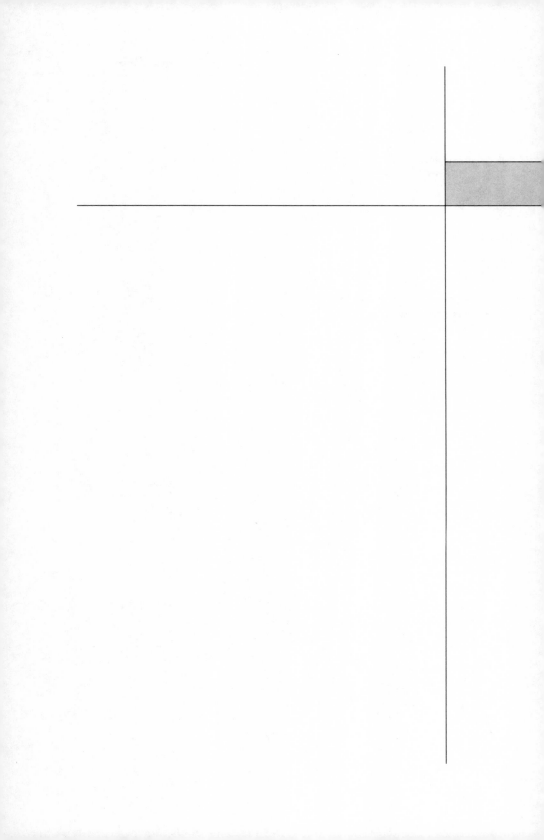

INDEX OF NAMES

Page numbers in **bold** reference illustrations.

CPSIA information can be obtained at www.ICGtesting.com
Printed in the USA
BVOW05s1746190815

413972BV00002B/5/P